I0820193

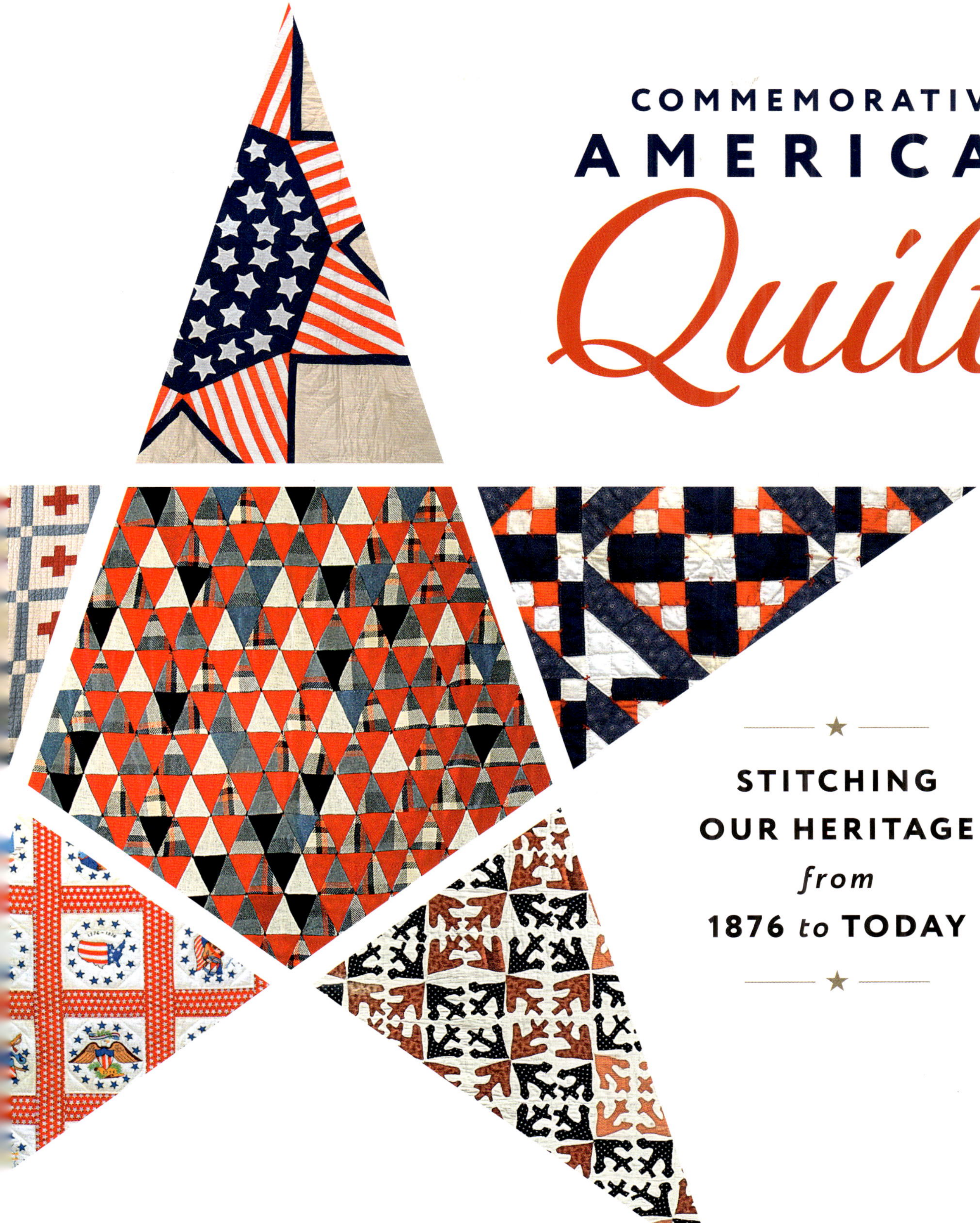

COMMEMORATIVE AMERICAN *Quilts*

STITCHING OUR HERITAGE *from* 1876 *to* TODAY

SANDRA SIDER

Foreword by **PAMELA WEEKS**

Other Schiffer Craft Books by the Author:

Quarantine Quilts: Creativity in the Midst of Chaos, Sandra Sider, Foreword by Meg Cox, ISBN 978-0-7643-6201-9

Deeds Not Words: Celebrating 100 Years of Women's Suffrage, Sandra Sider and Pamela Weeks, ISBN 978-0-7643-5917-0

The Quilting Power Grid: A Design Skillbook for Beginning Modern Quilters, with 50 Example Projects, ISBN 978-0-7643-6550-8

Other Schiffer Craft Books on Related Subjects:

Quilts of Valor: A 50-State Salute, Quilts of Valor Foundation, Contributing authors Ann Parsons Holte, Renelda Peldunas-Harter, Ann Rehbein, Sue Reich, Foreword by Marianne Fons, ISBN 978-0-7643-5630-8

Art Quilts Unfolding: 50 Years of Innovation, Sandra Sider, editor, Nancy Bavor, Lisa Ellis, Martha Sielman, SAQA (Studio Art Quilt Associates, Inc.), ISBN 978-0-7643-5626-1

Quilts Presidential and Patriotic, Sue Reich, ISBN 978-0-7643-5041-2

Sections of chapter 7 previously appeared in the author's self-published book *Pioneering Quilt Artists, 1960–1980: A New Direction in American Art*, 2010.

Library of Congress Control Number: 2025939956

Designed by Lindsay Hess
Back cover design by Christine B. Stuermer
Type set in Quinn Text / Circe / Elaina

ISBN: 978-0-7643-7131-8
ePub: 978-1-5073-0638-3
Printed in India

Published by Schiffer Craft
An imprint of Schiffer Publishing, Ltd.
4880 Lower Valley Road
Atglen, PA 19310
Phone: (610) 593-1777; Fax: (610) 593-2002
Email: Info@schifferbooks.com
Web: www.schifferbooks.com

Dedicated to

my Appalachian grandmother,
Virginia Dare (Morgan) Saunders (1884–1974).
I sleep under one of her many quilts.
And to my grandmother who lived
in the Midlands of South Carolina,
Lucie Vida (Gunter) Kneece (1887–1973).
She spun her own thread for tatting from
cotton grown on her farm.

20

211

167

69

192

184

201

228

Contents

2 **FOREWORD** by Pamela Weeks

4 **ACKNOWLEDGMENTS**

6 **INTRODUCTION**

14 ***Chapter 1:* PATRIOTISM IN CONTEXT**
How the US Centennial of 1876 changed quilting.

52 ***Chapter 2:* WOMEN AT WORK**
How women made the national 1876 event happen, and their contributions with quilts and other textiles.

68 ***Chapter 3:* CRAZY QUILTS**
The part the US Centennial played in the burgeoning popularity of a highly decorative style of quilts.

94 ***Chapter 4:* ALL'S FAIR**
Quilt culture at the nineteenth- and twentieth-century world's fairs prior to 1976.

118 ***Chapter 5:* HISTORY REPEATS ITSELF**
The wide varieties of patriotic quilts, and how their place in history relates to US Bicentennial quilt making.

144 ***Chapter 6:* HAPPY BIRTHDAY, AMERICA**
The idea and pattern sources of Bicentennial quilts, including the impact of national quilting contests.

176 ***Chapter 7:* QUILTS IN VOGUE**
Why and how quilt making took off during the 1970s, including the US Bicentennial's influence.

200 ***Chapter 8:* TIME AFTER TIME**
The twentieth century's commemorative events observed through quilt making, by communities and by individual makers.

230 **CONCLUSION**
Our country's 250th birthday and the challenge to quilt makers.

232 **NOTES**

245 **BIBLIOGRAPHY**

247 **INDEX**

Foreword

★

BY PAMELA WEEKS

To say that the craft revival sparked by the US Bicentennial celebrations in 1976 shaped my life is not an exaggeration. Colonial revivals have sparked the American public's interest in history and craft at least three times since our country's founding. The first was the Centennial celebration in 1876. Ten million visitors toured the Philadelphia Centennial Exposition, seeing handcrafted and manufactured goods from all over the world. Embroidery, pottery, weaving, fashion, home goods, modern appliances—all wonders to behold. The second was sparked by the two hundredth anniversary of the birth of George Washington in 1932, concurrently driven by a commercial effort to sell more women's magazines offering refreshed quilting patterns, led by the naturalistic designs of Marie Webster. The third was the US Bicentennial. That craft revival was also fueled by the back-to-nature movement, based on the "old-timey ways of living," as well as the hippie movement. It seemed that everyone was weaving, quilting, or making crocheted granny squares.

In 1976, on the Fourth of July, I was working the top of the mountain chairlift at a ski area—Gunstock Recreation Area in Gilford, New Hampshire. At noon, we stopped the lift and listened. As proclaimed by President Gerald Ford, the church bells in the village below began to ring, celebrating the two hundredth anniversary of the signing of the Declaration of Independence. I was filled with awe and pride, knowing that people across the country were pausing to listen and reflect as bells rang everywhere in our country for a full two minutes.

During that 1976 to 1977 period, thanks to the multiple magazines featuring quilting patterns, I made my first patchwork pillow.

Since that, I've had several careers in the past fifty years, including real estate and restaurant management, but the most satisfying for me include my six years working in several capacities for the League of New Hampshire Craftsmen, and eight years leading ABC Quilts, a tiny New Hampshire–based nonprofit making quilts for babies born at risk, with a kids' quilting-based education program that included age-appropriate lessons for preventing drug abuse. Now, as the Binney Family Curator at the New England Quilt Museum, I'm enjoying my best job ever. I believe that the craft revival sparked by the US Bicentennial, and my choice to choose quilting as my artistic outlet, led me here.

When Sandra Sider invited me to write a foreword for this book and suggested we curate an exhibition related to it at the New England Quilt Museum, I accepted immediately, because of the importance of the Bicentennial craft revival in my life, and because of the scope of the material she has undertaken to reveal. In the 1990s I started paying attention to quilt history, and eventually the important role that commemorative quilts play in documenting local and national history as well as women's history. For example, in chapters 1 and 2, Sider analyzes the Centennial Exposition held in Philadelphia. The exhibitions were international, innovative, and commercial in nature and, thanks to a special committee composed of women, included women's work—textiles and household goods and clothing from all over the world. Sider explores the theory that something in this major event sparked the fad of crazy quilts, and also how the plethora of textiles on exhibition may have also influenced the quilting fads of multitudinous pieced and charm quilts.

Sider's wide and far-reaching scope here precedes Centennial-inspired quilts by including a few that commemorate the Civil War, and others that show support for early- and mid-nineteenth-century politicians. After a thorough investigation of the Centennial Exposition, she focuses on the twentieth century and takes us through the 1933 Sears Century of Progress national contest, which garnered 25,000 entries and offered major prize money. The explosion of Bicentennial quilts follows, as do other commemorative quilts—those made for anniversaries celebrating our national parks, major buildings, and the Emancipation Proclamation, to name just a few. With her guidance, we visit the creation of the major national quilt shows in the 1970s. In the 1980s and 1990s there were more contests, including the 1986 Statue of Liberty Centennial competition. There is so much contained here, and it's time for you to dive in.

In 2026, the New England Quilt Museum will host an exhibition related to this book. We are gathering quilts from the Centennial to the Bicentennial, with many created before, beyond, and in between, representing as many of the quilts and contests from Sider's research as we can fit on our walls. They commemorate and celebrate our country's founding, its anniversary, important places, events and people—these educate us as to the importance of those things, and, I hope, inspire us to create our own commemorative quilts.

Foreword writer Pamela Weeks is the Binney Family Curator of the New England Quilt Museum and has written and cowritten several books on quilt history, including *Civil War Quilts*.

Acknowledgments

The collectors, curators, registrars, archivists, artists, photographers, and quilt guild officers who kindly helped me with this book are too numerous to list but have my gratitude. I want especially to thank Vicky Bevan, archivist for the Royal School of Needlework in London, as well as Susan Kay-Williams, former chief executive and archivist. I am also very grateful to staff members of the International Quilt Museum, especially Carolyn Ducey and Sarah Walcott. Karey Bresenhan and Nancy O'Bryant Puentes generously shared with me their vast knowledge of quilt culture during the wonderful years I worked for them as curator of the Texas Quilt Museum. Quilt artist Teresa Barkley's influence pervades my book, not only with images of her fascinating commemorative quilts but also of her impressive collection of textile souvenirs. Discussions of the book's various subjects with Barbara Brackman, Marianne Fons, Paula Nadelstern, Sue Reich, Luana Rubin, Bill Volckening, and Teresa Duryea Wong sharpened my focus and sent me down several productive avenues. My best advocate since I began this book has been my editor at Schiffer Publishing, Sandra Korinchak, whom I cannot thank enough for her avid attention to this project. Finally, Pamela Weeks has encouraged me through every step of this challenging yet exhilarating journey, and I look forward to visiting our 2026 New England Quilt Museum exhibition, *Commemorative American Quilts: Stitching Our Heritage from 1876 to Today.*

Introduction

In 1876, the United States commemorated one hundred years as a nation, a span of time far beyond the average lifetime of its populace. Few people lived past the age of fifty, with a century representing a very impressive length of time.

Because tickets were sold for the one hundredth anniversary events, the Philadelphia Centennial Commission was able to count an astounding total of more than ten million visitors, including foreigners. The word "anniversary" means the turning of years, and reaching one hundred in 1876 meant more than it might mean today, when the US has more than 95,000 centenarians.

But no human can live anything close to the age of two hundred, lending the concept of the US Bicentennial in 1976 a level of excitement like that of the Centennial.[1] "People find something mystical about numbers, especially those that end with zeros."[2] Think of the significance of a fiftieth wedding anniversary. . . . We feel a sense of accomplishment, even when the event commemorates nothing more than the passing of time. For a nation, however, that time span encapsulates controversy, struggle, pride, and a shared heritage, good or bad.

On a smaller scale, excitement over a major anniversary applies to residents of states, counties, cities, towns, and many other aspects of American life. "The importance of local pride should never be underestimated in a country which still promotes its pioneering spirit and where state identity is continually stressed."[3] When beginning to work on my book, I expected to locate unpublished quilts filled with patriotic imagery for the US Centennial and Bicentennial, and of course I knew about several of the commemorative quilt contests, such as the famous 1933 Century of Progress, the 1986 Statue of Liberty quilts, and the Columbus turmoil of 1992. But I was surprised and delighted by quilts commemorating anniversaries of our national parks, Grand Central Terminal, the Emancipation Proclamation, railroads and wagon trains, barns, and several sesquicentennials (150 years), semiquincentennials (250 years), and tricentennials (300 years).

This book focuses almost exclusively on quilts, a consummately American art form, as expressions of patriotism, protest, celebration, and commemoration. Possibly because Centennial quilts were intended

Courtesy of Julie Silber Quilts, Berkeley, California.

George Washington souvenir bookmark (ca. 1876), woven silk

▶ Mary E. Carswell, *Grand Army of the Republic Quilt* (1885), 84 x 84 in.

Courtesy of the Mattatuck Museum, Waterbury, CT; Collection of the Mattatuck Museum, x72.352

mainly as enhanced souvenirs, rather than to use on beds, many of them evidently survived in much-better condition than we see in some of their contemporary quilts created for functional use.[4]

We begin by discussing in **chapter 1** the hope for national unity promulgated by those planning the Centennial in the late 1860s. (This starting point is, of course, later than quilts made during the Civil War.) We know of several quilts beautifully symbolizing that hope for unity through imagery and materials. Mary E. Carswell, a member of the Women's Relief Corps from Waterbury, Connecticut, created her conciliatory statement in 1885, the *Grand Army of the Republic Quilt*. Her album quilt of forty-nine squares, filled with military emblems, incorporated pieces of silk from the maker's friends in both the southern and northern states, literally patching together regional differences. This quilt struck a chord during Reconstruction, garnering newspaper coverage in several cities.

Why did quilts appeal so deeply to so many as commemorative objects? Their relatively large size certainly provided an ample canvas for display, especially for the souvenir textiles accompanying the Centennial—so much better than keeping the bandanas and handkerchiefs folded away in a drawer. As far as we can tell, extant Centennial quilts, like many crazy quilts, stemmed from the creative efforts of individual makers or of a single household, within the constraints of women's domestic culture. Both the Centennial and Bicentennial honored Revolutionary War history, with quilt making recognized as a valid component of historic Americana. By the time we reach the Bicentennial, collaborative album quilts imbued with community spirit appeared like open books celebrating people, places, and events through time in a specific locale. Quilt contests added to

By the time we reach the Bicentennial, collaborative album quilts imbued with community spirit appeared like open books celebrating people, places, and events through time in a specific locale.

the excitement of commemorations, encouraging quilters throughout the US. Although not connected to any sort of large-scale anniversary and thus outside the focus of this book, the *NAMES Project AIDS Memorial Quilt*, begun in the 1980s, today the most monumental piece of collaborative textile art on the planet, has further confirmed quilts as powerful commemorative objects in the modern world.

Our country has a long tradition of town and county fairs, chiefly Agricultural Society fairs, reaching as far back as the early 1800s.

The official census of 1870 documented that approximately 15 percent of the entire population was not born in the US, and that even more people were first-generation Americans.

In 1841 the first New York State Fair was held in Syracuse, ushering in state fairs that gradually spread throughout the US. While we do not know for certain exactly when the first awards (called "premiums") were given for needlework, we do know that Agricultural Society fairs were presenting premiums for quilts by 1846.[5] Quilts have always been a competitive component of such fairs in this country, often garnering monetary prizes for the winners and personal pride in award ribbons. But these early fairs in the US were modest events, usually lasting for only one or two days, and the quilts represented personal taste and private purpose. Where did the idea originate for an entire country to host a large-scale public exhibition lasting for months, in which other countries were invited to publicize their products and share aspects of their culture?

While not commemorating a span of time, Prince Albert's Great Exhibition of 1851, held from May to October, can be described as the first world's fair. Its main building alone delighted visitors: the grandiose Crystal Palace constructed of glass and iron in London's Hyde Park. Nearly 14,000 exhibitors, 6,861 from Great Britain and 520 from the colonies, attracted six million visitors who brought in the 1851 equivalent of $2 million in ticket sales.[6] The event made a profit of 186,000 British pounds, a huge financial success (millions in today's currency). These proceeds funded the establishment of several major museums in London and encouraged other countries to host similar fairs.

Chapter 1 sets the historical scene for the US Centennial of 1876, considering what the concept of "patriotism" meant at the time. The country had experienced growing pains, notably the Civil War and the struggles for African Americans, Native Americans, Asian Americans, and women to achieve the full rights of citizenship. With the official census of 1870 documenting the fact that approximately 15 percent of the entire population was not born in the US, and that even more people were first-generation Americans, we realize that much of the country in 1876 was still adjusting to the political reality of being, or becoming, American. Also considering that millions of white Southerners only recently (and reluctantly) had returned to

the Union, and that many African Americans lived in a state of turmoil during Reconstruction, we can perhaps understand why the Centennial was planned as a dual-purpose commemoration of a unified country as well as of US advancements in industry. Images on fabric of Centennial buildings, founding documents, and portraits of historic figures represented the country's strength and purpose, tangible history stitched into quilts.

In **chapter 2**, we explore the participation and contributions of women in 1876 events associated with quilts and other textiles, which included the simultaneous work of both the Women's Centennial Executive Committee (WCEC), which raised money for the occasion, and the Women's Christian Temperance Union, which held its first International Temperance Conference in Philadelphia during the Centennial summer, with quiltlike political banners decorating the speakers' platform. Many of the women suffragists served as volunteers and lecturers in the Temperance Union. Not only did the WCEC do the lion's share of private fundraising for the Centennial in general, but this group singlehandedly raised the money to construct the Women's Pavilion, with definite feminist overtones in their endeavor. The organizational abilities of women devoted to these two groups resulted in success at the national level for both initiatives.

Crazy quilts are the subject of **chapter 3** as we discuss the part that the Centennial may have played in the burgeoning popularity of this highly decorative style of quilts a few years after the exhibitions closed. Enthusiasm for the Centennial market drove the US textile industry in the months immediately preceding the Philadelphia exhibition, as mills printed mainly cotton fabrics designed to celebrate 1876 along with silks in several weights. By 1876, the US silk industry had been thriving for quite some time. Booths in the Centennial fairgrounds displayed bolt after bolt of fabrics along with threads that

Booths in the Centennial fairgrounds displayed bolt after bolt of fabrics along with threads, the newest models of sewing machines, and tools for hand stitching.

would have appealed to quilters who could afford them, and wholesalers were able to place their orders on-site. Merchants also offered the newest models of sewing machines as well as equipment and tools for hand stitching. The sheer volume of fabric available after the Centennial in this country, and the remnants sold by dry-goods merchants via mail order, provided plenty of swatches for most anyone who needed fabric for a crazy quilt. Other impetuses for the craze included the Gilded Age penchant for excessive domestic ornamentation, influenced by English embroidery; the possible influence of Japanese textile screens; and fairyland imagery.

Chapter 4 considers quilt culture pertaining to world's fairs and other international expositions in the US, and events commemorating several states and cities prior to 1976. Because quilts were made almost exclusively by women, the buildings constructed specifically for, and chiefly funded by, women hold our attention. These sites offered exhibitions of needlework, often including quilts, and occasionally tools and equipment for sewing. Several of these fairs also had a "Negro Building" where quilts could be viewed. While some journalists argued against segregating work by African Americans, others praised the concept of showcasing these accomplishments instead of letting them be subsumed into huge exhibition halls. Until World War II, the major fairs featured historical displays as well as the latest examples of women's work.

To contextualize patriotic themes and imagery in Bicentennial quilts, **chapter 5** investigates varieties of patriotic quilts prior to 1976, such as the many handmade quilts presented as gifts to the US presidents. While some of these quilts cannot be described as outstanding examples of quilting artistry, they claim an important place as American folk art, originating from the hearts of the people making them—scout troops, religious and civic women's auxiliaries, schoolchildren, et al. Judging by the quilts for which images are available, many of the community quilts gifted to our presidents were in album format, since various people contributed individual squares containing text and image.

Many of the group quilts created for the Bicentennial were in album format, a style that also served the groups celebrating alternative topics.

As you might imagine, both World War I and World War II prompted outpourings of patriotic quilts, some of which were auctioned or raffled to raise money for our troops in Europe, while others honored soldiers returning to their families. The pictorial pieces included images of pieced and appliquéd poppies, for which patterns appeared in numerous newspapers. During World War II, "V" for Victory quilts proliferated across the country, along with quilts symbolizing Victory gardens.

As with presidential quilts, many of the group quilts created for the 1976 Bicentennial were in album format as quilters in communities throughout the US commemorated the two hundredth anniversary of the signing of our Declaration of Independence from Great Britain. This format also offered a pictorial platform for groups celebrating alternative topics or expressing political protests. **Chapter 6** discusses the sources of Bicentennial quilts, including those prompted by contests sponsored by Mountain Mist and other entities. State fairs and National Grange events welcomed Bicentennial quilts in special competitions offering monetary prizes and ribbons. Bicentennial quilts celebrating the US overlapped with other occasions, such as Colorado's state centennial and the bicentennial of Putnam County in New York. Images of Americana and from American history filled commercial cotton fabrics and found their way into Bicentennial quilts exhibited in events across the country. According to the government's *Index of Bicentennial Activities*, more than 150 of the events funded by federal grants involved quilt exhibitions and contests. The themes differed, from blatantly patriotic endeavors to exhibitions of antique quilts as part of American cultural history.

Chapter 7 tackles the phenomenon of why and how quilt making took off during the 1970s, exploring possible connections with the Bicentennial. We delve into books, periodicals, workshops, classes, and lectures to study the quilt-making impetus coinciding with the Bicentennial era, tracking the slowly evolving development of quilts as contemporary art. Simultaneously, exhibitions in major museums presented quilts of all types to receptive viewers (and reviewers), from dramatically graphic antiques to art quilts constructed with new techniques and new materials. These exhibitions suggested that in the world of quilt making, there is no limit to the imaginative possibilities.

As time passed during the twentieth century, many celebratory dates unfolded in America, often commemorated with a quilt or quilt exhibition. **Chapter 8** surveys several such occasions observed through quilt making, by communities as well as by individual makers, including a nationwide contest. The Great American Quilt Festival of 1986 commemorated the centennial of the Statue of Liberty. A gift from the people of France honoring the democratic principles of the people of the US, the statue had captured the attention of America as early as 1876. In that year, to help raise money for the statue's pedestal, funded by contributions from individuals in the US, France shipped her hand holding the torch to the Philadelphia Centennial, where it was prominently displayed. Thus, two of the major commemorative events in America were linked by this iconic symbol of freedom that appeared on hundreds of quilts submitted for the competition. Somewhat ironically, few of the women who entered quilts in that contest would have experienced in 1886 the "freedom" that the statue symbolized, a point made by Susan B. Anthony with her bullhorn, sailing around New York Harbor during the statue's unveiling. Our country's 250th birthday in 2026 challenges quilt makers to grapple with the complex story of our quarter millennium. Shall we dwell on the past or look to the future?

CHAPTER 1

Patriotism in Context

★

This chapter discusses the historical context of America in the years immediately leading up to the 1876 Centennial events, to understand more fully what quilters were celebrating in their commemorative patriotic creations. We will also delve into quilt culture pertaining to the 1889 centennial of the US presidency, as well as George Washington's birthday bicentennial in 1932. As our first president, he remains a political icon.

◀ Martha Washington bandana, ca. 1876, one of several souvenir textiles commemorating her in a matching set with her husband, popular images that were stitched into quilts

▶ *George Washington Quilt*, ca. 1876, 89.5 x 79.5 in., printed cotton

Recent research on Reconstruction in the US has reminded us, as Paul Cimbala and Randall M. Miller explain, that "'the war' did not end with Lee's surrender at Appomattox and Lincoln's assassination in Washington. Much unfinished business remained. Northerners and Southerners still struggled with what the war demanded of them during the 'peace.' Frederick Douglass, for one, observed after the passage of the Thirteenth Amendment by which slavery was abolished that the work of liberty continued. So, too, did the work of binding up the nation's wounds."[1]

Centennial quilts and commercial fabrics celebrating the Union through cloth imagery of flags, historical figures, and symbols such as the Liberty Bell and eagle, along with the dates "1776–1876," seemed to serve that very purpose. This patriotic imagery appeared on banners, bandanas, and objects on display throughout the Centennial Exhibition, and as mentioned in one of the catalogs, "It is quite fitting and natural that at the present time, when we are celebrating our Centennial, that our manufacturers, in producing simply ornamental figures, should desire to typify, by every means in their

The Metropolitan Museum of Art, New York, 1985.347

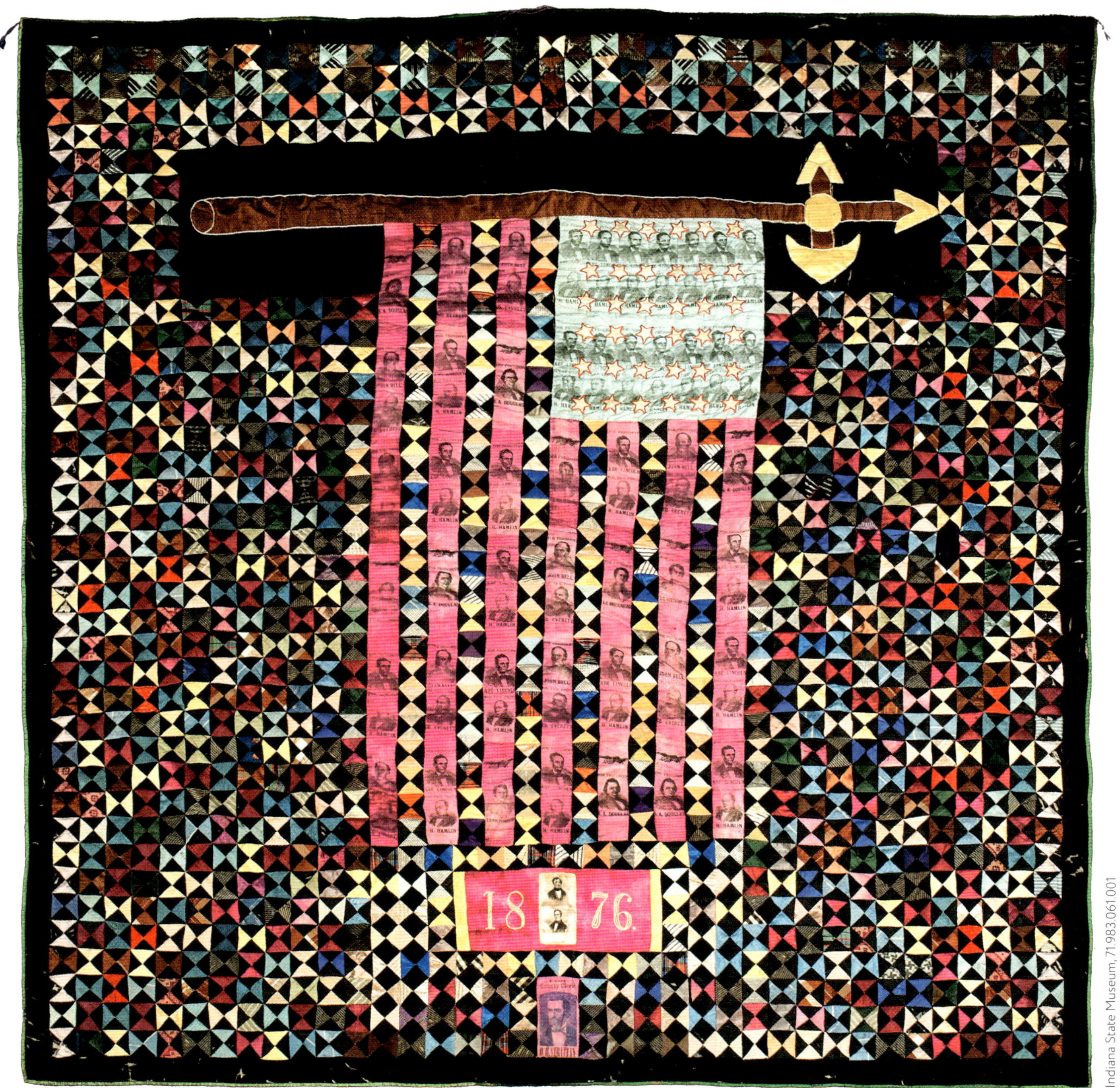

Indiana State Museum, 71.983.061.001

◀ Margaret E. Frentz (New Albany, Indiana), *Lincoln Flag Commemorative Quilt*, 1876, 72 × 68 in.

power, the eventful hundred years of the nation's history. The theme is a grand one, capable of being treated in a thousand different ways and viewed from a thousand different standpoints; and therefore the number of groups which are to be seen in the Exhibition illustrative is, perhaps, larger than of any other subject."[2]

The Centennial's overarching theme emphasized peace, epitomized in an official "Song of the Centennial" by Joaquin Miller, American poet and frontiersman:

Peace on earth and harvest time!
Hail the day but heal the scars!
Heavens blue, yon bannered stars
Blending in the far sublime,
Sing peace on earth and harvest time!

Peal the cannon! clang the bell!
Wave the banners! Bow and pray.
Turn in gratitude to-day
To mighty men who fought and fell—
To Him who doeth all things well.

Peace on earth and harvest time!
The farmer sings: the battle-field
Bears on her breast a gleaming shield
Of corn that clangs in rippled rhyme—
Lo! peace on earth and harvest time![3]

Disturbingly, especially for today's readers, the song was to be sung during the festivities by a minstrel performer.

While the makers' names and places of production for many of the extant Centennial quilts remain unknown, it is not surprising that most of those quilts whose makers or locations are identified resided in the Northeast and Midwest, not the Confederate states, where the word "Union" could evoke hostility and resistance against federal military supervision, which continued well past 1877, when the troops were recalled. In the western part of the country, US Centennial quilts evidently were rare. Except for California (1850), Oregon (1859), Nevada (1864), and Colorado (1876, the Centennial State), none of the other western states were part of the Union until after 1888.

Southerners, however, did not lack in patriotism for their own cause, including quilts auctioned in fundraising efforts and especially quilts made for soldiers. Leaders

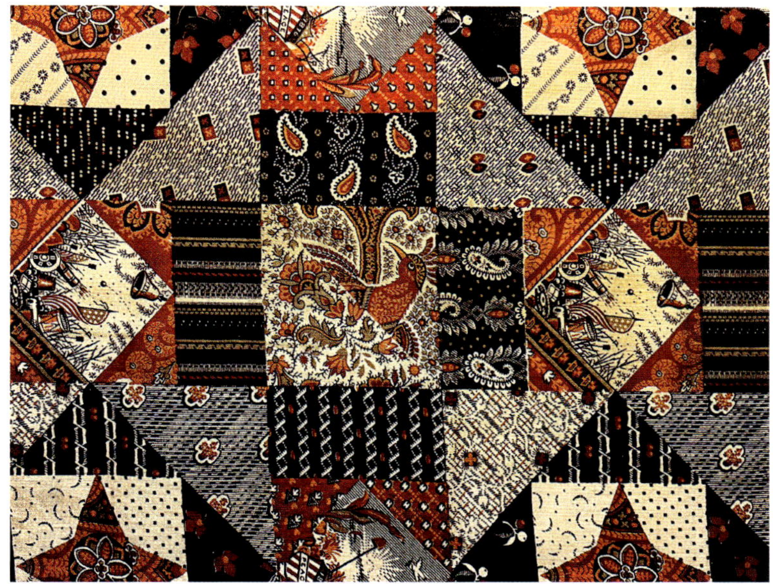
Collection of Pamela Weeks

Centennial fabric depicting Liberty Bell and other symbols, ca. 1876.

Collection of Pamela Weeks

Centennial fabric depicting dates of 1776–1876

of the Confederacy were celebrated in quilts made in the South. As Beebe informs us, "The women of the Confederacy used needle and thread to vote support for their President. The Museum of the Confederacy in Richmond, Virginia, is home to the *Davis Stars* quilt. . . . Completed circa 1864, the *Davis Stars* quilt is attributed to various women, including Varina Howell Davis, wife of the Confederate President, Jefferson Davis. *Davis Stars* is a fine art quilt of silk and wool featuring piecework, embroidery, and quilting in a tumbling block and stars pattern. The *Davis Stars* quilt depicts numerous motifs of the Confederacy."[4] As the US slowly moved toward its Centennial year, a new emphasis on national unity prompted Lucinda Ward Honstain, a quilt maker living in Brooklyn, to celebrate the hoped-for reconciliation of North and South. *The Reconciliation Quilt*, shown below, epitomizes in fabric one woman's 1867 political sentiments. Beebe explains that the quilt's title derives from the block that portrays the release of Jefferson Davis to his daughter, who is holding an American flag.[5]

▸ Possibly Gertrude Knappenberger (Pennsylvania), *Centennial Quilt*, 1876, 82.5 x 74.5 in.

▾ Lucinda Ward Honstain (Brooklyn, New York), *Reconciliation Quilt*, 1867, 97 × 84.5 in.

International Quilt Museum, University of Nebraska–Lincoln, 2001.011.0001

American Folk Art Museum, New York

New England Quilt Museum: Gift of the Binney Family, 1991.25

◀ Mary Haddy, *Centennial Quilt* (Cape Cod, Massachusetts?), 1876, 88 × 86 in. The anchor motifs may suggest involvement with the shipping or fishing industry or symbolize hope and steadfastness, especially as applied to a seafaring family.

PRIDE IN AMERICA AMID INDIGENOUS FIASCO

Western regions were territories during the national push toward western explosion—so-called "Manifest Destiny"—including broad areas labeled as Indian Territory. A map printed in 1876 that was compiled from official records of the General Land Office, Department of the Interior, and other sources depicts territories of more than a dozen Native American nations bordered by Arkansas, Kansas, and what is now West Texas. White settlers, with the support of state and federal governments, assumed that it was their right to seize Indian land. With passage of the Fourteenth Amendment in 1868, the US granted citizenship to those (males) born within its borders. Historical studies largely focus on what citizenship may have meant to Black men, but this change of status also applied to Native Americans, who discovered to their chagrin that "citizenship denotes incorporation into the civic and political body of the United States; it therefore exists in tensions, and sometimes stands in outright opposition, to a bedrock imperative of Indigenous politics: sovereignty."[6] Although the Fifteenth Amendment, in 1870, granted the right to vote regardless of race, color, or previous condition of servitude, in practice that evidently did not apply to Native Americans. In January 1876, the US government ordered all Native Americans to relocate to reservations throughout the West.

Until 1871, the federal government as well as several state governments had been encroaching on Native American lands through numerous treaties. In that year, Congress passed a law forbidding any

Library of Congress Prints and Photographs Division

Stride of the Century, ca. 1876, Currier & Ives, New York, lithographic print on paper. The figure is Brother Jonathan, a precursor of Uncle Sam.

further treaties between tribal representatives and the federal government, instead making unilateral decisions to control the locations of various tribes, often with military force. These wars continued until 1918, the last official battle between an Indian tribe and the US Army. While it was devastating for Native American nations, the US Army protecting the assumed rights of white settlers validated those "rights," with officers who led attacks against tribal forces obtaining recognition in the press as national heroes.

General Custer, for example, repeatedly appeared in regional and national newspapers that documented his (perhaps exaggerated) exploits, such as the harrowing rescue of two white women captured by the Cheyenne.[7] His death at the Battle of the Little Bighorn less than two weeks before the Fourth of July celebrations at the Centennial was mourned across the country as reports were published. "The news of the annihilation of the golden-maned boy general of Civil War fame and about 225 of his men reached Philadelphia on July 6, 1876, and dampened the patriotic enthusiasm of the throngs gathered there."[8] Even though our sympathy today lies with the fallen warriors of that encounter as much as with the soldiers, in 1876, Native Americans were largely viewed as "semi-barbarians" and their subjugation as a cause for celebration. Several paintings in the Centennial art gallery reinforced this stereotypical assumption, within the context of an overwhelming Eurocentric narrative. Custer's defeat galvanized the US military in their assaults against Native Americans, eventually facilitating statehood for Montana, North and South Dakota, and other states. Centennial quilts were created in this national mood of colonialism, with patriotism stoked with pride in America's continental expansion.

UNIFYING AMERICA

In the early 1870s, quilters outside the former Confederacy had other, more-plausible reasons to be proud of their country, such as the 1871 Treaty of Washington negotiated by President Grant and the secretary of state. At the time, this treaty was a cause célèbre demanding that Great Britain pay claims to the US because of the construction of three Confederate warships in Liverpool that had attacked Union shipping in the Indian Ocean as well as in the Atlantic. One of these ships was the infamous *Alabama*, which sank sixty-four ships until it was attacked and sunk in 1864. The arbitration tribunal that convened in Geneva consisted of members appointed by Queen Victoria, the king of Italy, the emperor of Brazil, the president of the Swiss Confederation, and President Grant. The tribunal awarded $15.5 million (more than $387 million today) in damages to the US, a major coup that enhanced the international reputation of Grant as well as of the US.[9]

The Civil War diminished the international standing of the US, especially since it resulted in Great Britain and France supporting the Confederacy in the conflict. But after the war ended, with the first transatlantic cable to the US in 1866 and the first transcontinental railroad in 1869, the US appeared unified and was recognized as an international player. The Centennial Exhibition of 1876 amplified US accomplishments, impressing members of the press and exhibitors from thirty-four

Souvenir bandana, 1876, with President Grant depicted in the upper right corner

Collection of Teresa Barkley

nations and twenty colonies with the innovation and ingenuity of technical innovations. US inventions that were showcased included the telephone, typewriter, sewing machine, and massive Corliss steam engine, which powered the fair's entire array of some two hundred buildings.

As the first world's fair in this country, the event presented the US as a world leader embracing the concept of "liberty," guided by a war-hero president in his second term. Philadelphia's 1876 Exhibition was also a triumph in that its commission and other backers overcame the devastating bank failures of 1873, when the New York stock market crashed and fortunes were lost, partly due to the collapse of the gold market. The economic depression lasted for five years. In the years leading up to 1876, fundraisers sold stock certificates in the name of the Centennial itself. In 1871, Congress had approved a bill establishing the Centennial Commission, with the president appointing a commissioner from each state who would convene in Philadelphia. They had nine meetings between 1872 and 1879, with the vast majority of the Centennial work delegated to committees, including the fundraising. Although Congress had approved the Centennial Exhibition, no federal funds were allocated for expenses of the exhibition or as compensation for the commissioners. Congress did lend $1.5 million for the exhibition, repaid after the event closed.[10]

SPECIAL DAYS AND SPECIAL BUILDINGS AT THE 1876 CENTENNIAL

Success of the exhibition was spurred by exhibitions and products from the District of Columbia and US states, each highlighted in its own building: Arkansas, California, Colorado, Connecticut, Delaware, Illinois, Indiana, Iowa, Kansas (together in the same large building with Colorado), Maryland, Massachusetts, Michigan, Mississippi, Missouri, New Hampshire, New Jersey, New York, Ohio, Pennsylvania, Rhode Island, Vermont, West Virginia, and Wisconsin. Special "state days" were celebrated throughout the run of the exhibition. Governors or other state officials, along with military bands, singers, orators, and Centennial authorities, attended opening ceremonies of the state houses, many of which were grand structures erected with funding appropriated by each state. Even the more modest state buildings had interesting neighbors, such as the Vermont building, located behind the Turkish bazaar, which displayed exotic textiles and even-more-exotic dancers.

State houses featured diverse styles of architecture, including numerous details looking to the past, such as Mississippi's log house. "Massachusetts brought before

▼ Souvenir bandana, 1876, with Liberty depicted in lower right corner

Collection of Teresa Barkley

Massachusetts building, in J. S. Ingram, *The Centennial Exposition, Described and Illustrated,* engraved illustration, facing p. 608

Connecticut building, in J. S. Ingram, *The Centennial Exposition, Described and Illustrated*, engraved illustration, facing p. 608

the world, as her State Building, a specimen of Colonial architecture, quaint-looking, derived partly from the English and partly from the French, and it attracted considerable attention. This was one of the few of the State buildings which adopted as their model the style of houses common to Colonial times. It is one of the largest and best appointed State buildings on the grounds."[11] Old-timey appearances graced other state buildings, notably that of Connecticut, which had "a strong wooden porch, built in the old fashion of a hundred years ago. . . . The wood used within and without was Connecticut pine, which was stained to give the dark look of age."[12] The interior furnishings included an old flax wheel and antique furniture. This is not to say that everyone was enamored of the "good old days." A woman writing for *Godey's Lady's Book* in 1876 described her reaction to an antique spinning wheel she saw displayed in a home: "To me it recalls vividly the old times which were not so very good as they now sound, when the house linen and the personal wear came twisted and untwisted between weary fingers through weeks and months of toil. . . . For the decencies of life, aside from the comforts, continuous and wearisome labor was necessary, and that with almost no mechanical aids."[13]

While most of the state buildings simply publicized their own products, others were lavishly decorated, such as the governor of Massachusetts's reception room, which was "very richly furnished, with paintings on the walls, a handsome Japanese screen and a number of other ornamental objects."[14] Kansas outdid the other states in unique ornamentation with an iconic "Liberty Bell" 6 feet in diameter, suspended from the roof, "made of grain stalks, the crack being represented by dark millet, and the clapper consisting of a long slender gourd for the tongue, and a turnip-shaped pumpkin for the hammer."[15] From California's paintings around its dome's interior of eagles depicted on state flags to Arkansas's extravagant display of red, white, and blue bunting festooned from the roof and radiating in every direction, quilters would have found an abundance of patriotic inspiration in the state buildings. In the Ohio sign-in register, we can see that multitudes of people flocked to the Centennial from all over the state, from major cities and small towns.[16]

Contemporaneous newspapers reported on the crowds of women who visited the Centennial Exhibition, including the special "Women's Day" promoted especially for women. That day in early November happened to be the date when the men were away voting in our national election, forbidden to women, who were not fully recognized as US citizens at the time. Women's Day may have been proclaimed as some sort of attempt at amelioration after a group of famous suffragists disrupted the official Centennial celebration at Independence Hall in Philadelphia on July 4, 1876. Rising from their seats, they distributed several hundred updated copies of the "Declaration of the Rights of Women" from the National Woman Suffrage Association.

They then exited the hall, going outside to a bandstand where Susan B. Anthony read aloud from the "Declaration of the Rights of Women": "And now, at the close of a hundred years, as the hour hand of the great clock that marks the centuries points to 1876, we declare our faith in the principles of self-government; our full equality with man in natural rights; that woman was made

Interior of Kansas state display, in J. S. Ingram, *The Centennial Exposition, Described and Illustrated*, engraved frontispiece

Collection of Sandra Sider

Women's Day on November 7th, Mrs. Gillespie's reception in the Women's Pavilion, engraving printed on paper

Collection of Teresa Barkley

Declaration of Independence souvenir bandana, 1876

first for her own happiness, with the absolute right to herself—to all the opportunities and advantages life affords for her complete development; and we deny that dogma of the centuries, incorporated in the codes of nations—that woman was made for man—her best interests, in all cases, to be sacrificed to his will. We ask of our rulers, at this hour, no special favors, no special privileges, no special legislation. We ask justice, we ask equality. We ask that all the civil and political rights that belong to citizens of the United States, be guaranteed to us and our daughters forever."[17] One of the association's most memorable actions was this disruption of the official Fourth of July ceremony, especially since it was staged immediately after the Declaration of Independence was read during the Centennial celebration—a special day indeed that included other enthusiastic suffragist events covered by the press.[18]

AFRICAN AMERICANS AND THE 1876 CENTENNIAL

It is virtually impossible to determine whether Black quilters made any of the anonymous Centennial quilts (the narrative will be different for the 1976 Bicentennial). From primary sources, we do know that enslaved women and girls worked on quilts throughout the early history of the US, for their owners as well as for use in their own dwellings. House slaves are documented as being employed in quilting, and enslaved seamstresses were especially valued in the marketplace.[19] Because African Americans were treated shabbily or ignored by white organizers of the Centennial event, it seems unlikely that these quilters would have been enthusiastic about celebrating the one hundredth anniversary of the Declaration of Independence. We do have an intriguing mosaic quilt quite possibly created by Elizabeth Keckley, a Black woman who had been Mary Todd Lincoln's dressmaker during the presidency of Abraham Lincoln and had saved luxurious fabric scraps.[20] Dating from the late 1860s or 1870s, the *Mary Todd Lincoln Quilt* features a center square depicting a flag, the word "Liberty," and an eagle stitched in silver thread (now heavily tarnished). "Liberty" could refer to several concepts: the fact that Keckley was a free woman; the Emancipation Proclamation of 1863, ratified in 1865 as the Thirteenth Amendment; and the Centennial celebration.

During the multiyear construction project for the Centennial, we have no extant record of African Americans being employed, in spite of their extremely high unemployment rate in Philadelphia resulting from the economic depression. During the Centennial itself, African Americans evidently were employed only in menial jobs, not even as guards. "Pennsylvania judge William D. Kelly, a long-time champion of civil rights, pleaded with the Centennial Commission to fill this serious gap in the exhibition by inviting Frederick Douglass to read the Emancipation Proclamation after the Declaration of Independence was read on the Fourth of July. Later that same day, he should deliver an address from the platform of Memorial Hall, portraying the contributions of African Americans in the War for Independence and for the preservation of the Union during the Civil War."[21] Nothing came of this suggestion, and Douglass was not permitted to speak during the opening ceremony in May 1876. He even had trouble making his way past the guards to reach the grandstand, even though by that date he was one of the most famous orators in America.

Only a few works of art credited to Black artists were on view at the Centennial Exhibition. Edmonia Lewis's life-sized *Death of Cleopatra*, a remarkable marble statue of an African queen made in Rome and shipped to Philadelphia for the Centennial, was a popular favorite.[22] Members of the press and other writers praised the sculpture for its realism: "The face of the figure was really fine in its naturalness and the gracefulness of the lines."[23] Lewis also may have sculpted the elaborate base for a statue of Richard Allen, first bishop of the African Methodist Episcopal Church (AME), who established his church in Philadelphia in 1794.[24] His portrait bust was commissioned from Alfred White, a Cincinnati artist identified in the press as African American. The unveiling was to have been at the Centennial Exhibition on the Fourth of July, but the work was delayed while the sculptor waited for marble to arrive. The AME Church eagerly waited the sculpture's delivery for several weeks, only to learn that a railway accident had destroyed the pedestal, leaving only the bust intact. A new pedestal was hurriedly constructed, with the unveiling in Fairmount Park just a few days before the Centennial event closed. Nevertheless, several hundred African Americans attended the ceremony honoring the first monument erected by their community to honor one of their own. "The monument to Allen was the most highly publicized Black presence at the Centennial Exposition and kept before the public the idea of the essential American-ness of the nation's Black population."[25]

★

Several hundred African Americans attended the ceremony honoring the first monument erected by their community to honor one of their own.

★

A life-sized statue of *The Freed Slave* holding aloft a copy of the Emancipation Proclamation was by a European artist, Francesco Pezzicar. His life-sized statue of a scantily clad Black man on view in Memorial Hall was not treated favorably by members of the press. Fernando Miranda's wood engraving illustrating the statue was published in *Leslie's Illustrated Historical Register* documenting the 1876 Centennial. Interestingly, the engraving depicts a dozen well-dressed Black visitors clustered around *The Freed Slave*—if we can construe this as visual evidence.[26] The Centennial Exhibition was a memorable event conceived by and for white people, with Black contributions to American ingenuity largely bypassed, such as inventions by Henry Blair, Solomon Brown, Henry Boyd, and Lewis Latimer, who worked with both Alexander Graham Bell and Thomas Edison.

African Americans, especially in the South, suffered the violence of extreme racism during Reconstruction. Disputed statewide elections fomented by racial injustice, such as in Louisiana during 1870, foreshadowed the hotly contested presidential election of 1876. For quilters who traveled from all over the US to be excited and inspired by patriotic

I ORDER AND DECLARE THAT
BE FREE
UPON THIS ACT
A LINCOLN
1 JANUARY 1863
163

◀ Fernando Miranda's engraving of Francesco Pezzicar's sculpture *The Freed Slave, in Frank Leslie's Illustrated Historical Register*, 1877, engraved illustration, p. 133

fervor, the American political scene at that time was discouraging. The Fifteenth Amendment (1870), which enfranchised Black men, resulted in several hundred winning state and national seats. The Black vote also helped elect Grant to a second term as president in 1872. But that year also witnessed the Amnesty Act, through which Congress gave many thousands of former Confederate officials and soldiers the right to vote and hold office. Former rebels, including many slave owners, gradually began to replace African Americans in federal, state, and local offices during the Reconstruction period, which allegedly was supposed to help protect and support freed slaves. Between 1872 and 1876, several massacres of African Americans in the South by former Confederates overturned the goals of Reconstruction, especially with the Ku Klux Klan doing its worst. One of the results was Jim Crow law in this country for nearly a century. This was the US in which quilters were creating their Centennial quilts, perhaps oblivious to the sociopolitical reality, but perhaps in hopes of America living up to its promise.

AMERICAN TEXTILES AND THE TEXTILE INDUSTRY

At the beginning of the nineteenth century, the United States was very much an agricultural society. As Ferrero, Hedges, and Silver remind us, "Vast numbers of women [along with men in some tasks] performed the age-old, pre-industrial tasks associated with textiles. They planted and grew flax and cotton, spun thread, wove cloth, and sewed the garments, household linens, and bed quilts that were either necessary for the survival or desirable for the comfort of a family."[27] Children, mostly girls, were taught to sew at home, and this meant sewing by hand until the availability of the sewing machine in the 1850s. When girls began attending female academies in the 1820s and 1830s, sewing was part of the curriculum, especially quilt making and decorative embroidery. While some young women chafed against the discipline, many of them documented their pride in creating quilts and other stitched items.[28] These processes began to involve home ("family") sewing machines more than a decade before the Centennial.

The Singer Manufacturing Company, which won awards at the 1876 Exhibition, dominated the national and international markets during the following decade. Their print ads sang the company's praises, boasting that Singer sold approximately 230,000 more machines in 1878 than in 1870, with 1878 being a banner year for sales as Singer captured the world market share. Even if many of those sold were industrial

Singer building at the Centennial, in *Frank Leslie's Illustrated Historical Register*, 1877, engraved illustration, p. 102

machines, we still might assume that many of them were sewing machines for home use. With the advent of the sewing machine, the thread industry was challenged with inventing a strong, smooth thread that would easily pass through the needle. With machine sewing requiring twice as much thread as hand sewing—such as the machine running stitch used to piece quilts—and even more thread in most decorative machine stitching, thread-spinning factories had a financial incentive to produce appropriate thread.[29] Available threads presented numerous problems for machine sewing. They were too thin and weak, too thick, too wiry, or simply too expensive for most people. Better cotton thread solved the problem, specifically a six-cord thread consisting of three two-ply strands, which we see advertised on trade cards throughout the last quarter of the nineteenth century.

Exhibitions and demonstrations at the Centennial showcased sewing machines, one of the largest being Wheeler & Wilson's installation, an extensive display of their old and new family machines, some in operation by steam, others by foot, together with an elaborate and tasteful assortment of needlework. Ingram described the models: "The wood-work was exceedingly rich. Six full cabinets in Gothic, Queen Anne and Chinese styles of native black walnut, oak, ash, holly, maple, satin-red wood, etc., rivaled in taste any display in the Exhibition."[30] Along with improved thread, the sewing-machine industry could boast an improved, award-winning needle invented by a woman, Mrs. A. G. Suplee of San Francisco, on display in the Women's Pavilion. Her invention was an open-eye, easy-threading needle."[31]

As an article in *Textile History* documents, "By 1870 the Philadelphia textile manufacturers, including those of Germantown (at the northwestern edge of the city), were enlarging their firms, creating more extensive marketing and production systems, adding partners, generating new lines of goods, building new mills or additions, and opening sales offices in other cities. Handloom operators began to buy the buildings they had been leasing, to add looms and experiment with more complex and valuable products."[32]

▸ Singer sewing machine advertisement, ca. 1878, printed broadside

Coats cotton spool threads, in Frank Leslie's *Illustrated Historical Register*, 1877, engraved illustration, p. 307

Wheeler & Wilson sewing machines, in J. S. Ingram, *The Centennial Exposition, Described and Illustrated*, engraved illustration, facing p. 158

Some Very Hard Nuts to Crack.

☞ 1

Companies have sprung up in every part of the Union for making an "Imitation Singer Machine."

Why are not similar companies formed for making Imitations of other Sewing Machines?

The public will draw its own inference. *Gold is continually counterfeited; brass and tin never!*

2

The Singer has taken the FIRST Prize over ALL competitors more than TWO HUNDRED TIMES. ***Why?***

☞ 3

After the Chicago Fire the Relief Committee undertook to furnish sewing machines to the needy women of that city. Applicants were permitted to choose from six different kinds of machines. 2,944 applicants were furnished with machines; 2,427 chose Singer Machines, and 517 distributed their choice among the five other kinds of machines! These girls were to EARN THEIR LIVING on these machines. ***Why did they take Singers?***

☞ 4

THE PEOPLE'S AWARD TO THE "SINGER."

The people bought Singer Machines as follows:

1870 . . . . . . **127,833** Singer Machines.
1878 . . . . **356,432** " "

Many of the manufacturers of other Machines refuse to state their sales! WHY?

73,620 More Singers sold in 1878 than in Any Previous Year.

Three-Quarters of all the Sewing Machines sola throughout the world in 1878 *were "Singers."*

THE SINGER MANUFACTURING CO.,

52 Orange Street,

NEW HAVEN, CONN.

Collection of Sandra Sider

These chiefly consisted of knit goods—especially hosiery—along with the spinning of wool and silk, and some cotton textiles. Ten years later: "It is well known that Philadelphia is the greatest manufacturing city of the world. . . . The census now being taken will show that the value of the products for the present year from the various manufactories of our city will reach the grand total of $600,000,000. To this the textile manufacturers will contribute: in woolens and cottons of the general table, $48,500,000; . . . in silks and mixed goods $7,000,000."[33] Added to this production were carpets, hosiery, knit goods, and worsted yarn, making the grand total for textiles higher than for any other category of manufacturing in the city. No wonder that the textile industry commanded an abundance of exhibition space at the Philadelphia Centennial. Quilters could see fabrics in new colors, motifs, and textures, with wholesalers placing orders for yardage at numerous booths. This world's fair also functioned as a trade fair.

Cotton textiles printed with patchwork designs ("cheater cloth" in quilters' lingo) became popular following the Centennial, and not only in the US. In her research on patchwork prints, Deborah Kraak found that "the hundredth anniversary of the United States' declaration of independence from England made 1876 a watershed year in the history of American decorative arts, due to the impact of certain displays at the Centennial Exposition, held in Philadelphia. . . . The Centennial Exposition celebrated America's colonial history. Displays of artifacts from the Revolutionary War era included the very popular re[-]creation of a colonial kitchen as conceived by the 1870s.

Courtesy of the Free Library of Philadelphia, Print and Picture Collection

Centennial booth of William Simpson Sons

The accompanying nostalgia for objects that reflected America's idealized, rural, and hand-crafted past—the so-called 'Colonial Revival'—may have played a role in the sudden late-nineteenth[-]century burst of production of American printed cloth that imitated handmade patchwork."[34]

The rustic New England log house with

Courtesy of the Free Library of Philadelphia, Print and Picture Collection

Centennial booth of Pacific Mills

Rustic house interior, in *Frank Leslie's Illustrated Historical Register*, 1877, engraved illustration, p. 90

its colonial kitchen consisted of two rooms. The bedroom featured a quilt on the bed. Ingram reported, "There was an old-fashioned kitchen, too, where a boiled dinner, beans, brown bread and old-fashioned puddings were prepared and served up for company in old-fashioned style every day from 12 p.m. to 3 p.m. About twenty ladies, dressed in the costume of a hundred years ago, did the honors of this establishment."[35] The quilt seems to have been a simple one-patch in a checkerboard pattern, as far as we can tell by a section of the quilt draped over the edge of the bed, as illustrated in an engraving.

Even though woven coverlets far outnumbered patchwork quilts prior to the 1780s in colonial America, the making of quilts and quilted clothing was included in colonial revival projects. When we consider this colonial movement over the course of several decades, it is obvious that images of handmade textiles were imbued with the colonial past.[36] This country's history fed into the patriotic excitement of 1876.

CENTENNIAL QUILTS

Several companies, notably the Cocheco Manufacturing Company of Dover, New Hampshire, produced patchwork-printed textiles and patriotic commercial motifs for the Centennial. The Smithsonian Institution owns a bed-sized quilt consisting of thirty squares and twelve half squares, sashed together with white stars on a blue

SUPPLEMENT, JULY 15, 1876.] HARPER'S WEEKLY. 58

Library of Congress Prints and Photographs Division

Colonial artifacts and activities in the New England log house at the Centennial, *Harper's Weekly*, July 15, 1876, engraving, p. 585

background (T10090). John Bradbury, a dry-goods merchant in New York City, received the fabrics as samples. His wife, Emily; her mother, Maria Silsby Robertson; and their daughter Harriet created the quilt in Charleston, New Hampshire, in 1876. Harriet donated their Centennial quilt to the museum in 1948.[37] According to the Smithsonian's website, "The center of the back of the quilt contains a cotton kerchief that contains the text of the Declaration of Independence surrounded by the Liberty Bell and the seals of thirteen colonies linked by the names of the patriots of the Revolutionary cause."

Patriotic imagery on cloth, mentioned at the beginning of this chapter, extended beyond cotton yardage. The United States exhibits in Machinery Hall included jacquard looms being operated by the Phoenix Silk Manufacturing Company of Paterson, New Jersey. One of the larger looms produced Centennial bookmarks depicting Presidents Washington, Lincoln, and Grant, among other luminaries. Ingram described their popularity: "The weaving was exquisite, and it was no matter of surprise that they could not produce them fast enough to meet the demands of the hungry visitors to the Centennial, all of whom wanted to take home something made in the Exhibition."[38] In addition to all types of bookmarks collected by attendees for their scrapbooks, fabric bookmarks were saved by quilt makers, who stitched them into crazy quilts during subsequent decades. Other textile souvenirs included woven images of the Centennial buildings in rectangular format, with warp ends of the silk threads as fringe. One of the local Philadelphia silk mills specializing in woven ribbons, Werner Itschner & Company, was perfectly situated to provide souvenir textiles. Centennial imagery also appeared as lithographs printed on fabric.

While curators and dealers rarely identify crazy quilts containing 1876 souvenirs as "Centennial" quilts, especially for those completed during the later nineteenth and early twentieth centuries, it obviously was important for the makers to commemorate the significance of the Centennial, and the significance of the fact that they—or perhaps an elderly or deceased relative—had been present at the 1876 Exhibition. It was a watershed event in American history. How should we define a "Centennial" quilt pertaining to the 1876 event? Evidently the textile industry was offering patriotic quilts at this time, such as the white "Marseilles" quilt bordered in red and blue, advertised by Montgomery Ward in its 1875 catalog (#279, for $3.00).

Here we are focusing on quilts made personally, by an individual, family, or community. We have examples of quilts featuring only the word "Centennial" made around the time of the late 1870s and early 1880s, which curators and collectors assume to be commemorating the one hundredth anniversary of the

The fabric bookmarks collected by attendees were saved by quilt makers, who stitched them into crazy quilts during subsequent decades.

Declaration of Independence, and that seems reasonable, so close to the 1876 date. But what about an undated quilt stitched with only "Centennial" from the late 1880s or early 1890s? It could be celebrating the centennial of the US Constitution, adopted in 1788, the centennial of the US presidency in 1889, the Cotton Centennial in 1884, and possibly other events discussed later.

Another category of quilt that may have been associated with the 1876 Centennial is pieced quilts whose designs emulate or reference woven colonial coverlets in red and white, blue and white, or red, white, and blue (the obvious patriotic combination). We can also welcome as Centennial quilts the works consisting wholly or mostly of Centennial yardage ("centennial calico" as advertised in newspapers), even those completed years after the event. Some of the most visually exciting Centennial quilts incorporate the souvenir bandanas and handkerchiefs, several of which were offered in more than one colorway. Judging by the evidence in quilts, these textile souvenirs were printed as yardage and then cut apart.[39] As a recent study of such bandanas has shown, "As a communication medium known early in its history as a 'little banner,' the bandana became an informal and economical means of promoting what might capture the public's attention. Living in a technological environment where mass production is taken for granted, we can only imagine a quasi-industrial society's fascination for a hand-loomed square of fabric printed with an illustration—something to value and to save."[40] Or something to feature in a commemorative quilt.

Souvenir textiles had several variations of the American eagle, some carrying the *"E pluribus unum"* motto of the US ("one from many"), along with stars, the Liberty Bell, the US flag, many flags of other countries exhibiting in Philadelphia, and especially bandanas with a large US flag front and center, bordered by numerous small flags of other nations. That particular bandana was cut up in various ways to be sewn into quilts. The text of the Declaration of Independence bordered with names of Revolutionary War heroes was printed on a bandana (see page 27), with other bandanas depicting buildings at the exhibition, individually or in a group.

Memorial Hall, housing the art gallery, had its own bandana showing attendees arriving on foot and via horseback, carriage, coach, and the Fairmount Park horse-drawn trolley. Another bandana titled "International Exhibition 1876" featured the Art Gallery near the top, the Horticultural Building below, and the monumental Main Building in the center, each building in its own cartouche. A rondel in each corner had portraits of Washington and Grant and allegorical imagery. One of the allegories presented a female figure placing laurel

▶ Blanche Wiggin Staples Robinson (Lowell, Massachusetts), *Lowell Crazy Quilt*, 1893–1904, 72 × 60 in. The center medallion is a printed silk bandana from the 1893 Chicago World's Fair (see chapter 4).

New England Quilt Museum: Gift of Judith D. Hall, 1989.02

Ribbon depicting 1876 Women's Pavilion, detail in *Lowell Crazy Quilt*, woven silk

New England Quilt Museum: Gift of Judith D. Hall, 1989.02

wreaths on the heads of two female figures, probably symbolizing Industry and Art. Judging by the similarity of this tableau to that at the top of the Centennial stock certificate, we can assume that the central figure probably was meant to be Liberty (see page 24).

Other portraits also appeared on souvenir bandanas, with George and Martha Washington depicted in at least two different styles of bandanas designed from two different portraits. In both examples, the portraits obviously were meant to be a matching pair, having the same decorations, size, and format. As we shall see in chapter 2, Martha Washington was something of an icon for the Women's Committee. Her head in profile was struck on one of the fund-raising souvenir Centennial medals produced in the Mint Exhibit and the Philadelphia

▼ *Pieced Centennial Flag Print Quilt* verso, ca. 1876–ca. 1893. 90.5 × 96.5 in. This quilt includes souvenir textiles from the 1876 Centennial and the 1893 Chicago World's Fair.

Collection of Shelburne Museum, gift of J. Watson Webb Jr., 1952-571; photography by Andy Duback

Mint, the molds being destroyed soon after the exhibition closed.

If we look at the souvenir bandanas in Centennial quilts, we can summarize various ways in which quilters used these textile objects, which evidently were marketed nationwide. Often we find a single bandana in the center of a pieced quilt, almost as if the bandana could have been added to a completed quilt top. The overall quilt patterns containing one bandana usually are quite simple, such as small pinwheel or tumbler blocks. Other makers positioned their bandanas in the corners or stitched them into the backing of a quilt. Quilters also used uncut bandana yardage for their quilt backing. In a few examples, the bandanas are combined with flag textiles in especially striking arrays.

We find strips of Centennial fabrics pieced

▼ *Pieced Centennial Flag Print Quilt*, ca. 1876–ca. 1893, 90.5 × 98 in.

Collection of Shelburne Museum, gift of J. Watson Webb, Jr. 1952-571; photography by Andy Duback

Centennial Center Medallion Eagle, 1876

Collection of International Quilt Festival, 2010.01

Indigo Trapunto Quilt, ca. 1876, 81.5 × 79.5 in.

Collection of Teresa Barkley

▲ Memorial Hall souvenir bandana, 1876

From *Quilts and Quiltmakers Covering Connecticut* by the Connecticut Quilt Search Project (Atglen, PA: Schiffer, 2001), 109

Laura Electa Seymour (Bristol, Connecticut), Centennial bandanas on verso of pictorial quilt, ca. 1876–1890, 52 × 46.5 in. This quilter attended the 1876 Centennial, signing her name in the Connecticut Building's visitors' book on November 1, 1876.

as sashing in commemorative quilts. Repeated motifs of drums, eagles, shields, musical notation, and flags create emphatic visual rhythm in vertical, horizontal, and diagonal motion. The motifs include actual musical notation for songs such as the "The Star-Spangled Banner" and "Hail, Columbia!"[41] Both songs held patriotic relevance in 1876, since "The Star-Spangled Banner" was not proclaimed as the official US national anthem until the 1930s, and the original music for "Hail, Columbia!" (under a different title) was performed at George Washington's inauguration. "Hail, Columbia!" would have been especially appropriate for a country attempting to unite in peace after the horrors of civil war, even though the theme of the song is victory against the British. Here is the refrain:

Firm, united let us be,
Rallying round our liberty,
As a band of brothers joined,
Peace and safety we shall find.

Centennial quilt makers used appliqué for various purposes, especially to highlight "1876" or "1776–1876," as well as the words "Liberty" and "Independence," and to depict the Liberty Bell. In some instances, quilters meticulously fuzzy-cut the national coats of arms and flags from souvenir bandanas, blanketing the quilt with these colorful images. As we might expect, the American eagle is a pervasive image, sometimes with attention to detail and other times in a charming folk-art silhouette. Stars are ubiquitous, from multitudinous printed stars in background fabric, to pieced stars bordering the surface, to a large medallion star dominating the entire quilt design. In just about any way we might imagine, Americans, mainly women, commemorated their Centennial patriotism by making quilts. When we consider that most of them did not yet enjoy the full rights of American citizenship, their work assumes an aura of admirable civility.

CELEBRATING THE US PRESIDENCY

Centennial of the Presidency in 1889

The American presidency began in 1789 with the inauguration of George Washington at Federal Hall in New York City, the first capital of the US. With foreign dignitaries, members of Congress, military honor guards, and hundreds of spectators attending, the inauguration was a momentous event celebrating the creation of a new country.

★

President Harrison gave a speech near a large wooden statue of Washington, physically linking his presidency to that of the first president.

★

Washington's words of humility in both of his inaugural addresses set a precedent for deferring to the law and supporting the citizenry whom the president represents. In 1889, Benjamin Harrison reiterated the importance of "the people" as witnesses, in a gesture intended to unify Americans.[42] That gesture of unification encompassed four new states that would join the union later that year—Montana, North Dakota, South Dakota, and Washington.

On his journey from Mount Vernon to

New York in 1789, George Washington made special arrangements to enter Philadelphia, as witnessed by a newspaper reporter: "Washington left his carriage and mounted a fine white horse, on which he rode into the city. Triumphal arches spanned the streets, and decorations of evergreens and flags hid the fronts of the houses. The boats on the rivers were bedecked with the gayest colors, and everywhere there were eulogistic and patriotic mottoes."[43] The image of Washington seated on his horse or standing beside it appeared on portraits printed on fabric and sewn into quilts, also embroidered and appliquéd in quilts. Washington's iconic status was emphasized by Harrison at his inauguration and documented by a journalist: "Our people will not fail at this time to recall the incidents which accompanied the institution of the government under the constitution, or to find inspiration and guidance in the teachings and examples of Washington and his great associates."[44] Harrison, known for his support of Native Americans and his vociferous antiracist stance, seemed to embody American idealism, helping to make him a popular figure.

In the spring of 1889, cities across the country staged events to mark the centennial of the presidency, also celebrating the American union. New York outdid itself, constructing a monumental temporary triumphal arch in Washington Square that was later replaced by the permanent monument. Thousands of people attended the three-day-long celebration. President Harrison gave a speech in front of the arch, overlooked by a large wooden statue of Washington, physically linking his presidency to that of the first president. But a shadow was cast over the centennial by the New York State Woman Suffrage Association. Their request for events honoring Martha Washington and other influential first ladies was denied. At their convention in New York, they declared, "As the men of the nation are to meet to celebrate the Washington centennial the women desire to honor the memories of historic women who shared the dangers and hardships of the struggle for American independence, and by their constancy contributed to the success of the Revolution."[45] The speakers included Susan B. Anthony.

Sometime around 1889, a textile company printed yardage of joined bust portraits of Washington and Harrison featuring US flags, eagles, and stars. The fabric was designed so that it could be cut into bandana-sized rectangles, and quilters incorporated these images into various quilt formats, from lap-sized to bed quilts. Although the commemorative fabric as a bandana usually graced the front of a quilt, the yardage was also used for backing, such as in a crazy quilt owned by the Benjamin Harrison Presidential Site. We also have an example of the presidential portraits standing alone in the center of a pieced quilt.[46] Through the medium of fabric, with both portraits of equal size and quality, quilters elevated Harrison to the historic status of Washington during this centennial celebration.

Fundraising Banner Honoring Theodore Roosevelt

To raise money for their church, the Ladies Society of the First Presbyterian Church stitched two similar patriotic banners with appliquéd flags, one around 1890 (also owned by the Smithsonian) and the other during the presidency of Theodore Roosevelt. Such

Collection of International Quilt Festival, N111

Division of Home and Community Life, National Museum of American History, Smithsonian Institution, 1979.1019.02, Gift of Emilie Noakes Manley

Ladies Society of the First Presbyterian Church (New York, New York), *Patriotic Banner*, 1905–1910, 87 × 106 in.

projects suggest that patriotism prompted by the Centennial flowed into the twentieth century. We might assume that the fund-raising success of the first banner encouraged the group to raffle a second banner several years later. Depicted here is the later banner, described by the donor as an autograph quilt. The US flag bears the inked signatures of President Roosevelt and his cabinet members, with embroidery enhancing the signatures. The red-and-white silk rays in the center have the names of each state along with inked signatures of the governors. Judging by metal rings sewn on the top edge, we can assume that the banner was meant to be hung for display.

◀ *Presidents' Medallion Quilt*, ca. 1889, 81 × 80.5 in.

George Washington's Birthday Bicentennial in 1932

Unlike the lackluster interest of the US Congress in the 1876 Centennial, the federal government generously funded the George Washington Bicentennial Commission, charging it with organizing nationwide celebrations for this event. The commission originated in 1924 with a resolution from President Coolidge and was formalized in 1927. Coolidge gave a speech praising George Washington in the House of Representatives that was broadcast via the new medium of radio to millions of listeners here and abroad.

By the time the bicentennial year of 1932 arrived, the entire world had been plunged into the worst depression on record. In this country, even though more than one-quarter of the workforce was unemployed and funding was difficult, the commission managed to succeed in its purpose. Many thousands of celebrations were held across the country, and quilters had access to commemorative fabric featuring images associated with Washington, issued by textile companies for his bicentennial. Several newspapers published patterns for quilts honoring both Martha and George Washington.

"All organizations—religious, civic, social, fraternal—were offered the assistance of the Commission in planning programs for the bicentennial year. . . . Particular stress was laid on the fact that the celebration was to last nearly a year and that the people were not expected to attend any national exposition."[47] With this emphasis, the commission obviously realized that few Americans had discretionary money for traveling to a national event, and that localizing the celebrations created the possibility of stimulating local economies. Patriotic fervor was stirred at the national level by several events, commencing on February 22, the date of Washington's birth. President Hoover gave a speech in Congress, then stood on the Capitol steps in an astonishing event, as reported by a New Jersey newspaper, "for the singing of 'America' by a chorus of ten thousand voices. It is expected that millions of people will join in this 'sing' as it comes over the air."[48] The widespread communication of commemorative events via radio, television, and eventually the internet would enhance their inclusivity while providing a national forum for dissent during the coming century.

Carrie A. Hall (Leavenworth, Kansas), *George Washington Bi-Centennial Quilt*, 1932, 98 × 85 in. Stylized hatchets surrounding the silhouetted portrait refer to the legend of Washington as a boy chopping down a cherry tree and confessing to the deed "I cannot tell a lie."

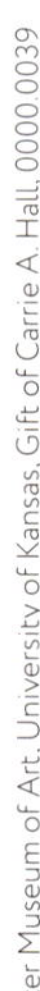

Spencer Museum of Art, University of Kansas, Gift of Carrie A. Hall, 0000.0039

CHAPTER 2

Women at Work

As early as 1875, reports of women planning to participate in the various Centennial celebrations appeared in newspapers and magazines, and textile manufacturers began to market fabrics with Centennial motifs and themes. A female columnist for *Harper's Bazaar* commented, "We do take a warm interest in the Centenary observations, not only because, in our opinion, we have earned the right to do so, but because we hold the anniversary as commemorative of the vast change and improvement in the condition of women within a hundred years."[1] Organizations, events, and publications directed by women would have been of interest to many of the millions of women visiting the 1876 Centennial Exhibition. Let's begin with the Women's Centennial Executive Committee, without which adequate funds would not have been collected for all aspects of the exhibition, including the Women's Pavilion they constructed in Fairmount Park. We will focus here on textile inspirations there and elsewhere in the exhibition, following the footsteps of women visitors. As always throughout this book, my goal is to situate quilt makers and quilts within their cultural contexts.

Collection of Sandra Sider

Women's Executive Committee for the Centennial, 1876, engraving on paper. Mrs. Gillespie is seated, writing at the table. The tired-looking woman with her hand on the mantel is holding her fundraising collection basket. Illustrations on the wall depict the Women's Pavilion as a work in progress.

Elizabeth Duane Gillespie, great-granddaughter of Deborah and Benjamin Franklin and a member of the Philadelphia elite, served tirelessly as president of the Women's Committee. As she wrote toward the end of the nineteenth century in her autobiography, "It seems not unwise to recall the noble part borne by the women of the country between the years of 1872 and 1876. I speak mainly of the women because they received little praise for their stupendous work, though, in the language of the Philadelphia *Ledger* of April 9, 1877, 'There was a time when the greater portion of the interest felt in the Centennial Exhibition outside of Philadelphia was the result of their exertions. The women of this country were their zealous friends while the men were indifferent.'"[2] While not all men were indifferent to planning the Centennial in Philadelphia, many in Congress proved extremely recalcitrant.

Following Gillespie's recommendation in the first meeting of the ward chairwomen, contributors were permitted to share the purchase price, like groups today buying lottery tickets. She wrote, "Not one of those who so largely contribute to the prosperity of our city (we mean the working women) is to be overlooked. Factories are to be visited, and the operatives are to be invited to band together and take shares of stock, so that, if possible, each shall have an interest in the success of the undertaking. . . . We invite you to unite with us in this work, for we are assured that this Exhibition will not only be the means of demonstrating the great advantages that the world reaps from women's work, but will place her work on a higher level. Every subscription that you gather will be but another stone added to the building of the pedestal on which the American woman is destined to stand; and in helping ourselves we shall help the women in other lands, where now it is no uncommon sight to see a woman and a cow harnessed together to a plough and a man driving them."[5] Gillespie's proto-feminist vision extended beyond the US, reaching out to the empress of Brazil to inaugurate the Women's Pavilion. Men had inaugurated all other buildings at the exhibition.

Centennial stock certificate, 1876, in *Frank Leslie's Illustrated Historical Register*, 1877, engraved illustration, p. 30

While needlework of all types abounded in the Women's Pavilion and elsewhere, Gillespie wanted to inspire working women at the Centennial to explore additional avenues of employment. She explained, "We desired to give to the mass of women, who were laboring by the needle and gaining only a scanty subsistence, the opportunity to see what women were capable of attaining unto in other and higher branches of industry; and to do this effectually, we felt that these exhibits must find place in a special space set apart for them alone. We did not shrink from competition with the works of men, but we sought to show our more timid sisters that some women had outstripped them in the race for useful and remunerative employment, and to encourage them to the perseverance sure to be followed by a larger measure of success."[6] Originally, ample space was to have been reserved in several locations, particularly in the Main Building, for work exclusively by women, who were in charge of fundraising for the entire Centennial Exhibition.

One of the first fundraising events in Fairmount Park commemorated another centennial—the famous Boston Tea Party, which took place in December 1773. Gillespie conceived of selling tickets to an actual tea party in Centennial Exhibition buildings that already had been completed, with commemorative teacups sold as souvenirs. Each member of the Women's Committee attending the event honored the memory of Martha Washington by wearing a replica of her cap and neck kerchief. *Godey's Lady's Book* reported that "reverent" viewers flocked to see a quilt created from remnants of Martha Washington's dresses that had been worn at official state receptions. It was prominently displayed above the sales tables.[7] This centennial tea party was so successful

1873 Tea Party ticket, in Gillespie, *Book of Remembrance*, engraved illustration, facing p. 283

that it was repeated in the Capitol Rotunda in 1874 as other fundraising concepts developed from Gillespie visiting several states to organize their Women's Committees. Many of them involved festivities honoring George Washington. Gillespie summarized their accomplishment: "By the close of the year 1874 organizations were formed in nearly all the States then in the Union, and the women were planning and giving entertainments, half the proceeds of which in the States outside of Philadelphia were invested in the 'stock of the Centennial Exhibition.' The other half was retained by the Managers towards the fitting out and care, during the Exhibition, of the portion of the buildings to be set apart for the exhibition of women's work."[8] These women raised $81,050 from the sale of Centennial stock and $3,630 by selling commemorative medals.

Elizabeth Duane Gillespie in "Martha Washington" costume for tea party, December 1873, photo by Gutekunst in her *Book of Remembrance*, facing p. 285

The Centennial funding also benefited from a project suggested by Gillespie, the 1876 *National Cookery Book*, to demonstrate

Women's Pavilion interior, 1876, in *Frank Leslie's Illustrated Historical Register*, engraved illustration, p. 94

Collection of Sandra Sider

Women's Pavilion exterior with sewing-machine advertisement, 1876, engraved illustration

Collection of Sandra Sider

Women's Pavilion interior, 1876, Centennial Photographic Co., Philadelphia, stereoscopic photograph

the unity of American women.[9] The call for submissions for this fascinating book stated, "No receipt [i.e., recipe] will be considered too homely, if characteristic of the country. Dishes peculiar to rich and poor—to hunting, fishing, or exploring expeditions, or to camp-life, etc. are desired. If comical and at the same time good, so much the better. Our aim is to give the true savor of American life in all its varieties."[10] Each dish was required to use items available only in the US, with no "foreign" recipes allowed. Gillespie considered this publication as an expression of American patriotism, unifying the country. A humorous editorial hand can be seen occasionally; for example, in the introduction to cooking turkey: "The turkey is a true son of the soil. *He* has never been asked for his naturalization papers! When Columbus launched his three caravels, he was an old inhabitant, and strutted and gobbled his unmolested way along the whole Atlantic seaboard."[11] This book surely must be the first nationwide cookbook of the US, with entries including Kansas Cocoanut Pound Cake, Idaho Miners' Bread, Virginia Brunswick Stew, Michigan Brook Trout, and Native American Oneida Boiled Mud Turtle—a culinary crazy quilt.

THE WOMEN'S PAVILION

In June 1875, less than a year before the exhibition was to open, Gillespie received a shattering letter from the director-general of the exhibition, explaining that the enthusiasm from so many foreign countries about exhibiting in the Main Building would leave no space for women's work. He wrote, "In view of this fact, and recognizing the noble and efficient work the women of this country have already accomplished in behalf of the Centennial Celebration, we feel encouraged to make the suggestion that it would be a most worthy and attractive feature of the Exhibition if they could secure a sufficient sum for the construction of a separate building in the Park, which, with the articles they might contribute of their handiwork, would most fittingly represent the position, energy, and accomplishments of the women of America."[12]

We can never know whether he expected (or wanted) the Women's Committee to succeed. The task seemed daunting. Gillespie quickly overcame her initial disappointment and anger, rising to the challenge and networking nationally. She also claimed the portion of funding previously collected for the women's display areas in the Main Building. The various committees raised $45,419 of additional funds in time to have the Women's Pavilion designed, constructed, and filled with work by women before May 1876. In addition, they raised the money for the music played at the opening and closing ceremonies, for publishing a weekly newspaper, and for erecting a schoolhouse next to the Pavilion, where experimental kindergarten classes were conducted.

The building was described at the time as "a noble monument of the energy and patriotism of the women of America. . . . The pavilion is located on Belmont Avenue, near the Horticultural grounds, and covers an area of 30,000 square feet. The whole structure is built of wood, in a modern and ornate style of architecture."[13] In the January 1876 issue of *Godey's Lady's Book*, the frontispiece featured the Women's Pavilion exterior in a full-page engraving, with an editorial note that assuredly encouraged visitors to visit the Pavilion: "This is certainly one of the finest buildings of its size that has been erected out there [in Fairmount Park], and reflects great credit on the taste of the ladies having it in charge" (p. 95). Published in Philadelphia, *Godey's* had easy access for press coverage of the exhibition.

Visitors to the Pavilion could find women at work on several tasks, as described by Gillespie: "Having space enough, we decided to have looms in one corner for ribbons and silks, and women weavers in charge of them. . . . The fertile brain of a woman writer, Mrs. S. C. F. Hallowell, suggested the propriety of having a newspaper edited and printed within our walls. This plan was adopted and was most successful, it proved. It was published weekly; its name was the *New Century for Women*."[14] This newspaper included reviews and descriptions of Centennial displays, including a regular column on "The House We Live In," covering details of the Women's Pavilion. We know that bed quilts were on view, for example, from Brabant (now part of the Netherlands or Belgium) and Brazil, but we have very few mentions of quilts displayed in that venue.

The Pavilion displayed sculpture, painting, literature, engraving, lithography, and inventions, as well as needlework.[15] Commentators such as Frank Leslie admired the textiles while emphasizing that the purpose of the Women's Pavilion was, in essence, to suggest wider avenues of female employment and profit outside the home. Items such as quilts definitely were kept in the domestic sphere, as Leslie testified: "A home piece of embroidery is a quilt sent by a lady from Alabama. It is white and rose-colored satin. On the white ground are embroidered 1,500 roses and rosebuds, in each of which there are 500 to 900 stitches. Seven thousand

▸ *Philadelphia Centennial Exhibition Quilt*, 1876–1900, 87 × 88 in.

Art Institute of Chicago, 1977.187

skeins of silk were used in this work, and a lady was engaged upon it eighteen months."[16]

Some of the more popular textiles in the Pavilion had elements of glamour and exoticism, such as the pieces sent from the British royal family and from Brazil, as described by Leslie: "The Royal School of Needlework of England has made many contributions, including work done by members of the Royal family. A satin skirt, closely embroidered, from a design by the Princess Louise . . . is the property of Queen Victoria. . . . The display of lace and embroidery is large and very valuable. The ladies of Brazil have contributed extensively in this direction. Some lacework and certain embroidered cushions will well repay careful observation."[17] While other buildings also showcased needlework, such as embroidery in gold and silver from Egypt and Turkey decorating jackets, hats, slippers, tablecloths, and more, the massive amount of textile handwork in the Women's Pavilion equaled anything else that quilters might have seen.

Beyond the Pavilion, quilt makers could peruse the latest in commercial fabrics in several locations. The exhibition catalog listed fabrics in the William Simpson & Sons factory in Philadelphia: "Calico prints in mourning, fancy, and shirting styles . . . solid blacks, Berlin solids of all colors, aniline blacks, mourning prints, silver grays, Eddystone chocolates, hair cloth chevlots, and fancy prints. These styles are all fast colors, and are printed on the best extra 64 square cloth."[18] Pacific Mills in Lawrence, Massachusetts, displayed "poplins, alpacas, serges, cashmeres, reps, jacquards, cretonnes, jaconets, and crépe."[19] Many of these fabrics could be used in quilt making. Rep, also called rip fabric, is finely woven with tiny ribs across the width, usually of silk, cotton, or wool; cretonnes are fairly heavy, used mostly for upholstery; jaconet is lightweight cotton, like lawn or cambric, with a smooth hand.

CHARM QUILTS AND MULTITUDINOUS QUILTS

According to quilt historian Sue Reich, "The rage for making charm quilts and quilts with thousands of pieces began shortly before our country's Centennial celebration."[20] Charm quilts usually contain no duplicate scraps of fabric, with friends and family members often exchanging scraps as they participate in the challenge of not duplicating fabrics. In the past, quilters also used mill scraps and remnants sold in batches by merchants. During the years immediately leading up to the 1876 Centennial Exhibition, mills in the northeastern US offered fabrics featuring the centennial themes mentioned above, along with their usual woven and printed cottons. The Centennial may have fueled charm quilt popularity. Fabric mills produced a number of dated commemorative Centennial prints for the fair. A quilter named Hannah Kendall used commemorative prints for 1876 in a signature quilt she exhibited at the exposition.[21] With the Centennial events having been held in Philadelphia, it's no surprise that "a good number of Pennsylvania charm quilts often feature Centennial prints highlighting the years 1776 and 1876 with the eagle, stars, cannon, flags, Liberty Bell, and Liberty cap in the design."[22]

Charm quilts fall within the category of what Reich has dubbed "multitudinous" quilts, which have several hundreds, and often thousands, of small pieces. While working on the documentation index for

Connecticut quilts in 2000, she discovered evidence in an 1882 issue of the *Willimantic Chronicle* that quilters openly competed to outdo each other in the number of fabric pieces stitched into a quilt.[23] Because the pieces were necessarily quite small, quilters also took pride when they were able to complete such projects without the aid of eyeglasses, an impressive accomplishment for older makers. The competitive spirit of prize entrants in the 1876 World's Fair was preceded and perhaps influenced by the atmosphere of New England state fairs in the previous two decades, as studied by Linda Borish: "Organizers of the fair wanted women to be a visible part of the event, whether with their families or with a co-ed group. These men wanted women to be both spectators and competitors. Fair boosters wanted the fair sex to become a top attraction at fairs in the mid-nineteenth century. . . . Reformers and profit-oriented fair managers appealed to women to contribute to the health of the fairs by competing in exhibitions. Agricultural fairs highlighted female competition, a pivotal part of the fair-going leisure experience. Rural improvers wanted women to compete for prizes at the agricultural fair through the display of domestic skills in public. These competitions integrated work and leisure, yet extended farm women's proficiency in the domestic sphere to the public sphere, where they could gain social prestige and recognition."[24] With newspapers reporting the names of women winning first prizes, they were indeed entering the public sphere.

★

During the years immediately leading up to the 1876 Centennial Exhibition, mills in the northeastern US produced fabrics featuring the centennial themes.

1876 INTERNATIONAL TEMPERANCE CONFERENCE

The oldest continuous women's organization in this country is the Women's Christian Temperance Union (WCTU), officially founded in Ohio in 1874 as an outgrowth of the Women's Temperance Crusade. Earlier in the century, various localized groups had railed against the excessive consumption of alcohol and its potentially damaging effects on society. The WCTU preached the extreme position of total abstinence, praying and singing in front of saloons, marching in temperance parades, lobbying local government officials, and asking people, especially men, to sign abstinence pledges. Between 1874 and 1876, the WCTU proselytized in numerous states, creating local and regional groups. Statewide conferences began to be held, loosely affiliated with the national office. The WCTU became so powerfully persuasive, even before women could vote on such matters, that Congress passed the Eighteenth Amendment in 1918, prohibiting any manufacturing, sale, or transportation of liquor in the US as well as its territories. Debates and lobbying about this amendment contributed to the two-year delay in Congress of passing the Nineteenth Amendment, supporting women's suffrage.

In June 1876, the first International

Temperance Conference convened in Philadelphia, as documented in a nine-hundred-page book: "A happy occasion gave birth to this volume. The celebration of the first centenary of American Independence by an International Exhibition of arts and industries brought together many intelligent representatives from many countries. Among these were men and women from every land in which the Temperance Reform has an organized existence. A Conference of these friends of the Reform was held in Philadelphia which lasted through four busy days. At that large and influential Conference the papers which compose this volume were prepared or presented."[25] Although Frances E. Willard presented at the conference as an officer of the WCTU, she was not permitted to mention political issues, such as women's suffrage.

In October 1876, Willard spoke at the International Temperance Convention of Women held in Newark, New Jersey, fully voicing her women's agenda. At this conference, while the Centennial events in Philadelphia continued to underscore American unity, the WCTU motto "For God and Home and Native Land" was first endorsed nationally. Previously the motto had been endorsed by the Chicago WCTU and the WCTU of the State of Illinois.[26] In that same year, Ohio WCTU members led by their president, Mrs. H. C. McCabe, created an album quilt known as the *Crusade Mystery Quilt* to raise money for the organization. She invited the original crusaders to contribute blocks, with their autographs and slogans as desired, resulting in thirty or forty names inscribed in many of the seventy-six 9-inch-square blocks. The piece

WCTU textile banners, in Willard, *Glimpses of Fifty Years*, color lithograph, between pp. 456 and 457

is multilayered: the decorative side with cotton batting and backing, then another layer of batting between the backing and the neutral-colored signature blocks, making the quilt sturdy and double sided. With tabs for hanging sewn along the top, this work obviously was not meant as a bed quilt, but rather as a banner to rally spectators.[27] Several of the solid-colored blocks on the decorative side are embroidered or appliquéd with patriotic motifs. Both patriotism and religion are important themes in this quilt. The initial fundraising efforts brought in approximately $400 (more than $11,000 today). The quilt's center contained a secret message for women of the future, to be opened and read in the bicentennial year of 1976.[28]

Its purpose has been analyzed as twofold: "The *Crusade Quilt* was a means to circumvent a political system that disavowed a woman's right or ability to speak or function in the public sphere; the quilt—traditionally a symbol of the private world of home and family—served as a forum for women to voice their concerns publicly about the problems related to excessive alcohol consumption. In addition, this quilt served as a vehicle of persuasion, promoting strength and perseverance in the temperance cause."[29] The *Crusade Mystery Quilt* was displayed at several WCTU meetings and was also on view in the Women's Pavilion at the Centennial Exhibition.[30] In her autobiography, Willard mentioned seeing the quilt hanging at the national WCTU convention in Baltimore: "It was a beautiful evidence of woman's skill and taste in needle handicraft, and as it hung in graceful folds from the gallery, was a banner of which no body of men or women need have been ashamed."[31] Political protest couched in the vocabulary of domesticity softened the message while simultaneously driving it home.

The 1876 quilt's center contained a secret message for women of the future, to be opened and read in the bicentennial year of 1976.

After Frances E. Willard was elected WCTU president in 1879, she insisted that the call for women's suffrage be included in the social reform platform. At the time, she used the argument that women should be able to vote against the manufacture and consumption of alcohol, to promote a safe home environment for mothers and children. Moral virtues of home and mother love powered the WCTU movement. Her ancillary purpose was to claim universal women's rights, including equal pay for equal work. Under Willard's guidance and motto of "Do Everything," issues such as prostitution, working conditions (especially for textile workers), public health, and world peace made their way into the WCTU's agenda. The larger WCTU gatherings featured decorative fringed "battle flags"—decorated banners, and occasionally quilts, flanking and behind the podium along with the US flag. As county and state fairs became popular across the country during the later nineteenth century, booths run by local chapters of the WCTU spread the message, with quilts used as fundraisers, especially signature quilts. Quilts celebrated the passage of state prohibition amendments, with the blue-and-white color combination in patterns such as *Drunkard's Path* expressing sympathy with the temperance movement.[32]

Tenets of the WCTU closely aligned with nineteenth-century aspects of the colonial revival movement, notably the entrenched domesticity of women as reenacted during various events and popularized in magazine imagery.[33] In this early stage of colonial revivalism, embracing heritage was part of the appeal of needlework projects—returning to the "good old days" of the so-called simple life and perceived gentility of America's founding generation.

QUILTS IN NEWSPAPERS

Between 1876 and 1886, the word "quilt" appeared more than 400,000 times in newspapers published in the US and its territories (according to Newspapers.com). Even though many of these hits probably do not relate to actual textiles, such as "a patchwork quilt of farmland," many of them assuredly do. The hits can be divided among mentions of a quilted garment, quilter(s), quilt(ing), and quilt(s). The frequency of hits ranges from nearly 28,000 for Pennsylvania and more than 23,000 for Kansas to 134 for Rhode Island.

Many of the hits from newspapers published in the same location refer to the same quilt or article on quilts. Also, the hits include mentions of quilts and quilting in fiction published by the newspapers, quilts listed in advertisements, and "knitted quilts" that we would describe as blankets or coverlets. Even after we disallow the distribution of hits as reflective of actual quilt production, a look at what makers had available for reading about quilts on a regular basis in the decade following the 1876 Centennial should provide some insights into quilt culture of the time. For geographic diversity, let's look at newspapers published in California, Montana, Louisiana, Kansas, Missouri, Texas, Tennessee, Pennsylvania, and New York.

As in several other states by the 1880s, California was holding state fairs, largely for agricultural expositions, but with social and cultural aspects such as pie-baking contests and showcases of domestic textiles. (Fairs in the US had no entertainment midway as such until the 1890s.) The 1883 fair in Sacramento exhibited an array of quilts, the majority made of silk, with several described as patchwork or pieced, plus a "crazy quilt, which is justly entitled to its name."[34] In 1886, the Santa Barbara County Fair exhibited quilts in a category titled "Women's Work," listed separately from the "Fine Arts" category for that event in the newspaper. Almost all the works were fiber or textiles, including a 116-year-old quilt, plus "Bertha M Wright, a little woman of 4 years, showed a quilt made by herself."[35]

Major quilting news traveled from coast to coast, such as an 1885 article about the quilt industry published in New York City and reprinted on the front page of the California *Merced Express*, in San Francisco's *Daily Examiner*, and several other newspapers across the country. Readers were informed about an impressive number of cotton quilts produced in an industrial setting in eastern Connecticut, with detailed information about the quilt fabrics and fillings, wages paid to the quilting-machine operators, the most popular color combinations, and more, as reported, "The world has not totally abandoned the homely calico quilt; the old-time favorite was never more popular than at the present. But its manufacture is no longer the prerogative and monopoly of the gentler sex, and its character has undergone a marvelous change. . . . [These] New England quilts are sold in great numbers in even the warmest of the Southern States, throughout the West, in Mexico, Canada, and the West Indies, as well as in the different cities of the South American States."[36]

The 1886 Santa Barbara County Fair displayed a 116-year-old quilt, plus "Bertha M Wright, a little woman of 4 years, showed a quilt made by herself."

Montana, not yet a state in these years, reeled from divisive territorial politics on the road to statehood, powerfully described in a quilt simile that referred to a young woman in Pennsylvania who allegedly lost her mind while working on her crazy quilt, printed in Butte: "We recommend this incident to . . . our Republican friends, who are endeavoring to make a covering for the torn, mangled and bleeding remains of their party in this country. . . . They cannot agree and the thing they call a covering that will embrace the factions of the party looks very much like a political crazy quilt."[37] Studying the premiums, or prizes, awarded at the 1885 Helena agricultural fair reveals several divisions for women's handwork, including, as in most other fairs, a category for quilts. First prizes were awarded for patchwork quilts in silk and in cotton, another for crazy quilts, and for a silk cradle quilt.[38]

Usually we find only the names of the women who created the quilts in these accounts, but a quilter named Mollie Williams residing in St. Joseph had her moment of fame, as reported in Missoula: "Some three years ago she conceived the idea of making a quilt and went to work. She began to write letters to prominent ladies of the United States, asking for a small bit of a dress. Hundreds of letters were written, and let it be said to the credit of the noble women of America, they responded almost without an exception."[39] This three-year project for a crazy quilt incorporated fabrics of all sorts, from calico to the richest silks.

In Monroe, Louisiana, the *Quachita Telegraph* alerted local quilt makers to a new fad via a column by the New York correspondent for the *Chicago News*: "This year the rage is for the 'Oscar crazy quilt.' On a piece of cambric half a yard square there is basted a sun-flower [emblem of Oscar Wilde] . . . or a lily, or daisy, or pansy." After the squares were filled in with odd bits of velvet and silk, they were joined together with black velvet ribbon decorated with hand embroidery. The writer went on to report that "this serves to revive the homely industry of quilt-making, and a prominent society lady tells me that one of the novelties here next season will be the sociable quilting bee."[40]

The *Times-Picayune* in New Orleans reprinted an article from the *National Republican* in Washington, DC, in high praise of a quilt by Mrs. John C. Mumford, wife of the clerk at the Arlington Hotel—actually a crazy quilt in blocks, described as a "patchwork quilt that is not merely a quilt, but a work of art. It is a poem in patches—a symphony in samples of silk and satin." Consisting mainly of silk, the quilt contained about a thousand fragments sent to the maker, including, supposedly, a piece from the White House curtains and from the lining of Thomas Jefferson's carriage. The writer repeatedly emphasized the artistry of Mrs. Mumford's quilt.[41] In a column titled "Woman and Home, Various Phases of

★

For her crazy quilt, Mollie Williams wrote letters to prominent ladies of the US, asking for a small bit of a dress. (1884)

Woman's Work," for *The Times* of Shreveport, readers were informed about a solar-system quilt by Mrs. M. Baker of Lone Tree, Iowa, that she worked on for seven years, "She went to Chicago to view the comet and sun spots through the telescope that she might locate them accurately."[42]

At the 1883 Osage County Fair in Kansas, visitors could view quilts entered in the competition, which featured several entries in the Log Cabin pattern, including examples pieced with wool fabric. Readers may have wondered why this "very attractive display" of "Textile Fabrics" was not part of the "Fine Arts" competition, when that category exhibited such items as artificial flowers, a feather wreath, and a geological collection.[43] Several Log Cabin quilts also stood out at the Sedgwick County Fair, attended by some five thousand people.[44] The reporter covering a fair in Fort Scott, Kansas, praised the installation of quilts on view, "The quilt department was an interesting feature. There were plain quilts, checkered quilts, diamond and log cabin quilts, diagonal quilts and crazy quilts, so a lady said to your informant. The arrangement was tasty and the various designs blended harmoniously together, making it withal very pleasing to the eye."[45]

The aesthetics of quilt making occasionally were discussed in detail, with an essay from the *Philadelphia Times* reprinted in Leavenworth: "Many things combine with the special interest of the patches themselves to make up the fascination of the work. There are the brightness of the color, the pleasure of the invention and combination, the kind of unexpectedness in the result as the pieces are fitting in, all redeeming it from being merely mechanical work, besides the pleasure of making something really pretty and useful."[46]

Missouri quilters thinking of making an autograph quilt could have been inspired if not awed by an autograph quilt begun by Mary Birch Dudley in the 1850s and probably completed shortly after the end of the Civil War. In 1880, a St. Louis newspaper reprinted a long article from the *St. Joseph Gazette* documenting the quilt's history. While the writer praised the quilt for the many prizes it had won, the story's real attraction may have been the words from "distinguished Americans" (all males) quoted in the article. Dudley had asked them to sign their autographs on pieces of linen, and several included notes from the donors. Judging by her choice of subjects, she was a Union sympathizer. She stitched the message from Garrett Davis, a member of Congress from Kentucky who was instrumental in preventing Kentucky from seceding, into the beak of an eagle: "The women of America! I invoke them to give their prompt and steady influence to uphold and protect the civil and religious liberty of their country." Robert C. Winthrop, who had been a US senator from Massachusetts, wrote, "The Union: To be cherished in all our hearts, to be defended by all our hands."[47]

A newspaper in Ironton, Missouri, reprinted precise instructions from the *New York Herald* for how to make an embroidered and appliquéd Noah's Ark quilt: "The animals are all in couples, and form a long procession marching round the entire quilt, marching round toward the ark. . . . The lady asks her friends and neighbors to work the pairs of animals, usually giving them some choice in the matter. Some of these quilts are very amusing, and really worth keeping." The

Metropolitan Museum of Art, 1981.1136.783

▲ Valentine copying Kate Greenaway figures, ca. 1880, 2.5 × 6 in., white card with embossed figures, green printed background

writer suggested that a child's coloring book might be used for the animal motifs, with paper templates serving as models for the fabrics. To help make the animals "true to nature," scraps of leather and fur could be added. Though this project was titled "The Latest Kink of Fashionable Lovers of Fancy Work," we might wonder whether it was indeed a fad, or if the writer was attempting to start one.[48]

Articles about raffles for fundraising quilts can be found in numerous sources, such as the report about a silk quilt donated by "Grandma Hans" to benefit the Bayland Orphan's Home in Galveston, Texas, founded in 1866 for orphaned children of Confederate veterans: "This quilt is a most gorgeous thing, pieced by the old lady herself from scraps of silk. . . . It is very large and the blending of color is certainly rich and pleasing. The labor it cost this charitable woman to put all these little scraps of silk together can hardly be comprehended by one who has not engaged in a similar task."[49] Her raffle raised $75 for the orphanage (more than $2,000 today). Galveston quilters were invited to view another beauty on view at a local gallery: "It is a combination quilt made by Mrs. Kate Scranton, who proposes to put it up for raffle. The center of the design shows a star faced upon a Maltese cross. Surrounding this are gathered fern leaves, and outside of this there are yet a series of combinations in perspective, the whole being fringed with Kate Greenaway figures in Kensington [embroidery] work."[50] In this context, a "combination" quilt probably meant several techniques—piecing, appliqué, and embroidery. Quilts with multitudinous pieces sometimes were displayed as curiosities, such as in a Houston venue organized as a ladies' loan exhibition in which a bed quilt containing 10,000 pieces accompanied, allegedly, a square of plush that covered the block where Mary, Queen of Scots, was beheaded; a sliver of wood from George Washington's coffin; and a piece of "marble" from the pyramids of Egypt.[51]

Crazy quilts had their own popular appeal, as evidenced by an 1885 Memphis exhibition in Crosby's Dime Museum. These "dime" museums, charging ten cents as the entry fee, appealed to working-class people. W. E. Crosby, the Tennessee impresario in charge of this particular exhibition of some one hundred crazy quilts, had assumed that the craze was dying out, but "then the fact was suddenly developed that many ladies were still working seriously at quilts of this style . . . and plenty of ladies called to see when the exhibition was to be opened as they wanted to line or finish quilts."[52] This reviewer mentioned that several men and one boy had entered quilts in the competition, and that every quilt had a history worth regarding. Advertisements for quilting tools in Tennessee suggest that a ready market existed for them, such as the Fraley Quilting Attachment sold by J. L. Simpson & Co. This tool, also called a quilting frame, was connected to a family sewing machine, saving many hours that would have been spent in hand quilting, "This arrangement is more accurate and more endurable than hand work, and it only takes about two hours to make a quilt."[53]

In Pennsylvania by 1884, crazy quilts were perceived as supplanting patchwork and sampler quilts in women's domestic sphere, "bed-clothes being made in great factories." This reporter had a keen appreciation of the contained crazy-quilt aesthetic, consisting of patches assembled in a series of squares to be sewn together: "Occasionally, the combination of colors thus wrought, are gorgeous in their contradictions of shade, and when the zig-zag seams are embroidered, their excentricity [*sic*] presents colors of a very fantastic character. And when the patches are combined in a quilt, formed of silk, satin, brocade, velvet and all the makes of the mostly fabrics, the whole is magnificent in appearance."[54] Readers in Pennsylvania learned that factory-made down quilts were competing with "blankets" for warmth in cold weather, as evidenced in a local newspaper: "In 1872 the first quilts made of goose down were imported into Philadelphia, and the trade has ever since been steadily increasing."[55] During the decades immediately following the 1876 Centennial, women who could afford goose-down quilts may have felt free to indulge in less utilitarian quilt projects such as crazy quilts and silk Log Cabin quilts, which often had no batting.

The Masonic Temple in New York City at 23rd Street and Sixth Avenue exhibited more than two thousand crazy quilts and similar fancy work in 1885. The exhibition included a detailed description of imagery in the "G.A.R" (Grand Army of the Republic) album quilt by Mrs. N. W. Carswell of Waterbury, illustrated in this book's introduction. This historically important, densely illustrated quilt—actually not a crazy quilt, although categorized as such—featured all the presidents' names stitched in the quilt's border.[56] Interestingly, in the exhibition review appearing in the *New York Times*, the writer mentions a crazy quilt on view supposedly 150 years old, and another seventy-five years old featuring the monogram of George Washington.[57] These two pieces would have been anomalies in the history of American crazy quilts and probably were patchwork quilts without the highly decorative embroidery of true Gilded Age crazy quilts, which appeared in significant numbers during the 1880s. Quilt historian Barbara Brackman remarked in a 2024 phone interview that the 1885 exhibition included a remarkable number of crazy quilts for the time, since the fad had begun only a few years earlier. It seems that making crazy quilts indeed had captured the attention of the quilt-making public.

CHAPTER 3

Crazy Quilts

American crazy quilts, many of them masterpieces of orderly disorder, began to appear in noticeable quantity by the mid-1880s, being identified in newspapers as "crazy quilts" around 1882.[1] They continued to be made through World War I, then sporadically until the 1940s, chiefly of wool or cotton instead of silk and velvet in the later years. Most of the extravagantly decorated crazy quilts were completed in the earlier decades—as far as we can tell from known examples. Several of these were described in chapter 2 from articles in newspapers. For the purpose of this book, the Gilded Age (or Victorian) crazy quilts we discuss are defined as constructed from asymmetrical patches of luxury fabrics, heavily decorated with embroidery, mostly done by hand, and occasionally containing three-dimensional objects. In some examples, the maker contained the patches within squares to organize the composition. We will consider quilts made by chiefly by women, according to nineteenth-century sources.

Except in rare instances, crazy quilts have no batting, or filler, but instead a foundation fabric or fabrics to secure the patches, and a backing fabric sometimes connected to the quilt top by tacking or tying. Occasionally a crazy quilt has a decorative border, such as velvet strips, lozenges, or a ruffle. Many crazy quilts are smaller than bed-sized quilts, because they were intended as throws to display over a piece of furniture or as lap quilts. Usually constructed of silk and velvet fabrics, and often rather fragile, they cannot easily be cleaned, especially those featuring three-dimensional objects such

▸ *Crazy Quilt*, 1885, 57 × 66 in., made by the hat trimmers of the Soft Department of Beckerle & Co., Danbury

▾ Detail, *Crazy Quilt*

From *Quilts and Quiltmakers Covering Connecticut* by the Connecticut Quilt Search Project (Atglen, PA: Schiffer, 2001), 98

From *Quilts and Quiltmakers Covering Connecticut* by the Connecticut Quilt Search Project (Atglen, PA: Schiffer, 2001), 99

Metropolitan Museum of Art, 1983.349

as commemorative ribbons, badges, buttons, taxidermy, and paper or cardboard items, including photographs and cards.

Asymmetrical patterning in quilts was nothing new earlier in the nineteenth century. Quilters in the United States were creating irregularly pieced quilts containing numerous small pieces. Today we categorize them as "tile" or "kaleidoscope" quilts, without the extravagant embellishment found in crazy quilts. These styles of quilts, along with unembellished crazy quilts, continued to be made throughout the nineteenth century and into the twentieth. With the fact that such a large number of quilts are in museums, along with the assumption that many more probably have been lost, then the ubiquity becomes impressive. In this chapter, we consider the various factors that possibly "fueled its explosion in the 1880s,"[2] including the US Centennial of 1876. We also discuss crazy quilts as an expression of and possibly in reaction to Gilded Age sensibility in the US.

GILDED AGE STYLE

A few ornate crazy quilts constructed of silks and velvets feature embroidered dates earlier than 1880, usually along with other dates, suggesting that the dates refer to events other than the date of completion of each quilt—perhaps the birth dates of children, year of a marriage, or death dates.[3] In crazy quilts, more is more, in response to the Gilded Age's love of bric-a-brac and surface ornamentation. While magazines such as *Peterson's* featured "fancy work" in the 1870s decorated with silk embroidery that "seems to be a precursor to Victorian Crazywork," this handwork was smaller than quilts, mainly the size of cushions.[4] Several contemporaneous sources referred to such collaged surfaces as Japan or Japanese work (discussed below), and these creations evidently helped open the floodgates to crazy quilts.

◀ Tamar Horton Harris North (North's Landing, Indiana), *Crazy Quilt*, ca. 1877, 54.5 × 55 in., a memorial quilt for her daughter Grace

Gilded Age style was, as described by Robert Shaw, "eclectic in the extreme, and many women decorated their homes in a mix of contemporary designs. . . . Crazy quilts are emblematic of this late-Victorian eclecticism, drawing bits and pieces from a host of different influences and design ideas."[5] Designed to appear somewhat haphazard, crazy quilts actually created a sense of unity from rambling variety, an elaborate repurposing of materials in fabric collage.[6] There definitely was method in the "madness."

At the height of the crazy-quilt fad in this country, poets, misogynistic pundits, and others often suggested the term "crazy" to describe those creating the quilts, in the word's more negative connotations, using it as an adjective for the makers instead of for (or in addition to) the quilts. A newspaper reporter in 1883 went even further and published an "interview," supposedly with a quilt maker, having her respond to a question about why the style is called a "crazy quilt" by saying, "Because the pattern is crooked, confused, and confounded: because there's an infatuation in the work itself: because to see one is to want to make one: because in our search for pieces we drive dressmakers, milliners and dry goods clerks crazy."[7] The "interviewee" goes on to describe women desperate for silk scraps who ask to cut off bonnet strings from the wearers, remove the silk lining from men's hats, and beg for their silk cravats.[8]

Crazy quilts may have been welcomed in society, such as during an Atlanta event reported in 1883: "There will be a display of crazy quilts, some of the most exquisite specimens of such work having been promised. The crazy quilt is the talk of the day."[9] But we might consider whether such fine needlework was taken seriously by the public at an event where the main attraction was a bubble-blowing contest in which prizes would be awarded for the highest bubble and the most bubbles blown in five minutes. Satiric poems published in magazines and newspapers also indicate disparagement of crazy-quilt makers. and in satiric poems ridiculing the makers:

And where is the wife who so vauntingly swore
That nothing on earth her affections
could smother?
She crept from your side at the chiming of four
And is down in the parlor at work on
another.
Your breakfasts are spoiled,
And your dinner half-boiled,
And your efforts to get a square
supper are foiled
By the crazy-quilt mania that fiendishly
raves,
And to which all the women are absolute
slaves.[10]

We might also question the reliability of "reporters" and other writers relying on sensationalism to sell newspapers and other publications. A story that seems outrageous may be just that—a story. Nevertheless, we have crazy quilts actually made of silk material that was produced for hat linings, completed in 1885 in Danbury, Connecticut, by a group of professional hat trimmers at Beckerle & Co. Lady managers in charge of fundraising efforts to build a hospital in Danbury had reached out to women working in the local hat factories, who created two elegant crazy quilts for the quite successful benefit raffle.[11]

Royal School of Art Needlework curtain door, 1875–1876, embroidered silk, designed by Walter Crane, in Smith, *The Masterpieces of the Centennial Exhibition Illustrated, vol. 2*, engraved illustration, p. 177

THE ROYAL SCHOOL OF ART NEEDLEWORK

Quilt historians generally agree that the penchant for exquisitely embroidered crazy quilts began to be popular in the 1880s, tapering off in the early twentieth century. The death of Queen Victoria in 1901, and the subsequent shift from intricately decorated home interiors to the harmonious effects of new twentieth-century style, may have contributed to the crazy quilt's drop in popularity at the time.[12] But how and why did the craze flourish? This question has been mulled over for decades, with quilt historians determining that crazy quilts gradually mushroomed partly as a result of several factors. Robert Shaw summarized several influences from the 1876 Centennial Exhibition, notably Candace Wheeler's inspiration for needlework from the Royal School of Art Needlework displays.[13] Founded only four years before the 1876 celebration, the Royal School of Art Needlework in London had a large

Royal School of Art Needlework booth, 1876, Centennial Photographic Co., Philadelphia, stereoscopic photograph

Collection of Sandra Sider

VITA BREVIS
ROYAL SCHOOL
OF
ART NEEDLEWORK
SALVE

booth in the Main Building of the Philadelphia Exhibition. Designed as an impressively tall, freestanding structure, the booth was entered via a monumental embroidered silk hanging with an opening down the center, a curtain door. A life-sized female figure on each side held curved ribbons embroidered with the words for "hello" and "goodbye" in Latin. Visitors had to part the curtain to enter.[14]

This curtain door presented the applied art of textiles in several aspects, symbolically as well as literally. Immediately above the entrance, a scene depicted the three Fates of the ancient world, who were thought to allot the span of each human life: Clotho, who spins the threads ("cloth" may have derived from her name); Lachesis, who weaves each life; and Atropos, who cuts the thread of life. Imagery flanking both curtain-door figures featured mermaids, monkeys, and many birds, including the peacock and chicken embroidered in quite a few crazy quilts. Immediately above the three Fates were baskets of flowers, and above them sat four female figures, each in her own fictive architectural niche. Visual documentation of the curtain is unclear, but these figures appear to be four of the Muses. One seems to be painting or sketching, and another is playing a musical instrument—typical activities of creative women who were fortunate enough to have leisure time.

Unlike most of the other exhibits in the Main Building, with their advertising focused mainly on wholesalers and other male attendees, the booth of the Royal School of Art Needlework evidently was designed to attract women. Measuring 12 by 12 feet, the interior must have been a sort of magical space, full of gorgeously embroidered textiles. "The exhibit of Kensington Embroidery all unwittingly sowed the seed not only of great results, but in decorative art worked in many other directions. The exhibits of art needlework . . . exactly fitted it to experiment by all the dreaming forces of the American woman. They were good needlewomen and sensitive to art influences by nature, and initiative capacity which belongs to power and feeling enabled them at once to seize upon this mode of expression and make it their own."[15]

Professor Walter Smith, a British art critic and educator who resided in the US, encouraged the teaching of "industrial art"—applied art that could help people learn skills enabling them to earn a living. He wrote the second volume of *The Masterpieces of the Centennial Exhibition* (1876), which includes engraved illustrations of numerous selected pieces, with particular praise for the Royal School of Art Needlework: "We are please[d] to see that this kind of work is finding favor among the women of this country, and that already schools of design and needlework are forming in several of our cities. We believe that as soon as the absurd prejudice, too long obtaining among the decayed gentility classes in this country, against manual labor for women has been overcome, that a new and powerful impetus will be given to the progress of all branches of decorative art among us. The field is an extensive one, and one peculiarly fitted for women to work with profit and success."[16] While we hardly know of any "profit" for their makers gained from creating crazy quilts, the best examples certainly can be judged as successful examples of textile excellence.

Candace Wheeler, photographic portrait by Saxony & Company, ca. 1870

Candace Wheeler, an artist and ardent feminist, admired the Royal School of Art Needlework for its goal of teaching "gentlewomen" who had fallen upon hard times the skill of art embroidery, by which she hoped they could support themselves through needlework. Because the school was located at that time in Kensington (west of central London), the work usually was called Kensington embroidery. In her autobiography, Wheeler explained that the school "was fortunately connected with an impulse toward the revival of many of the medieval arts, which in the past had enriched the life and history of England. . . . Happily the revival had been shorn of medievalism by the cleverness of the men who were leading it. The designs of artists like Burne-Jones, Morris, and above all, the direct and graceful work of Walter Crane, founded always upon figures of growth skillfully chosen and carefully adapted to needlework, gave great value to the new revival of embroidery."[17] Walter Crane was the artist who designed the curtain door for the booth in Philadelphia, as well as the embroidered screens at the entrance and other pieces inside the booth.

While touring the Centennial Exhibition, this intrepid woman became determined to establish a similar school in New York City, which she did, with branches eventually set up in Boston, Chicago, and Philadelphia. Between 1881 and 1900, Wheeler published dozens of embroidery designs in *Harper's Bazar* and other ladies' magazines, chiefly floral motifs and decorative details. She sometimes commented that—even when the motifs were intended by Wheeler to be grouped in embroidery—the maker should feel free to single out a motif to use individually (as they often appear in crazy-quilt patches). When offering instructions for embroidering larger pieces, such as curtain doors (and I would add crazy quilts), she taught that "the inevitable moral of artistic needle-work is that you must treat is as poetry and not as prose. It is like a book or picture: it is rest and enjoyment for the mind."[18]

In Robert Shaw's view, "Many crazy quilts were, in essence, textile scrapbooks—amalgams of fabric, images, and keepsakes of sentimental value to the maker or the person for whom the quilt was made. Women personalized their crazy quilts by incorporating bits and pieces of used clothing and dress fabric, embroidered and appliquéd

Metropolitan Museum of Art, 2007342

Crazy Quilt (New England), ca. 1880–1885, 80 × 80 in., pieced in cotton instead of silk, as an album of thirty-six blocks. The fabrics include printed cheater cloth resembling patchwork, and the imagery depicts motifs often embroidered in crazy quilts, such as a butterfly, peacock, fan, and horseshoe.

renderings of people, buildings, and pets, and needlework signatures, dates and phrases into their compositions."[19] Flowers, vines, and leaves almost always enliven the visual field, with abundantly textured embroidery stitches decorating the edges of every fragment during the heyday of crazy quilts. This era experienced the effects of the aesthetic movement, or art for art's sake, which valued beauty rather than function. As Cindy Brick summarized the situation, "By the time Crazy patchwork came to the fore, she [the homemaker] was already surrounded by the trappings of various decorative movements, most of which used rich, textural materials, lavish embroidery, laces and other handwork, and a variety of interesting surfaces."[20]

Wheeler was only one of the millions of women who visited the Centennial Exhibition in 1876. Touring the various exhibitions, women learned about the latest materials and tools available for quilt making, especially needles, fabrics, and embroidery threads, and saw improved inks, paints, and pens for those who might wish to include handwritten texts and painted images on their quilts. Editors of the ladies' magazines were quick to capitalize on the growing interest in crazy quilts, publishing patterns that suggested not only how to arrange fabric scraps but also which embroidery stitches to use. Penny McMorris identified several crazy quilts that copied motifs and entire patterns from these very publications.[21]

PATTERNS FOR CRAZY QUILTS

By 1890, manufacturers of sewing machines, whose businesses had skyrocketed after the Centennial Exhibition, were including patterns for crazy quilts as well as examples of decorative stitching that could accomplish machine embroidery. A trade card from the Singer Sewing Machine Company, obviously targeted at women, illustrated numerous stitches on one side, with many of them shown stitched over the seams of fancywork patches on the other side. One of the patches states, "Have you seen the new Improved Family Singer Sewing Machine," and in the center of the card we see an image of the "Latest and Best" sewing machine.[22] The industry also offered machine-embroidered motifs for appliqué, such as flowers, birds, and spiderwebs, along with stamping kits. J. F. Ingalls in Lynn, Massachusetts, offered a kit for a complete alphabet and designs for daisies, roses, vines, etc. with a box of powder and a stamping pad.[23]

Individual authors jumped on the embroidery bandwagon. One of the authors wrote a handbook on ornamental stitches, independently published in 1885, that was reprinted in several periodicals. Part of the text, copied from an 1884 book titled *Kensington Embroidery and the Colors of Flowers*, informed readers that "the ornamenting of seams with fancy stitches in bright-colored silks gives a very pleasing effect, and the illustrations of the stitches in this book give an idea of the different ways in which they can be worked. Of course no directions can be given as to the colors to be used, as this is where the taste of the worker is displayed."[24] He went on to give precise instructions on "How to Do Kensington Painting," which required a stiff, hollow pen (perhaps similar to a tjanting), squeezing paints directly from the tubes onto a palette for mixing. Keeping in line with his theme of stitchery, Parker then explained that after the painting for a motif is completed, the maker should "scratch the petal or leaf over with the point of the pen to give it the appearance of stitches, always remembering to make the lines run toward the centre, as in embroidery."[25]

Trendsetters in interior design, including Candace Wheeler, were leaving fancywork behind to embrace principles of functionalism as part of the Arts & Crafts movement by 1900, although handcrafts were endorsed to offset the gross industrialization of the workplace. Jane Przybysz has discovered that "proponents of woman's suffrage, dress reform, and home economics all sought to distance themselves from images of sentimentality and feminine excess they associated with Victorian fancywork."[26] In addition, immersing oneself in the creation of a hand-stitched crazy quilt came to be derided as a colossal waste of time for middle-class and affluent women, who instead could be improving their minds, helping in their local communities, and lobbying for women's suffrage. Nevertheless, the fad for crazy quilts burned intensely across the US for nearly twenty-five years.

Marin Hanson's research has revealed that the fancy handwork of crazy quilts and colonial revival quilts expressed nostalgia "for a simpler, pre-industrial time and looked to non-Western, pre-modern cultures for inspiration."[27] It's ironic that while the Centennial Exhibition's main purpose was to show the world that the US had become an industrial power, several of the sites drawing the largest crowds harkened back to historical periods—the "old-timey" processes, materials, and styles—complete with costumed reenactors. The final two decades of the nineteenth century seem to have been an ambivalent time for quilt makers, tempted by the ease of sewing machines and commercially produced ornamentation and patterns but continuing to embrace antimodern and exotic designs.[28]

POPULARITY OF JAPANESE STYLE

A few quilt historians have credited the visual influence of objects in the Japanese exhibitions, especially the crazing assumed to have been present in some of their glazes. *Ornamental Stitches*, published in 1884, claimed, "Crazy Patchwork has now become so popular as to require but little instruction. As the name mentions, it is sewing together odd bits of Silk, Satin, Plush [velvet], etc. in a 'haphazard' sort of way, so that the angles may somewhat imitate the craze or crackle of old china, from which all this kind of work derives its name."[29] We know that women flooded into the Japanese Pavilion, one of the most visited areas of the entire exhibition. I have not yet found, however, any firsthand documentation, in text or image, of crackle-glazed porcelain in the pieces on display.

A visitor reporting on the exhibition commented, "The Japanese screens are among the most wonderful articles in their exhibition. In these the most astonishing effects are produced by combining embroidery with painting. . . . In embroidery the Japanese equal the world; and the work on the screens will be found to equal that displayed in the Woman's Pavilion."[30] Leslie's 1877 *Register* gave a fuller description: "These [the screens] are covered with gilt paper of peculiar texture, the ornamentation consisting of patches of various material fastened thereon. . . . The work is uniformly on a ground of silk, the designs being either painted, embroidered or quilted. . . . One process of ornamentation consists of the

▸ Florence Elizabeth Marvin (Brooklyn, New York), *Crazy Quilt with Animals*, 1886, 81.5 × 82.5 in., embellished with yarn flowers, glass beads, metal spangles, and a yellow glove. The animals include several owls seated on crescent moons, as well as barnyard animals.

Art Institute of Chicago, 2003.294

building up of figures by patient tailor work, layer after layer, of silken, woolen or other materials, these being sewed or glued upon each other."[31] Because several of these screens were rather large, their patchwork structure and ornamented surfaces doubtless gave viewers a fairly good idea of how those effects might produce similar visual interest in textile art.

The term in Japanese for screens featuring a seemingly random patchwork surface is *yosegire*, which means sewing together of different fragments. *Yosegire*, an antique process that "enjoyed a fashionable revival" in Japan by the 1830s, "grew out of a desire to preserve and prolong the life of valuable, and particularly imported textiles, but . . . women began to take pleasure in organizing patches of different colors, textures, and shapes into a pleasing design that they either used for clothing, or to make decorative cloths, or to enliven the appearance of a screen."[32] Japanese silk brocades produced at this time often incorporated a decorative technique that may have led those attending the Centennial Exhibition to think that the woven fabrics were embroidered, perhaps influencing the penchant for that handwork technique in crazy quilts.[33]

Another aspect of Japanese products in 1876 that may have appealed to designers of textiles were the asymmetrical decorations on ceramics, bronzes, and lacquer objects, especially surfaces swirling with floral motifs in different sizes, interspersed with small-scale geometric ornamentation and insects. Penny McMorris tells us, "It is obvious that the taste for Japanese design accounted in large part for the late-nineteenth-century passion in all of the arts, including needlework. Beauty became equated with the irregular, and adjectives such as *bizarre*, *strange*, and *odd* conveyed appeal and a sense of Oriental mystery."[34] In one of the catalogs describing a tall bronze vase, we read, "In the grotesques at the base and in the relief ornamentation on the sides we see that peculiar exaggeration and distortion of natural objects which many people prefer to the conventionalism obtaining with European artists."[35]

This sort of free-flowing, organic composition could have suggested that an oversized butterfly might be juxtaposed with a spray of tiny rosebuds, or a miniature owl with a large spiderweb—effects that

Japanese screen at the Centennial Exhibition, in *Frank Leslie's Illustrated Historical Register*, 1877, engraved illustration, p. 270

Japanese lacquerware at the Centennial Exhibition, in *Frank Leslie's Illustrated Historical Register*, 1877, engraved illustration, p. 25

we often see in crazy quilts—and in fairy tales (see below). Some of the ceramic and bronze objects in the Chinese exhibition had similar visual effects, but the sheer quantity of such pieces sent from Japan would certainly have caught the attention of viewers. Japan invested heavily in the Centennial Exhibition, taking advantage of this opportunity to promote its country's perceived superiority in the production of ceramics, metalwork, embroidery, and other goods. We should note that even prior to the latter 1850s, when Japan began trading with the West again after more than two hundred years of almost complete isolation, patterns featuring "Oriental" motifs were being offered in the ladies' magazines, with Chinese or Japanese sources usually not distinguished. Nevertheless, the 1876 Centennial Exhibition created a watershed event for America's fascination with Asian arts and crafts. As one of the catalogs remarked, "At the present day the desire for oriental shapes and patterns in furniture, household ware, room decorations, and textile fabrics has become so great that the manufacturers in this country and Europe have turned their attention largely to productions of this kind."[36]

Clarence Cook, an American art critic and arbiter of taste, published a series of essays on home decor in *Scribner's Monthly* around the time of the 1876 Exhibition that were published together in book format in 1878. A section on embroidery praised the current decorative handwork of women: "Now, on a pale sapphire silk, she made a flight of apple-blossom petals drift before the wind, at one side the branch that bore them, with its tips of leaves; or across one corner of a square of amber satin a geometric spider had woven her silver web, darting from tip to tip of the white rose-tree; or cat-o'-nine-tails against a blue-green water, with a rose-red mallow; or the neck and head of a duck sailing through her kingdom; or autumn leaves, sad colored, raining down against a weltering sky of gray; or hips and haws; or black elderberries, or—anything. The lady worked as she pleased, and had no fear of 'schools' or of 'laws' before her eyes. . . . It is almost inevitable that we should be thrown upon the Japanese for our first hints and instruction; their art is so perfect as decoration, their method so varied, and their materials suited to every subject and belonging to our own time. . . . And therefore it has a vitality for us, and knocks at *little secret doors* in our own natures."[37] The lady seems to have been embroidering fancywork very similar to that found on a crazy quilt. As early as 1882, the term "Japanese" quilt in fancywork was understood to mean a luxury crazy quilt. An 1882 article on "art needlework" explained: "When the present favorite style of quilt was introduced it was called the Japanese . . . and the Japanese is now generally known as the 'crazy' quilt. . . . The materials are the waste scraps that gather in every house, too small or too irregular to serve any other possible purpose. These are reinforced by the exchanging of scraps between acquaintances."[38]

About the time that stitching crazy quilts was becoming a very popular activity in American domestic circles, Gilbert and Sullivan opened their satirical operetta *The Mikado* in London, in March 1885. Set in a mythical Japanese town, the operetta conflated Japan and China through the names of characters, but the sets and costumes were in pure Japanese style, including the use of actual Japanese textiles. Dozens of companies were performing *The Mikado* across the US by the following year. Several textile mills printed fabrics illustrating various Japanese "embroidered" motifs, as well as cheater cloth meant to emulate Japanese-style patchwork.[39] Merchants such as J & P Coats helped spread the penchant for Japanese textile designs via trade cards depicting the main characters and their lush costumes. On one such card, the character Yum-Yum is seated on a spool of 200 yards of J & P Coats 50-weight thread, holding up another spool, and a card depicting *The Mikado* in an ornate kimono declares,

All people who have to do sewing
And don't use Coats' six cord thread,
Will be punished with cotton
That's snarly and rotten
And kinks, till they wish they were dead.

OTHER POSSIBLE INSPIRATIONS DURING THE CENTENNIAL

What other decorative textiles on view at the Centennial Exhibition, in addition to those in the Woman's Building, discussed in a previous chapter, could have inspired the embroidered details of American crazy quilts? In Smith's *Masterpieces* catalog, we learn that "all the great centres of lace manufacture were represented in the most satisfactory manner, and in many instances partially wrought specimens were exhibited, showing the way in which the work was

Whole-cloth quilt in *Mikado motifs*, ca. 1886 (production date of the printed cotton), 88 × 85 in., from the Cocheco Print Works, Dover, New Hampshire

Metropolitan Museum of Art, 1986.342

executed . . . [describing a piece of Belgian lace]. It is almost impossible to realize that this *fairy-like* creation, with its convoluted patterns, its garlands and flowers and ferns, has been wrought, stitch by stitch and inch by inch, by patient women, following a pattern thread by thread."[40] The author describes another display of Belgian lace in words that could be referring to a crazy quilt: "The profusion and variety of the flowers and ferns suggest the richness of tropical luxuriance, and they have been grouped and intermingled by the artist with charming grace and naturalness. An excellent feature of the design is the way in which the representation of the groups is arranged, so as to convey *as little idea as possible of sameness*, and to make the whole harmonious."[41] He describes a French lace shawl as "a graceful arrangement of ferns and flowers and grasses in *studied confusion*. . . . There is a suggestion of oriental richness."[42] Visitors also viewed sumptuous tapestries, densely decorated carpets, saddlebags embroidered in brilliant colors, silk fabrics woven in profusions of ornamental motifs, and much more.

If we look beyond the Japanese and Chinese exhibitions to highly decorative forms of nontextile art and craft on view, we can see that Smith described an abundance of inspirational motifs. A large "Moorish" inlaid wooden cabinet from Egypt "shows a freedom from mannerism and richness of fancy that can hardly be too commended."[43] A silver tea

Collection of Sandra Sider

Yum Yum trade card, 1880s–1890s

Collection of Sandra Sider

Mikado trade card, 1880s–1890s

Lace on display in the Brussels Exhibit, 1876, in Smith, *The Masterpieces of the Centennial Exhibition Illustrated*, vol. 2, engraved illustration, p. 205

set made Philadelphia "is decorated with repoussé work of the most elaborate description. Flowers, leaves and grasses twine and intermingle over its surface with all the luxuriance of nature."[44] From London came an elaborate, monumental tile mantelpiece combining human figures, geometric motifs, and "delicate vine-sprays with brilliantly plumaged birds darting in and out between the leaves."[45] These are only a few of the hundreds of objects in which surfaces echoed and promoted the Gilded Age *horror vacui* seen in crazy quilts. From booth to booth and from building to building, the 1876 Exhibition sparked the imaginations of millions of viewers.

THE SILK INDUSTRY

As we saw in chapter 1, the US textile industry in general experienced a boost from the Centennial, not only in the general market but also in fabrics and textile souvenirs produced specifically for the Centennial itself. Silk persisted throughout the last two decades of the nineteenth century as one of the main fabrics used in crazy quilts, along with velvet. Let's take a look at what was happening in the silk market, with a focus on silk manufacturing and marketing in the US.

Raw silk had been produced in the US colonies during the seventeenth century as a cottage industry. The production ebbed and flowed, depending on variables such as tariffs, wartime, bounties paid by Great Britain, etc. Silk farming in New England, South Carolina, and several other original thirteen colonies continued during the eighteenth century. Silk became a major industry in Georgia.[46] Savannah housed a nursery of mulberry trees, specialists arrived from Europe to teach sericulture, and enslaved people were ordered to Savannah to learn about producing raw silk. The early nineteenth century witnessed sericulture spreading into the Midwest, followed by a silk boom in the South during the 1830s. Many cocoon growers completed the manufacturing process by weaving the silk themselves, but not on an industrial basis.[47] By the 1860s, sericulture was practiced in California, where a French botanist founded the California Silk Center Association of Los Angeles. With congressional support and the increasing interest of women in silk farming, the US produced significant amounts of raw silk in the 1880s and early 1890s. Women established several associations for silk farming, such as the Women's Silk Culture Association of the United States, which operated a filature in Philadelphia.[48]

The first successful, large-scale silk-weaving mill was established in the 1840s in Paterson, New Jersey, which became a powerhouse of silk weaving and dyeing by the latter 1860s. In 1874 the value of US silk textiles almost equaled the value of the amount of silk being imported.[49] At the Centennial Exhibition, the Main Building housed the American silk displays. Other buildings featured aspects of the silk industry, including machines displayed in Machinery Hall and the Woman's Pavilion, plus an exhibition in Agricultural Hall of silkworms, cocoons, and a machine for silk reeling (slowly pulling filaments from cocoons), and a demonstration of cottage silk weaving by a woman in the log cabin.

Manufacturers of silk in the US united to create the Silk Association of America in 1872, based in New York City. For the 1876 Exhibition, Linus Pierpont Brockett wrote *The Silk Industry in America: A History, Prepared for the Centennial Exhibition*. This publication was not just a pamphlet but, rather, a book of more than 250 pages with twenty-three leaves of plates. Brockett was a well-published author who wrote about noteworthy people and events, including Abraham Lincoln, the conquest of Turkey, and heroic women of the Civil War. His book praising American silk no doubt was made available for purchase during the Centennial Exhibition. Except for the financial disaster of 1873, discussed in an earlier chapter, the silk business was booming. In the association's annual report for 1876, the tremendous increase of the amount of raw silk imported for silk weaving in the US between 1870 and 1875 testified to the robust nature of the industry, and thus the impressive amount of silk fabrics available for purchase, from 738,382 pounds in 1870 to 1,330,482 in 1875.

"The American silk exhibition at the Centennial was situated at the eastern entrance of the Main Exhibition Building, occupying a space of 117 feet along the central avenue or nave. It included 28 exhibitors, of whom 6 were from Paterson, N.J. Besides these, there were exhibits in Machinery Hall, three of which were from Paterson, N.J.; in the Women's Pavilion, exhibits from two exhibitors; and in Agricultural Hall, one exhibit from San Francisco, of California raw silk cocoons, silkworms feeding, silk reeling, etc.," according to Leslie's *Register*.[50] Foreign commission houses were seeking consignments of American silk, testifying to the satisfactory quality of silk being produced.[51] Among all other factors prompting the popularity of crazy quilts, an abundance of affordable domestic silk was not insignificant. Small wonder that so many dry-goods merchants were advertising to promote the purchase of silk. They were certainly marketing a lot of silk fabrics.

While doing research for this book, I kept thinking how satisfying it would be to discover a crazy quilt created specifically from the silk remnants of a particular dry-goods merchant. I kept finding sales advertisements for bags or boxes of such remnants, and popular accounts in magazines often spoofed the "mania" of quilt makers accused of harassing merchants for

★

Silk farming in New England, South Carolina, and several other original thirteen colonies continued during the eighteenth century.

★

Silk weaving in log cabin at the Centennial Exhibition, in *Frank Leslie's Illustrated Historical Register*, 1877, engraved illustration, p. 265

Collection of Sandra Sider

Silk remnants advertisement, from the Paris Silk Agency in New York City, in *Home Magazine*, 1880

"dress samples" of silk intended for their crazy quilts. Then I came across the crazy quilt completed 1889–1890 by Minnie Weinzweig Fligelman in Montana. Her daughters, Belle Winestine and Frieda Fligelman, donated her quilt to the Montana Historical Society in 1949, documenting their mother's narrative from stories told to them by their father, Herman Fligelman.

A dry-goods merchant who was residing in Boston, Herman heard about the booming economy of Helena, a town in Montana developing rapidly as a result of the local gold rush, and capital of the Montana Territory. Herman took the train to Helena, managed the New York Dry Goods Company, and changed its name to Fligelman's in 1885. He and Minnie met and married ca. 1888 in Minnesota, where communities of other Romanian Jews were residing by the mid-1880s. Evidently Herman had traveled east on a buying trip, bringing home a bride. The satin, velvet, and damask fabrics in Minnie's crazy quilt were remnants from her husband's store. She worked on the quilt while pregnant with their first daughter, born in 1890, probably completing it that same year since she quickly became pregnant again, had a difficult birth, and died soon afterward. Minnie's personal history enriches the content of her quilt—a young woman who lived to see Montana become a state in 1889, connecting her handwork to national patriotism with a prominent Liberty Bell positioned beneath a horseshoe with the words "Good Luck" embroidered above it and the symbol for Freemasonry inside the bell. Her words embroidered above the fan read "In Union There Is Strength," a motto taken from Aesop and perhaps referring to reciprocal support between the Order of the Eastern Star and Freemasons. Alternatively, or perhaps simultaneously, she might have been referring to the Union of the US that Montana had recently joined.

An article in a special 1986 issue of *The Clarion* discussed the importance of crazy quilts to the collector and dealer Margaret Cavigga: "Crazies are, perhaps, the most personal of quilts—Cavigga calls them 'memory quilts.' Indeed, many resembled sentimental scrapbooks made from pieces of wedding gowns, baby clothes, and hair ribbons. Others were stitched with birth and death dates forming a kind of family record."[52] Another aspect of crazy quilts enhancing such a needlework project in the eyes of disenfranchised women was a sort of escapism, through which women in the upper and middle classes who had time on their hands could turn to their crazy quilts to create their own visions of a fanciful world in a state of reverie. Everyone reading this book who has ever been engaged in an all-consuming creative project has experienced the effects of "losing oneself" in the work as time seems to stop.

FAIRYLAND AND FANCYWORK

Philanthropic fairs organized by women on a much-smaller scale than the Centennial Exhibition raised funds for numerous causes during the nineteenth century, including medical treatment for soldiers, abolition of slavery, women's suffrage, churches, animal rights, etc. They offered many types of products, including fancywork and other handmade items. Beverly Gordon adds, "Women's magazines of the late nineteenth century featured suggestions for fair booths. They stressed the creation of a fantasy environment—for example, 'dressing' not only the attendants but also the tables—literally, putting a skirt on them and festooning them with ribbons and drapery. The word 'fairyland' is repeated often in these descriptions."[53]

By the 1860s, fairy tales had reached a huge audience through stories serialized in magazines. Gordon explains the attraction: "The overarching fairyland idea was so much of a leitmotif in the second half of the nineteenth century that the term functioned as a code word, implying something appealing and magically transformed."[54] The textile industry capitalized on this theme by printing trade cards depicting sweet little fairies plying their goods, such as George E. Taplin in Montpelier, Vermont, handing out trade cards from his corner store offering "Fashionable Dry Goods." These words were stamped on the back of a trade card on which a winged fairy is using a large needle to stitch flowers. The card was issued by John English & Co. to advertise their "imperial diamond" needles.

In 1893 the Willimantic Linen Company in Connecticut, famous for the strength of its cotton thread used in sewing machines, commissioned Rose Terry Cooke to write *A Fairy at School*. This fanciful booklet narrated by the fairy queen follows a naughty fairy embedded in a bale of cotton through all the processes needed to produce strong cotton thread. The purpose of this trial is to teach the fairy the value of hard work, simultaneously advertising the superior quality of Willimantic cotton. At the end, the queen springs into the saddle of her Luna moth and speeds away to fairyland.

Fairyland as a cultural construct appeared in numerous popular theatrical performances, with special effects of lighting and costume to create a mysterious ambiance. Shakespeare's *A Midsummer Night's Dream*, featuring Queen Titania, King Oberon, and their fairy court, was a perfect example of fairyland personified by characters in the play. Two of the fairies are named Moth and

Collection of Sandra Sider

Fairy with needle on trade card, 1880s–1890s

Courtesy of the Montana Historical Society, x1949.04.01

Minnie Fligelman, *Crazy Quilt*, ca. 1889, 34 × 20 in.

Courtesy of the Montana Historical Society, x1949.04.01

Detail, Minnie Fligelman, *Crazy Quilt*

Cobweb, and these images in nature frequently appeared in crazy quilts. Depictions of fairies in their woodland environment also appeared in Gilded Age household accessories, such as table lamps, in which fairies were sometimes associated with moonlight and stars in a nocturnal setting. A similar nighttime effect can occasionally be seen in crazy quilts featuring the moon, stars, and nocturnal animals such as owls embroidered against dark fabrics (see image, page 79).

Above we mentioned the impressive quantity of silks in the US available for fancywork. Even more important, as we know from Gordon, was the "astonishing assortment of sophisticated fabrics that the textile industry was producing in the last part of the nineteenth century. Seemingly every hue was available, and each came in dozens of shades."[55] The reflective quality, sheen, and graphic texture of luxury fabrics added to the magical allure of a complex crazy quilt. The fairyland imagery in crazy quilts evoked a safe, happy place, far from the problems of America during the Industrial Age.[56] Women who were comfortable in their domestic arrangements could give themselves over to the delight of their fancywork projects when time allowed. For women who were not so fortunate, their crazy quilts may have been a welcome respite from daily care—and perhaps more than that.

WOMEN IN THE GILDED AGE

To conclude this chapter, let's consider crazy quilts within Gilded Age society in general. An American history scholar has defined this society: "Didacticism characterized Victorian expression as well as Victorian institutions. . . . It was a great age of prescriptive writing of all kinds: child-rearing manuals, books on household management, etiquette books, even joke books, to tell people how to be funny. It was also an age when poetry and fiction legitimated themselves by the morals they taught. 'Art for art's sake' was not a principle widely accepted among American Victorians; literature and the other arts were expected to benefit society by elevating or instructing their audiences."[57] Since crazy quilts have minimal, if any, didactic qualities, how did they fit into such a mindset in this country?

As Hedges sees it, "In the Victorian era, when middle-class women lost the productive role they had held in an earlier agricultural economy, quilts became more and more decorative, more and more examples of conspicuous waste in their often irresponsible use of expensive fabrics such as satin, lace, brocade and velvet. They became an inadvertently ironic sign of woman as consumer rather than producer, and of her confinement to a narrowed and less functional domestic sphere. They became a badge of her oppression and even an unfortunate safety valve that served to delay rebellion by diverting energy."[58] Let's think for a moment about a crazy quilt as a "safety valve" diverting a woman's energy. This concept probably would have appealed to the art critic who wrote *Masterpieces of the Centennial Exhibition*, in which he proclaimed, "Give our American women the same art facilities as their European sisters, and they will flock to the studios and let the ballot-box alone."[59]

The more scathing cartoons castigating female suffragists lambasted them for abandoning their "domestic sphere" because, according to Gordon, "The woman was seen as the embodiment of the home, and in turn the home was seen as an extension of both her corporeal and spiritual self. . . . This metaphoric relationship between house and body was expressed in popular language and imagery throughout the industrial age and can be traced in everything from fiction to advice literature. As Harriet Beecher Stowe put it in her novel *We and Our Neighbors* (1875), a married woman's character was made manifest in her home."[60] During the later nineteenth century, the dining room and parlor in a middle-class home reflected the wife's public persona as a "homebody," decked out "with richly colored silks and velvets, and both included more complex arrangements of drapery and trim:

Art Institute of Chicago, 1960.145

Crazy quilt block with moth, ca. 1884, 18 × 18 in.

Art Institute of Chicago, 1960.143

Crazy quilt block with crescent moon and star, ca. 1884, 17.5 × 17.5 in.

just as an evening dress in the 1880s was made with an elaborate system of drapery and ruchings . . . surface embellishment would follow the same pattern."[61] Here we are talking about women's domestic sphere—an environment and situation imposed upon women yet also managed and possibly manipulated by them.[62] The spider and spiderweb embroidered on numerous crazy quilts—evidently viewed as symbols of good luck—also could be considered as symbolizing the maker, stitching together her quilt like the spider spins its web. Rose Terry Cooke, a poet as well as an author of stories, published a poem equating the spider's creativity with her own process of writing. But the spider has another connotation, of spinning a web—actually the spider's home—like the Gilded Age woman organizing and embellishing her domestic environment in her own way.

If we can trust the hundreds of comments about crazy quilts in newspapers and magazines between the 1880s and early 1920s, the fad truly was popular and pervasive.[63] Like all original handwork created by an individual, crazy quilts bore the stamp of their makers, including their initials or name in some instances. Even crazy quilts incorporating commercial patterns printed in ladies' magazines reflected individuality in the selection of fabrics, colors, textures, size, and embellishment. These quilts were made for different purposes—memorials, celebrations, souvenirs, wedding and birthday gifts—but always intended as home decoration. As for the woman creating one, the completed quilt attested to her value in women's culture of the time. But who knows what was going through her mind as she took countless hours away from other household tasks, her crazy quilt the perfect excuse for what we now call "me" time:

Patchwork only, did you say
This mosaic quaint and gay,
Starred with dainty appliqué,
    In confusion mazy?
Sooth it hath a high-born air,
With an easeful charm and rare,
Lightening the weight of care.
    Wherefore call it crazy?[64]

CHAPTER 4

All's Fair

As the nineteenth century advanced, more occasions arose for commemorating significant expanses of time. Several of these celebrations served as vehicles to introduce new machinery and materials, and to sell products, boosting consumerism and capitalism, while rebuilding the US economy shattered by the Civil War, especially in the South. For the world's fairs held in this country, various US states and foreign countries constructed booths and houses, competing for the attention of the public and representatives of industry. Until the 1939 New York World's Fair, these Janus-like events looked both backward and forward in time as they encouraged viewers to consider past achievements and milestones, simultaneously applauding challenges overcome while pointing toward a brighter future literally illuminated by the magic of electrical and then neon installations. Entertainment for various segments of society added to the attraction.

Textiles composed important sections of most of these fairs in the US until World War II, with numerous exhibitions and souvenirs to attract and inspire quilters, including luxurious, exotic fabrics and needlework from foreign lands. Several of the events promoted national quilt contests. In this chapter we consider quilt culture pertaining to twelve of the major commemorative fairs in this country prior to the US Bicentennial in 1976.[1] To be sure, the US participated in other large-scale fairs, such as the 1895 Cotton States and International Exposition in Atlanta. This event included a Woman's Building exhibiting decorative textile arts and a Negro Building with a pictorial quilt by Harriet Powers on view. But our focus here is on commemorative events.

1884 COTTON CENTENNIAL

From December 1884 through May 1885, New Orleans, then the ninth-largest city in the US, hosted a world's fair known as the World's Industrial and Cotton Centennial Exposition. More than 1,100,000 people visited the event, held in what is now Audubon Park. Close to one-third of US cotton passed through the New Orleans Cotton Exchange during the later nineteenth century. The date of 1884 was selected because, according to extant records, 1784 witnessed the first shipment of US cotton to England. That

Courtesy of Julie Silber Quilts, Berkeley, California

Cotton Centennial souvenir bookmark, 1884, silk, woven at the exposition

Textile exhibits, ca. 1884, Edward Livingston Wilson, photographer. Interior view of Main Building at the World's Industrial and Cotton Centennial Exposition of 1884, held in New Orleans, Louisiana.

Historic New Orleans Collection, acc. no. 1982.127.6

cotton prior to 1784 and for decades later was produced with enslaved labor. The city of New Orleans was one of the largest slave markets in the US until Congress banned the importation of people with the intention of selling them into slavery in 1808. But by the mid-1880s, many African Americans in New Orleans found themselves experiencing the limited benefits of Reconstruction in advance of the Jim Crow statutes soon to come. They were invited to participate in the 1884 Cotton Centennial, segregated in the Colored People's Department, which proved to be a popular attraction for visitors of all races.[2]

Even though the exposition had a separate Woman's Department, the works by Black women had to be displayed in the Colored People's Department, which was allocated more than 34,000 square feet in a gallery of the Government Building totaling some 16,000 exhibits. Newspapers in New Orleans reported information about some of the displays: "A great deal of handiwork was displayed, including carving, carpentry, and so-called women's work, which consisted of needlework, quilting, and wax and hair work, along with other items. The Colored Ladies Centennial Association organized a display of contributions from women in New Orleans, which included quilts, rugs, paper flowers, clothing, lace, preserves, and antiques, among many other homemade creations."[3] Quilts included a Log Cabin, a diamond quilt made of 3,128 pieces, and a mosaic quilt, along with the "piece de résistance," created by seven women. Titled *African Beauty*, the quilt was "composed of eight squares, set in a fine dashingly designed border, and joined together by velvet embroidered strips."[4] The first grouping of women's work had been contributed from women across the country because most of the states participating had their own Black commissioners.

Along an extensive balcony above the mammoth 33-acre Main Building, visitors could easily view displays in the Woman's Department without being far from the main attractions below. Journalist Eugene Smalley dismissed the Woman's Department in his review for *Century Magazine*, criticized by Miki Pfeffer: "About the Woman's Department generally, Smalley judged its pretty alcoves as admirable and peaceful places but its displays of needlework and ornamentals as 'elaborate trifles' from genteel hands, examples of 'woman's play rather than woman's work.'"[5] In general, press coverage focused more on women's practical inventions and other items potentially useful for industry rather than domestic productions such as quilts, especially with male reviewers failing to understand that a woman's definition of work might be strikingly different from their own. The *Times-Picayune*, published by Eliza Nicholson, presented more-comprehensive and more-balanced reports, as did Mary Louise Booth, editor of *Harper's Bazar*. Nevertheless, reviewers questioned whether domestic productions such as quilts could have any market value that could supply income to their makers.

A correspondent for the *Atlanta Constitution* shared this revelation about a unique quilt at the exposition: "I went to the New Orleans Exposition and saw so many [crazy quilts] that I felt then that I never cared to see another, but the quilt I am going to tell you about is something different from anything you ever saw or heard of. . . . In the centre she had a large cream-white handkerchief with a deep crimson border. On this she painted a lion in the act of killing a deer. . . . On each side of the crimson border she had worked a vine in old gold silk. The rest of the quilt was made of all colored silk handkerchiefs—each handkerchief having been folded and cut in a three-corner piece, fit in according to taste. The whole had been bordered with a wide band of garnet silk. . . . It was very beautiful." Julia Ward Howe, the famous New England abolitionist and suffragist chosen to codirect the Woman's Department, seriously valued the ideas and activities of women.[6] Her celebrity status attracted a plethora of press attention and visitors to the department. Visitors also were drawn by music and ornamental banners in the booth of the Women's Christian Temperance Union, next door to the Woman's Department.

1893 WORLD'S COLUMBIAN FAIR

The first US commemoration of Christopher Columbus's "discovery" of the Americas occurred in 1792, his tercentenary, organized by members of the Massachusetts Historical Society paying tribute to the explorer.[7] Although 1892 was the four hundredth anniversary of Christopher Columbus landing on an island in the Caribbean and allegedly "discovering" the New World, the World's Columbian Fair opened late due to construction delays, with the grand opening in May 1893. The exposition closed at the end of October, tallying some twenty-seven million visitors, more than double the number of attendees at the 1876 Centennial in Philadelphia.

Textile designer and author Candace Wheeler, interior designer for the Woman's Building, commented on American art viewed by attendees: "English art-work is nearly always characterized by subdued and modified harmony, while that of America has vivid and striking notes which play upon a higher key, and still melt softly into each other as the perfect modulations of the best English art. I was very conscious of this during the year of my directorship of the Woman's Building and other exhibits at the World's Columbian Fair at Chicago, that place of wonderful comparisons of the art-work of the world. I could nearly always recognize work of American origin by its singing color-quality."[8] Wheeler specifically

Library of Congress Prints and Photographs Division

Woman's Building exterior, 1893, Chicago, J. F. Jarvis, publisher, stereoscopic photograph

Library of Congress Prints and Photographs Division

Woman's Building interior, 1893, Chicago

praised American embroidery, asserting, "It is among our own women that we find the highest grade of embroidery. The productions of the Americans are scholarly, but not academic. They are full of fresh originality, and the motto of our needlewomen seems to be that they must use the rules that have heretofore governed their art, but that they must not be hampered by them in their own fresh, spontaneous growth."[9]

Although needlework by Englishwomen on view was described as "old-fashioned," the *Chicago Tribune* praised "perhaps the most curious article in the collection . . . a patchwork quilt. It is composed of a large number of tiny pieces of print with scripture texts in eighteen different languages worked thereon in blue and red cotton."[10] This sort of novelty quilt seemed to catch the eye of reviewers, and perhaps also of quilters at the exposition. For several reviewers, domestic creations (such as quilts) were mentioned as not worth the effort of viewing in the Woman's Building. One reviewer, however, asserted that the building actually was worth visiting, because "there has been advancement in the industries and occupations since the time when women's work meant washing dishes, sweeping and dusting, spinning and weaving, and doing the family

Collection of Pamela Weeks

Columbian fabric depicting George Washington, Christopher Columbus, the Statue of Liberty, and abbreviations for the US states, ca. 1892

Library of Congress Prints and Photographs Division

A Southeast Asian woman (possibly Javanese) working with textiles at the 1893 Chicago fair, 1893

sewing. As a matter of very great fact the woman's building is one of the most attractive buildings on the grounds for both sexes. To be sure it is devoted to woman's work, but it is an astonishing revelation as well as an education to see how much of the work in this world is woman's work."[11] The assumption of "progress" in women's work since colonial times was paralleled in descriptions of work by African Americans, highly praised during the 1897 Tennessee Centennial (see below). While quilting was not included as a progressive activity, outstanding quilts nevertheless were praised by reporters and visitors alike. Various controversies in the press concerning exhibitions in the Woman's Building quite likely intrigued more attendees to visit it. By most accounts, the building was crowded throughout the run of the exposition.

Quilt historian Barbara Brackman, whose blog has been an inspiration for this book, researched quilts displayed at Chicago's world's fairs. From delving into archival material at the Chicago Historical Society, she determined that an official catalog of art and handcrafts in the 1893 Woman's Building had no mention whatsoever of quilts. There were, however, numerous pieces of textile art throughout the building, representing more than a dozen countries, notably extravagant embroidery in several formats, including a wall hanging from the Royal School of Needlework.[12] As in 1876, souvenir textiles were popular and found their way into quilts, and the textile industry marketed commemorative cotton yardage that was pieced into quilts.

Scattered references to quilts appeared in descriptions of a few state exhibits, including an antique quilt in the North Dakota exhibit allegedly by Mary, Queen of Scots, supposedly passed down through one of her maids of honor, which actually may have been a large embroidered textile. Brackman did locate one quilt in the Chicago Historical Society featuring a souvenir bandana from the exposition (#1952.161). She reported, "My original thesis that the fair would reflect the quilt-making activity has not been supported by the documentary evidence."[13] Researching more than four decades later with abundant online resources, I definitely can confirm her conclusion for the 1893 Exposition. While quilts created in the home environment achieved recognition and won premiums at county and state fairs, at the world's-fair level they sometimes were described by the press as old-fashioned, with attention focused instead on embroidery, weaving, lace making, tapestry, and decorative printing.

1897 TENNESSEE CENTENNIAL AND INTERNATIONAL EXPOSITION

Centennial Park in Nashville housed the Tennessee Centennial and International Exposition for six months in 1897, boosting civic pride and celebrating regional industry. Because this event was the first centennial celebration of a state being admitted to the Union, it attracted national press coverage. As happened several times in US history concerning ambitious commemorative events, the opening happened a year later than the actual centennial date, due to construction delays. In a triumph of technology, President McKinley fired up the Machinery Building from the White House via electric remote control. With more than one hundred buildings, the Tennessee Centennial attracted an impressive number of visitors for its location, nearly 1.8 million people. The attendance might have been much higher except for an epidemic of yellow fever assaulting the Gulf region that summer. During the height of the summer, demand for transportation to Nashville for the event soared, to the effect that the railroads added extra sections to trains and extra trains on the schedule, with freight trains limited to perishable goods only. Visitors could travel directly to the park on a special rail spur running from the Nashville station. One of the main attractions was a full-scale replica of the Parthenon in Athens, Greece, a venue for artwork. That temporary creation of a famous building from ancient Greece proved so popular that the city constructed a permanent version in the 1920s.

Quilts and aspects of quilt history could be viewed in several buildings of the Tennessee Centennial, including the Woman's Building, Negro Building, Education Building, Commerce Building, and Children's Building, which mounted a display from the Holston Institute, a Masonic school founded in 1886 near the city of Bristol. On view was a crazy

Woman's Building exterior, 1897, Nashville

Library of Congress Prints and Photographs Division

Negro Building exterior, 1897, Nashville

Library of Congress Prints and Photographs Division

Quilts in Negro Building (*seen at bottom*), 1897, Nashville, Keystone View Company, stereoscopic photograph

Library of Congress Prints and Photographs Division

quilt in the shape of Tennessee made by girls in the school, each county distinguished by its own patch of fabric.[14] The *Nashville Banner* mentioned that the Government Building, as part of its display of historical colonial objects, included "a piece of cloth that was hidden by a colonial dame from the British by being buried in the ground. The whole piece of cloth was afterwards made into a quilt and this bit offered for exhibition was taken from that."[15] Regardless of whether this story is true, the added value to a quilt fragment in the exhibition as a result of its supposed colonial history might have helped reinforce the late-nineteenth-century penchant for colonial style. From luxurious draperies and other elegant furnishings in the modern parlors to a colonial bedroom and sitting room reproducing a domicile that once headquartered George Washington, in this venue, according to the exposition catalog, "the noble women of Tennessee completed the chain which connects the history of the settlement on the Cumberland with the present city off Nashville."[16] This sort of vibrant connection with history typified centennial and bicentennial commemorations, inspiring quilt makers.

While the Woman's Building featured both embroidered needlework and quilts, press coverage seemed to focus more on embroidery than quilts. We do know that some of the quilts displayed during the US Centennial were offered for sale, including quilts in the Negro Building. The Boston Commissioners for the "Negro Department" in 1897 printed a circular containing a call for entries: "This is a rare chance for artists of the race [in Massachusetts] to show their work to the world. Any person possessing works of art will confer a great favor and help the cause by sending the same to us; the greatest care and safety will be used with these exhibits, and they will be returned free, or will be sold if the owner desires. . . . The Women's Board is the brightest feature of the Negro Department. It is hoped that all women's clubs and societies will co-operate with this board and send papers and documents on race progress, also fancy work, needle work, patch work, and quilts."[17] This building displayed some three hundred exhibitions from eighty-five cities. A stereoscopic photograph of the Negro Building's interior depicts the top edges of two large quilts hanging on a partition near the bottom of the image. The documentary booklet for 1897 has a page for each major building, with the text for the Negro Building patronizingly asserting a Black debt to whites: "The white race of the South has generously and wisely aided the Negro race to solve the problem of self-help. . . . The purpose of this department is to show the progress of the Negro race in America from the old plantation days to the present."[18] As usual in the attitudes of many whites toward African Americans at the time, there was a disconnect between the fact that it was white Americans who had forced them into the servitude from which they eventually were helped to "progress." The 1897 celebrations of Emancipation Day, with Booker T. Washington as a featured speaker representing Tuskegee Institute, drew large crowds of visitors to the building.

1904 LOUISIANA PURCHASE EXPOSITION

In 1803, the Louisiana Purchase granted to the US the possession of territories in the

Mississippi River basin extending from present-day Montana through the Texas Panhandle and ending in the eastern half of present-day Louisiana. The purchase for $15 million included sole jurisdiction of all Indian territories and, totaling more than 825,000 square miles, became the largest land deal in history. The city of St. Louis, Missouri, located at the eastern boundary of this former territory, began planning in 1889 for the centennial commemoration by offering city bonds for sale. Officially deemed the Louisiana Purchase Exposition, the event quickly became known as the St. Louis World's Fair. With a site of nearly 1,300 acres, the fair was almost double the area of the World's Columbian Exposition and included some 1,500 buildings. Partly because the 1904 Summer Olympic Games took place near the fairgrounds during the fair, attendance topped 19.5 million. This was the first time that the Olympic Games took place in the US, causing nationwide excitement.

Although no Women's Building was included among the many display areas, the St. Louis planners bowed to numerous public outcries from Missouri women and appointed Beverly H. Bonfoey, secretary of the 1904 World's Fair Commissioners, to select women's works for display. According to one report by St. Louis journalist Rose Marion, "Enough quilts to drive any other man crazy have been sent to him, but he only smiles and chooses [a] committee of women who will help him to pass on their many merits."[19] Bonfoey remarked that there were at least a carload of Missouri quilts alone—entirely too many to fit their allotted gallery space in the Missouri building—so he also assigned quilts to the Manufactures and Varied Industries Buildings. One of the quilts, a red, white, and blue composition by Mrs. Anna E. Carpenter of Ionia, impressed reviewers with its 25,653 pieces.[20] Quilts consisting of multitudinous pieces never failed to catch the eye of reporters and other fair attendees. In at least one instance, too much attention was paid by an unscrupulous viewer; press coverage of quilts at the fair described an act of vandalism: "The quilt is handmade and valued at $175. One large piece a foot square has been cut out of the quilt, while several smaller bits have been cut and torn from it. . . . The quilt was made by Mrs. Rhodes of Childress, Tex., and was placed in the Texas building for exhibition and sale. The material is very fine. It is a novel piece of work, the quilt being remarkable for the number of pieces it contains, which are said to be 58,588."[21]

Textile souvenirs featured several types of images. One small horizontal bandana depicted the Palace of Liberal Arts bordered with stars. A souvenir handkerchief listing the program of events for April 30 through May 2 had portraits of President Theodore Roosevelt and Governor David R. Frances,

▸ *Flag Quilt*, 1904, 74 × 75 in. The flag in the center seems to be that of Cuba, which possibly could be celebrating the Cuban athletes who won medals in St. Louis at the 1904 Summer Olympics, or honoring President Roosevelt, lauded as the hero of the Spanish-American War. On April 30, 1904, he sent a signal via telegraph to open the fair.

Palace of Liberal Arts souvenir textile, 5 × 7 in., 1904

Collection of Teresa Barkley

International Quilt Museum, University of Nebraska–Lincoln, 2017.018.0001

president of the exposition, along with portraits of Napoleon Bonaparte and Thomas Jefferson, who represented the US in the Louisiana Purchase. Visitors could also purchase jacquard-woven handkerchiefs of the main buildings as well as bandanas printed in several colors, such as a picture of the Cascade Gardens in blue and green with a multicolored floral border. Some of these textiles probably were incorporated into quilts, as was done after 1876 and 1893.

As the fair was closing in early December, St. Louis merchants purchased some of the works on display for their inventories. B. Nugent & Bro. Dry Goods Company took out a full-page ad in the December 4 *St. Louis Republic* announcing "first-class goods" from many prize exhibits currently being delivered to the store, perfect for holiday gifts. The business offered quilts and dress goods from the American section of the exhibitions.

1907 JAMESTOWN TER-CENTENNIAL EXPOSITION

The Jamestown Ter-Centennial (Tricentennial) Exposition of 1907 commemorated the first permanent English settlement founded in 1607, twelve years before the first enslaved Africans would be purchased there. Located at the harbor of Hampton Roads, quite close to the original Jamestown site, the exposition offered visitors the usual exhibition buildings as well as vistas of several fleets. US history and military displays dominated the main events, as documented in the event booklet: "Provision had been made for the greatest international and military celebration that the world has ever witnessed . . . and perhaps this marshal pageantry afloat and afield, by reason of its wondrous and spectacular interest, will be the most attractive feature of the great fair."[22] Hampton Roads was remembered for its part in the Revolutionary War and the War of 1812. Several speeches and other presentations emphasized America's miliary history, and the Department of State exhibited facsimiles of the founding documents along with portraits of founding fathers. The Smithsonian's display went much further back in time, featuring references to the aboriginal inhabitants of America. Because of Jamestown's historical association with Native Americans, the exposition used the midway, called the "War Path," to feature reenactments of mythologized events and a Wild West show. Members of the Pawmunkey tribe (part of the historic Powhatan Confederacy) performed in the reenactments, but groups of Plains Indians in feather headdresses and on horseback provided the other entertainment.

More than two dozen states erected buildings, several of which had decorative textiles on view, although I found no specific mention of quilts. The exposition had a

Textile, Silver, and Copper Building, 1906, Jamestown, color postcard

Collection of Sandra Sider

Collection of Teresa Barkley

Roosevelt souvenir handkerchief, ca. 1904

Collection of Teresa Barkley

Exposition bandana, 1904, depicting flags of the US and France

Textile, Silver, and Copper Building, where different types of fabric, sewing notions, and textile machinery were on display. A publication that categorized the classification of items exhibited, keyed to numbers that possibly indexed the items to locations in the exposition, included several groups of textiles, such as threads and fabrics of cotton (velvets and ribbons), of vegetable fibers other than cotton (damask and linen), and of animal fibers (dress goods of cotton mixed with silk). Silk and fabrics of silk had their own category, as did laces, embroidery, and trimmings.[23] As for textile souvenirs, visitors could purchase pillow slips and handkerchiefs depicting scenes from the exposition, as well as portraits of Pocahontas and John Smith, whom she allegedly rescued from death at the hands of her Powhatan tribe.[24]

Textiles were exhibited in the Negro Building. Events for the celebration of Negro Day on August 3 drew some eight thousand Black attendees at the Negro Building, where the Fisk Jubilee Singers performed and students from the Hampton Normal and Industrial Institute (now Hampton University) paraded on the field. A male quartet from the school sang "plantation melodies," and Booker T. Washington presented the main lecture, which doubtless drew the crowds. One reporter remarked, "Washington has cultivated with no small degree of success President Roosevelt's peculiar style of oratory, Mr. Roosevelt's gestures and head pose are readily observable in him,"[25] perhaps intending to describe a sort of homage. Although speakers such as Washington raised the daily attendance figures, the exposition failed financially. Only about three million people attended, fewer than half the number projected by the exposition's planners.

1926 SESQUICENTENNIAL OF THE UNITED STATES

Six years before the US sesquicentennial, the Nineteenth Amendment recognized the right of women to vote in federal elections. While bigotry and racism prevented many thousands of women from exercising that right for a very long time, the Nineteenth Amendment was a beginning for women across America. Unlike female visitors from the US at the 1876 Centennial, women in 1926 nominally were full citizens. As in 1876, Philadelphia hosted the event, titled the Sesquicentennial International Exposition, making it a world's fair, and women played an important role in that celebration. Even though the exposition failed financially and it took the city three years to repay all the debts, colonial revival displays in the Old High Street buildings organized by the Women's Committee successfully used eighteenth- and nineteenth-century artifacts, including quilts, to inform visitors about Philadelphia's history.

Newspapers often referred to the event as the "Sesqui," giving detailed descriptions of some of the state buildings. New Jersey constructed a replica of the 1759 military barracks in Trenton. The furnishings were intended to show visitors a taste of colonial style, including antique furniture and a patchwork quilt.[26] As ancillary displays for the Sesquicentennial, the city observed special short-term events, such as Revolutionary Day in July 1926, when the 1761 MacPherson Mansion in Fairmount Park was opened to the public. Most of the furnishings were gathered from collectors across the city, including items for the bedrooms, one of which featured the *Penn's Treaty with the Indians* quilt made by Martha Washington.[27] Typically for quilts on view during the exposition, they were meant to enhance the historicity of the event. The attitude of fair organizers toward American quilts as old-fashioned would be quite different for the next large-scale US commemoration in 1933.

Library of Congress Prints and Photographs Division

Negro Building, 1907, Jamestown, Keystone View Company, stereoscopic photograph

Between World War I and the early 1930s, the pioneering books on American quilt making by Marie Webster and Ruby Short McKim had become popular, with both women publishing quilt patterns and kits in magazines. Other enterprising women, such as Anne Orr, entered the market via magazines and newspapers, with quilt kits proliferating across the country. Orr, a native of Nashville, had been instrumental in organizing women to raise money for the Women's Pavilion at the Tennessee Centennial. She was editor of *Good Housekeeping* magazine from 1921 until World War II, publishing her articles on needlework.

Library of Congress Prints and Photographs Division

"America Welcomes the World," Sesquicentennial poster, 1926

1933 CENTURY OF PROGRESS

After the Black Hawk War in 1832 ended resistance from Native Americans, the town of Chicago was founded in 1833, making 1933 its centennial year. By that time, the city's population exceeded three million, with 25 percent unemployed—50 percent in the manufacturing sector—during the worst year of the Great Depression. But memberships to the fair had earlier been sold to some 118,000 Chicagoans, giving them access to the fair.[28] These funds, along with significant corporate sponsorships, made the Century of Progress events possible. Sears, Roebuck and Company, the mail-order retail giant based in Chicago, had opened its first on-site store in Chicago in 1925. Products included items for women as well as men, including sewing machines, notions, and fabric. In what turned out to be marketing genius, Sears opted to commemorate the Chicago centennial by sponsoring a contest for the best quilt maker in the country, resulting in an astonishing total of nearly 25,000 quilts submitted. Sears had advertised the Century of Progress Quilt Contest in its January 1933 catalog, mailed to twelve million subscribers across the country.[29]

Library of Congress Prints and Photographs Division

Monumental replica of the Liberty Bell, 1926, Philadelphia

As Barbara Brackman informs us, "Each Sears store sponsored a local contest with three winners. Their mail-order houses had similar contests. The winners at the local level were sent to ten district contests and the three best from each district were sent to Chicago."[30]

Monetary prizes rewarded the district (regional) winners. Prize money for the three top quilts nationally amounted to $1000, $500, and $300—significant money for 1933, and an incentive to enter the contest ($1,000 being worth more than $24,000 today). Although Sears offered a bonus of $200 if the first-place winner had entered a quilt with a Century of Progress theme, all three prize winners had used traditional patterns and kits sold by Sears. Judging by extant quilts and their patterns repeatedly published in magazines, those three patterns proliferated among quilt makers during the 1930s subsequent to the Century of Progress publicity.

Reporters were especially taken by unique modernistic quilts depicting the Century of Progress theme: "The new patch quilts are strictly 1933 and as daring and as breezy as the new skyline of the Century of Progress buildings are stunning . . . you will see a breath-taking gray quilt that tells the story of steel. . . . It is a most imposing sort of a quilt, rather cold and uncomfortable and a bit sinister . . . but one of the most unusual and remarkable creations ever displayed."[31] The finalist judges, including Anne Orr, preferred traditional patterns with extremely fine hand quilting. One quilt maker, Ida M. Stow of Park Ridge, Illinois, complained in

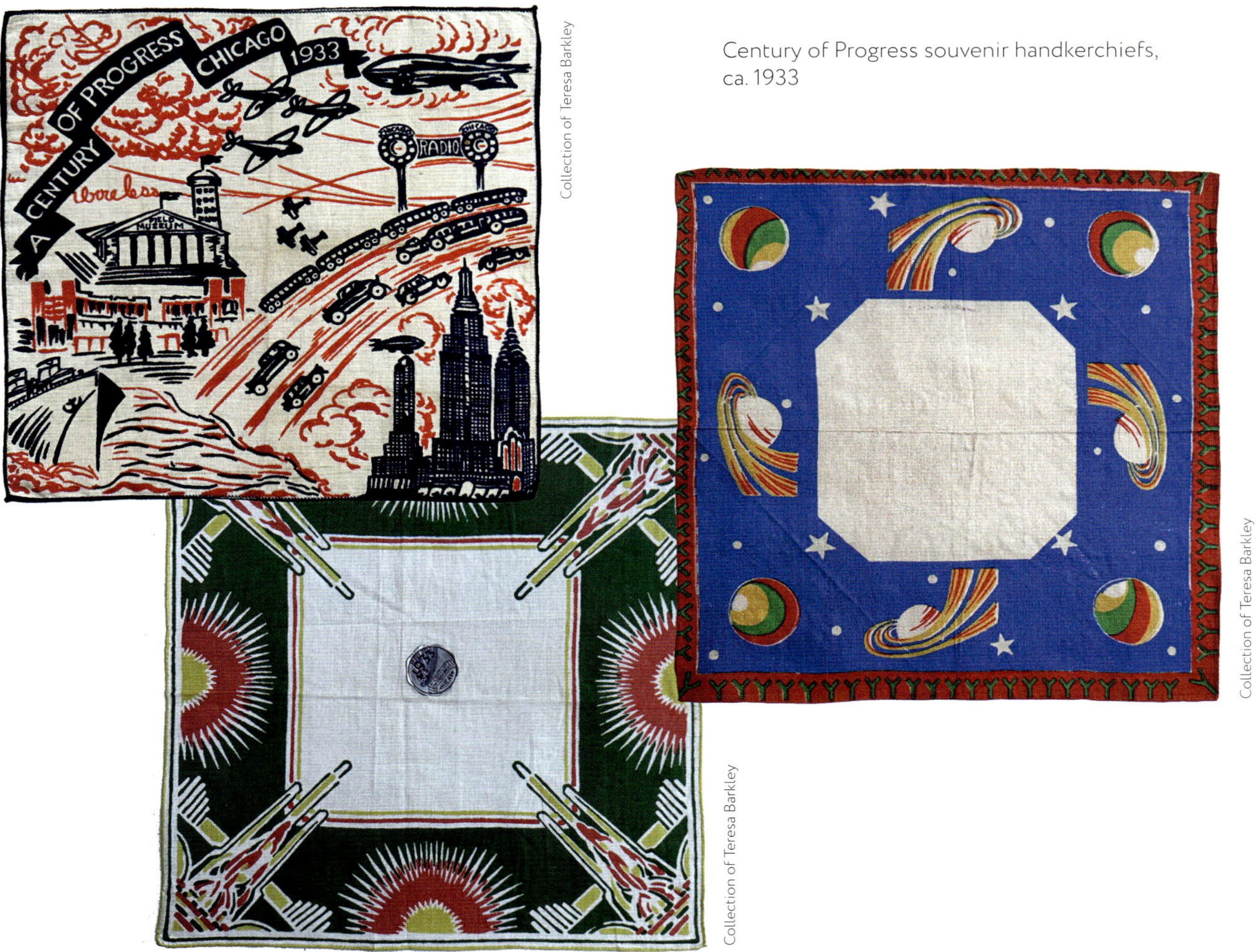

Century of Progress souvenir handkerchiefs, ca. 1933

Collection of Teresa Barkley

Collection of Teresa Barkley

Collection of Teresa Barkley

Collection of Sandra Sider

Sears Building, 1933, color postcard

a letter that the judges "were biased against the quilts that commemorated the fair in unique designs."[32]

Winning entries could be viewed in the Sears Building on the fairground. Individual Sears stores mounted exhibitions of regional winners, such as the 1933 "Century of Progress" show in their State Street venue in Chicago, displaying prize-winning quilts from eight states in the Midwest region.[33] The fact that the *Chicago Tribune* had a "patchwork quilt editor," Nancy Cabot (pen name of Loretta Leitner Rising), who wrote a daily column offering patterns and snippets of quilt history, testified to the popularity of the craft. At the state level, press reports on quilts selected to be shown in Chicago made big news, such as a quilt coming from Mississippi: "Representing many hours of tedious work, the patriotic quilt now on display in the show window of Downing-Locke store on Capitol Street is attracting much attention. The quilt made by Mrs. L. P. Roberts Sr. . . . was three months in the making. In the center of the quilt a huge map of the United States has been worked in with the flower of each state cleverly interwoven into the cloth. An American flag and the Eagle are the designs over the map, while around in the edges in various colors the seals of the various states have been worked into the design."[34] As if this work in cotton fabrics were not impressive enough, the quilter was proceeding to replicate her design in silk.

1936 TEXAS CENTENNIAL AND DALLAS EXPOSITION

Texas in the mid-1930s desperately needed an economic boost. The Panhandle was a veritable dust bowl, and other parts of the state suffered from a severe drought affecting both agriculture and cattle ranching. Even though the oil industry had been thriving, companies were ordered to limit production during the early 1930s. Times were hard for most Texans, and discretionary government funding could not pay for the entire fair. But like Chicago, Texas had begun planning for the Texas Centennial a few years before the Great Depression. In addition, companies such as Ford and DuPont funded their own ambitious exhibitions. Because of extensive fairground space used for the Texas State Fair, Dallas hosted the events. In fact, the Centennial coincided with the fiftieth anniversary of the state fair in that location. Art deco architecture erected in Fair Park for the Centennial was intended to become permanent parts of the site, with a total budget of $15 million. The concentration of fifty buildings, described as "severe in line and contour like Aztec architecture" with vistas of "stately simplicity,"[35] was like nothing the six million visitors had ever seen.

According to Suzanne Yabsley, "The dire economic situation of the time prompted quilting for practical reasons, while the

International Quilt Museum, University of Nebraska–Lincoln, 1997.007.0368

◀ Emma Mae Leonhard (Illinois), *From 1833 to 1933* quilt, ca. 1933, 86.5 × 78 in., alternating blocks featuring stylized art deco architecture at the Chicago World's Fair, also depicting fashion through the century, entered in the Sears contest

Texas Centennial (1936) inspired the making of special quilts."[36] Two of those quilts, created by African American makers, could be viewed in the Hall of Negro Life and Culture Building within Fine Arts, documented by Jesse O. Thomas: "'Lone Star' quilts, which in design represented a map of the State of Texas on which each county was designated, with the rivers and mountainous sections of the State brought out in bold relief."[37] Surprised not to find more mentions of Texas quilts on view, I sent an email inquiry to the Dolph Briscoe Center for American History at the University of Texas, Austin, which houses numerous boxes of archival material pertaining to the Texas Centennial. My inquiry revealed that the Texas Centennial Historical Contest called for "relics" made or used in Texas prior to 1900, with prizes awarded. Given the rich, diverse quilt culture of Texas, our largest state by far at the time, quilts or images of quilts should have been on view. That contest may have resulted in antique quilts being viewed by the visitors.[38]

Collection of Sandra Sider

Women's Museum, 1936, Dallas, postcard

1939–1940 NEW YORK WORLD'S FAIR

Opening on April 30, 1939, this world's fair commemorated the sesquicentennial of George Washington's first inauguration, which took place in New York City. Under the directorship of Robert Moses, the city reclaimed and transformed a wasteland in Flushing Meadows into fairgrounds. By 1940, Europe had entered World War II, which meant that some countries closed their exhibits before the second season. Nevertheless, the fair continued to attract visitors.

Even though the timing of the fair looked backward to the city's history, the official theme in 1939 was *The World of Tomorrow*. Previous world's fairs had emphasized the triumph of technology at the time and how it could make life at home and at work better. In 1939, technological inventions pointed to the future, such as promises made by RCA about television. At the fair, it captured moving images of people outside, then showed them inside the RCA Pavilion, a hint of possibilities to come when "tele" would become distances far away. NBC broadcast President Franklin Roosevelt opening the fair by boosting the signal to an aerial atop the Empire State Building. Numerous exhibitors installed "futuristic" rooms and machines, such as a Futuristic Kitchen. Automobile-manufacturing companies competed to publicize the cars and model roadways of tomorrow.

During its two seasons, the fair welcomed forty-five million attendees, with many New Yorkers attending more than once. The 375 buildings offered something for everyone, including the Textile Building, exhibiting fabrics, patterns, and textile equipment. The spherical Perisphere adjacent to the tall, spiky Trylon, symbols of the fair, appeared on textile souvenir bandanas and handkerchiefs incorporated into quilts. Cotton yardage printed for 1939 depicted miniature figures in traditional costumes, emphasizing the fair's international flavor, as well as a bird's-eye-view of the fairgrounds.

Macy's department store and *Good Housekeeping* magazine sponsored a nationwide 1939 World's Fair quilt contest titled *Better Living in The World of Tomorrow*, resulting in only 250 entrants. Quilt makers were required to submit work of their own original designs—quite unlike the 1933 Chicago contest—which may have discouraged quilters who preferred to follow traditional patterns. The first-place winner was Mrs. Elsie G. Heller from Allegheny, Pennsylvania, with her quilt *Power* described in the *New York Times* as "a dark gray cogwheel in the center with bolts of orange and flame-red lightning radiating from it. The field is beige, and torches and cornucopias are stitched into it."[39] After the city decided to extend the fair into 1940, another contest sponsored by the world's fair, titled *America Through the Needle's Eye*, opened the competition to work previously completed, as well as new work made specifically for the competition, with five divisions of textile art that included patchwork. Bertha Stenge of Chicago won the first prize in patchwork with her handsomely trapuntoed *Palm Leaf* quilt, which already had won first prizes at the Kentucky and Illinois State Fairs.[40]

1962 CENTURY 21 EXPOSITION

By the late 1950s, the US enjoyed a booming postwar economy as the Great Depression faded into memory. Quilt making as a home craft also diminished in many parts of the country as families purchased manufactured blankets and comforters. All eyes focused on the space race after President Kennedy announced in a special 1961 speech to Congress that the US should commit to putting a man on the moon and bringing him home safely within the decade. Just two months before the Century 21 Exposition opened in Seattle in 1962, John Glenn became the first American to orbit the earth. The textile industry marketed fabrics in the early 1960s featuring space-age motifs such as rockets, astronauts, planets, and flying saucers. It seemed as if the future was fast approaching, and close to ten million visitors journeyed to Seattle to see it. The exposition helped transform Seattle into an important nexus of international trade, the city's main goal for the fair. This world's fair had been in the planning stage as early as 1959, the fiftieth anniversary of the Alaska-Yukon-Pacific Exposition that took place in Seattle, demonstrating the city's potential for private investors and federal funding for such commemorative events.

In 1962 the Space Needle, with its revolving panoramic restaurant, attracted tourists by the hundreds. At the time, this 605-foot-high tower was the tallest structure west of the Mississippi. Its restaurant, named Eye of the Needle, emphasized the symbolism of a needle pointing to space. From the stationary observation deck above the restaurant, visitors could enjoy spectacular views of Mt. Rainier and the mountain ranges, Puget Sound, the city of Seattle, and the fairgrounds below. At a time when relatively few people traveled via air, seeing the earth from such a height provided a thrilling experience.

▸ Marie Mueller (Iowa), *Cornucopia* quilt, ca. 1933, 95 × 85 in., entered in the Sears contest

International Quilt Museum, University of Nebraska–Lincoln, 1997.007.0266

Among the millions of visitors, there must have been quite a few quilters. They would have had the opportunity to see and purchase arts and crafts in booths and houses erected by more than three dozen nations, with Asia strongly represented along with European countries in the Boulevards of the World.[41] The Filipino Pavilion offered an expansive area for commerce and industry, reported in the *Filipino Forum*: "In this section of the Pavilion, the focus is on the Philippines' major export products. Coconut, sugar, minerals, lumber, hemp, tobacco, textiles and embroideries, furniture and handicrafts, shell products, and processed fruits."[42] India also hosted a beautiful pavilion, displaying lengths of colorful silk and other textiles. In another pavilion for Interiors, Fashion, and Commerce, according to the exposition program, "the American Institute of Interior Designers coordinates a vast display of home and office furnishings. The fabrics and fashions are shown in the present and projected into the future."[43] These exhibitions would have intrigued quilt makers looking for new motifs and materials.

1964–1965 NEW YORK WORLD'S FAIR

The date of New York City's founding can be confusing, since it has two such dates: 1625 for the Dutch incorporation and 1664 for when the English renamed New Netherland as New York. In 1975 the date on the Seal of New York was changed from 1664 to 1625, meaning that the 1964 World's Fair commemorated the first triennial, based on 1664. Unlike the 1939 World's Fair, which occurred in the exact same location, the 1964 event had copious televised coverage of exhibitions and activities by eighty nations, some 350 private companies, and two dozen US states.

Like the 1939 fair, the city extended this event into a second season, totaling more than fifty million visitors. The gigantic steel Unisphere, depicting the earth's geographical areas, symbolized the theme of "Peace Through Understanding." I visited the fair as a teenager and still remember how people in the audience were amazed by the clunky AT&T Picturephone, and how awed I was by robotics exploring the "lunar surface" in Futurama II, hosted by General Motors and designed by Disney. My most vivid memories recall performers from other countries in their regional and national costumes, especially from Greece, the Ivory Coast, China, and Mexico.

Although the fair's publicity evidently had no mention of quilts on view, at least one state presented quilters at work, as an example of regional craft in West Virginia.[44] Some of

▸ Myrtle Louise Black Collord (Idaho), *World's Fair Map Quilt*, 1939, 71.5 × 87 in.

New York World's Fair souvenir handkerchief, 1965

Collection of Teresa Barkley

International Quilt Museum, University of Nebraska–Lincoln, 2022.003.0001

the other venues probably would have interested quilt makers, notably the India Pavilion, with its selection of saris, and the African Pavilion, selling native handicrafts, including textiles. Also, the Singer Bowl stadium, sponsored by the Singer Company, installed a large display space underneath the stadium, offering the latest fabrics, sewing projects, and Singer products.

1968 SAN ANTONIO WORLD'S FAIR

When San Antonio was founded in 1718 with its own presidio, the settlement served as a mission town near the eastern border of the Viceroyalty of New Spain in the Americas. After belonging to the Mexican Republic from 1821 to 1836, the city of San Antonio became part of the Republic of Texas until Sam Houston led Texas to statehood in 1845. Since the early eighteenth century, San Antonio's population has been largely Hispanic. For its semiquincentennial anniversary celebration, named Hemisfair, the city looked to its Hispanic neighbors in the Southern Hemisphere, thus the punning title of the event. More than six million people attended the fair, whose iconic image

Collection of Teresa Barkley

◀ Teresa Barkley (Maplewood, New Jersey), *Take Me to the Fair* quilt, 1989, 39 × 39 in., with 1939 World's Fair souvenir bandana in center

is the Tower of the Americas, dominating the skyline today. While its concrete shaft is the height of Seattle's Space Needle, the restaurants at the top bring the tower's height several feet higher.

IBM hosted two pavilions. In their Durango pavilion, visitors could experiment with two IBM display terminals to design textiles described in the souvenir guidebook: "These television-like units are each equipped with an electronic 'light pen.' Visitors can sit at the terminals and create individual fabric designs with the 'light pen.' The design is then woven by the loom under instructions from the computer. The four-inch swatch of fabric that results is then presented to the visitor that designed it."[45] What lover of textile design would not have enjoyed that experience? Fabrics could be purchased in several areas, such as the Thailand exhibition, showing fine silks, and in Las Plazas del Mundo market, offering various textiles, including handcrafts, from Latin American vendors.

Hemisfair had a Woman's Pavilion funded at the last minute, thanks to the efforts of local women. As the official fair guidebook explained, "The unifying theme that runs through Hemisfair '68 is the confluence of civilizations in the Americas: Man, the adventurer, explored the new untracked wilderness but it was woman, the home-maker, who civilized it. The Woman's Pavilion at Hemisfair was conceived in honor of that contribution. . . . The exhibit encompasses works of art and craft, evidence of woman's role in business, and her contributions to the performing arts."[46] The 1968 guidebook could not have made clearer the perceived cultural dichotomy between the purpose of "man" and "woman." None of the earlier fairs discussed had a "man's" building or pavilion, because the events focused almost exclusively on male accomplishments.

What is especially fascinating about women's participation in the San Antonio event is that it was planned after Title VII of the 1964 Civil Rights Act and the Supreme Court decision of 1965 demanding more rights for women, such as equal pay for equal work, encouraging the second wave of feminism in this country. In 1876 and 1893, separate buildings for women at the fairs and the women who organized them provided venues for suffragist activities, contributing to feminism's first wave. According to an article in *Southwestern Historical Quarterly*, "The Board of Lady Managers for 1893 represented every state and a growing nationwide network of women's clubs, through which they paid for the building, collected the artifacts that filled it, and organized a week-long Women's Congress that drew huge crowds . . . to hear lectures about women's contributions to virtually every aspect of life and thought."[47] In 1968, as America found itself on the verge of a cultural revolution involving gender, race, and other explosive topics, the 1968 Woman's Building epitomized the status quo—the doldrums of many women between World War II and the 1960s who had dropped the creativity of quilt making as, in the words of Robert Shaw, "out of sync with the modern world."[48] That attitude would soon change.

CHAPTER 5

History Repeats Itself

Events leading up to the 1976 US Bicentennial had several noteworthy similarities with what was happening between the 1860s and 1876. Although the economic recession of the early 1970s proved to be not as severe as that of 1873–1877, energy prices soared, oil was embargoed, and inflation raised the costs of daily living in general. Disillusionment with the government extended from the small towns of America to Washington, DC, itself. Unlike in the 1860s, we experienced no large-scale civil war at home, but we intervened in the civil war of Vietnam, resulting in the deaths of nearly 60,000 Americans and the societal upheaval of antiwar protests. Like reactions to the peace of 1865 when the fighting ended, people in this country breathed a sigh of relief in 1973, when our combat troops left Vietnam. After the scandal of Watergate, and President Nixon's resignation on the eve of the Bicentennial, the US needed a fresh focus. Both the Centennial and Bicentennial years seemed like new beginnings.

Concerning racial politics, Reconstruction, which lasted from 1865 to 1877, seemed to offer hope to African Americans but was accompanied by continued violence and discrimination. After this country reeled from the race riots of 1965 in Los Angeles, as well as those of 1967 in Newark and Detroit, the national outcry following the assassination of Martin Luther King Jr. in 1968 galvanized civil rights leaders. Both the Nixon and Ford administrations, which included Black advisors, attempted to improve conditions for school desegregation, voting, and Black colleges, among other initiatives.

The year 1876 had also brought into the spotlight the ongoing genocide of Native Americans, an issue that continued to prompt action on the part of the American Indian Movement (AIM), founded in 1968. Protesting broken treaties and federal encroachment on natural resources in what was supposed to have been Native American land, in 1973 members of AIM occupied the town of Wounded Knee in southwestern South Dakota, where the US military had massacred close to three hundred Lakota Sioux in 1890. Responding to various AIM demands, Congress passed the Indian Self-Determination and Education Act of 1975, which recognized additional tribal rights and provided federal funding. American women in 1876 found themselves almost three

Courtesy of the Woodrow Wilson Presidential Library, Staunton, Virginia

Red Cross Quilt, 1917, 85 × 73 in., made in Kansas

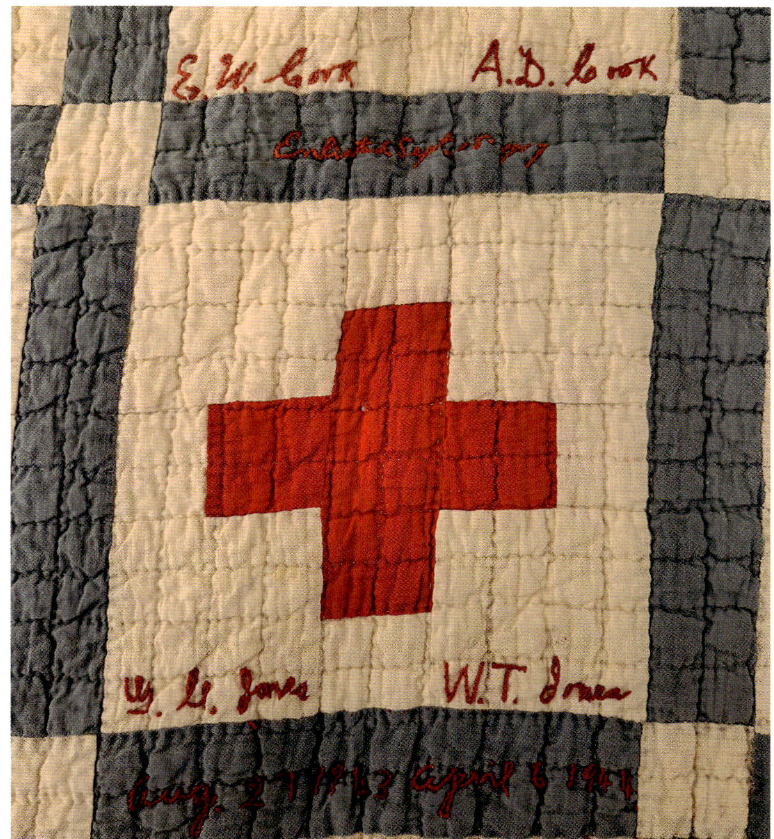

Courtesy of the Woodrow Wilson Presidential Library, Staunton, Virginia

Detail, *Red Cross Quilt*

decades past the 1848 proto-feminist *Declaration of Sentiments*, lobbying for their full rights of citizenship along with equal pay for equal work. The National Woman Suffrage Association, founded in 1869, was led by Susan B. Anthony and Elizabeth Cady Stanton. The National Organization for Women, founded in 1966, still lobbies for gender equality, including equal pay for equal work.

As a commemorative event, the 1876 Centennial overrode and even subsumed some of the above issues in a patriotic frenzy. As a lead-up to the Bicentennial, we consider how quilt making throughout the twentieth century prior to 1976 continued to encourage the tradition of patriotic self-expression, inevitably resulting in a deluge of Bicentennial quilts in 1976 and immediately afterward. These patriotic quilts, while not all commemorative, help contextualize the outpouring of 1976 quilts. We also explore different approaches to "patriotism" and patriotic feeling in American quilts. Between 1876 and 1976, the concept of patriotism became more complex and diverse. Just as the Centennial united most Americans in the midst of ongoing conflicts, the Bicentennial witnessed a nationwide fiesta, even during various protests.

PATRIOTISM IN PRESIDENTIAL QUILTS

Presenting quilts to the White House as tokens of presidential appreciation was documented as early as 1865, with a flag quilt made in California for Ulysses S. Grant. By the twentieth century, members of the press took note of such gifts. President Taft received, as reported in a Pittsburgh newspaper, "a red, white, and blue quilt from

S. H. Read of Merna, Neb., a civil war veteran 82 years old, who wrote that the quilt had been made entirely by hand and contained 5,982 separate pieces."[1] During the presidency of Woodrow Wilson, gifts from Americans included at least three quilts, one from a German American, Charles Miller, described by a journalist in Richmond: "It is intended as a gift from Mr. Miller to President-elect and Mrs. Wilson. It contains 1,600 patches of silk, some in the colors of Old Glory, others in the Princeton orange and black, a few in dark red and navy, the colors of Germany. Typical of the White House is an attractive counter-design in white."[2]

President Wilson received a Red Cross quilt made in Kansas around 1917 that includes embroidery reading "EW Cook, AD Cook, Enlisted Sept. 18, 1917," as well as names of two members of the Jones family who served in WWI. With a color palette of red, white, and blue, this quilt was created in patriotic mode. Edith Wilson, the first lady, was presented with a quilt consisting of multitudinous tobacco silks assembled in strips and depicting world leaders, flags, and other subjects.[3] Gifting a quilt to her at this time—during the final two years of Wilson's presidency—was like presenting a quilt to the president, who had suffered a debilitating stroke in 1919. Mrs. Wilson administered presidential business, interpreting his wishes for the cabinet and assigning decisions to various governmental officials.

President Harding's wife, Florence, had an interest in quilt making. She organized a quilt fundraising project in 1921 with the Whatsoever Circle of Kings Daughters in Marion, Ohio, to benefit a local hospital. During Warren G. Harding's presidential

Courtesy of the Woodrow Wilson Presidential Library, Staunton, Virginia

Tobacco Silks Quilt, ca. 1920, 91 × 68 in., made in Delaware

Courtesy of the Woodrow Wilson Presidential Library, Staunton, Virginia

Detail, *Tobacco Silks Quilt*

Collection of Teresa Barkley

Republican campaign handkerchief

Collection of Teresa Barkley

Democrat campaign handkerchief

campaign, Mrs. Harding gathered fifty-four autographs on fabric swatches of political luminaries such as Presidents Taft and Wilson, and Vice President and Mrs. Calvin Coolidge, plus authors, film stars, and others for the purpose of having them pieced into the "Harding front porch quilt." A cabinet member purchased the quilt for $150.[4] Assembling autograph quilts like this would become popular during the Bicentennial. Although not a quilt but a woolen blanket, the first edition of the Harding Jacquard Wool Blanket was presented to the president in 1923, when the Hardings visited the Pendleton factory in Oregon during a trip to dedicate part of the Old Oregon Trail. The blanket's geometric motifs in red, white, and blue became one of Pendleton's most popular designs, and the company continues to reproduce it today in the form of a quilt-like cotton coverlet.

We know from nineteenth-century quilt history that blocks with the letter "T" covering the surface often were created to indicate support of temperance and prohibition. The same sort of overall lettered motif honored some of our presidents, such as an "H" quilt from Ohio. Made around 1930, it celebrated the presidency of Herbert Hoover in forty-eight "H" blocks, white lettering on blue, with a red background.[5] The elephant and donkey, symbols of our two major political parties, appeared in patterns for quilt blocks, especially a year or two in advance of a presidential election—such as "A Very Democratic Donkey," published by the *Kansas City Star* shortly before the 1932 election.[6] Each party produced its own campaign textiles that were worked into quilts and other objects as patriotic symbols.

Library of Congress Prints and Photographs Division

National Recovery Act yoyo quilt in NRA office, Washington, DC

Franklin Delano Roosevelt served as president from 1933 until 1945, before term limits were ratified in 1951, steering the US through the Great Depression. To that end, he established the National Recovery Agency as part of his New Deal for America to help industry recover from the economic fiasco. Although the Supreme Court declared this aspect of the New Deal to be unconstitutional and shut it down in 1936, several of the goals were accomplished, with Roosevelt viewed as a hero by many workers. Textile companies printing feed-sack bags honored him in their motifs. We have several "NRA" quilts from that time featuring the blue eagle insignia of the agency, and at least one of them was gifted to the president.[7] The blue eagle became a symbol of patriotism nationwide for businesses supporting the recovery effort as shop owners posted the image on their packages and in their windows. They

▼ Franklin Roosevelt feed-sack fabric

Collection of Teresa Barkley

Courtesy of the Harry S. Truman Library and Museum

Alphabet Quilt, ca. 1945–1952, 83.5 × 64 in. Artifact #1960.

commercialized patriotic imagery like many businesses would do in 1976.

Of the three quilts owned by the Harry S. Truman Presidential Library & Museum, one was donated during his presidency (1945–1953), an alphabet quilt in patriotic colors. The alphabet letters quite probably were reddish, not pink as pictured above, which could have been caused by sun fading. The fact that the quilt has a sleeve on the back suggests that it was hanging on a wall, exposed to light and air. In the context of red, white, and blue ticking fabric used as horizontal sashing, this quilt seems much more like a patriotic quilt than first glance would indicate. Also, red was a very popular color to use for the lettering in alphabet quilts. President Eisenhower, 1953–1961, grew up with quilt making in Kansas, helping his mother in her sewing projects. The Dwight D. Eisenhower Library & Museum owns eleven quilts, including a variation of the *Windmill* pattern in red, white, and blue cotton, with tiny white stars in the blue triangles. Eisenhower grew up in the town of Abilene, Kansas, and worked in farming, involved with sustainable methods. The windmill is a popular symbol of Kansas, ubiquitous on farms during Eisenhower's youth. During the Bicentennial, quilts celebrating individual states often highlighted their state symbols.

President Kennedy received several quilts as gifts, including at least three with patriotic themes, during his two brief years in the White House before he was assassinated. One of the quilts was made by Mrs. Ethel Zinn (or Vinn, according to some sources) with the help of 4-H girls. Quilting in her nursing home in Wichita, Kansas, she presented the White House with a Kansas Centennial quilt, 1861–1961, combining appliquéd and pieced blocks.[8] President Lyndon Johnson also was gifted several quilts. During Richard Nixon's presidency, quilts with patriotic imagery were presented to the White House, including a presidential quilt that has a large blue (Republican) eagle in the center, surrounded by red stars on a white background, made by three Kentucky sisters.[9] In 1970, wives of the Republican members of the Eighty-Eighth Congress presented Pat Nixon with a huge quilt embroidered with signatures of their husbands.[10] In 1971, a group of senior citizens in Jones County, Mississippi, completed a red, white, and blue quilt and gifted it to the White House.[11] Regardless of political party affiliation, all these quilts—and they are representative of similar gifts—indicate attitudes of respect and admiration not only

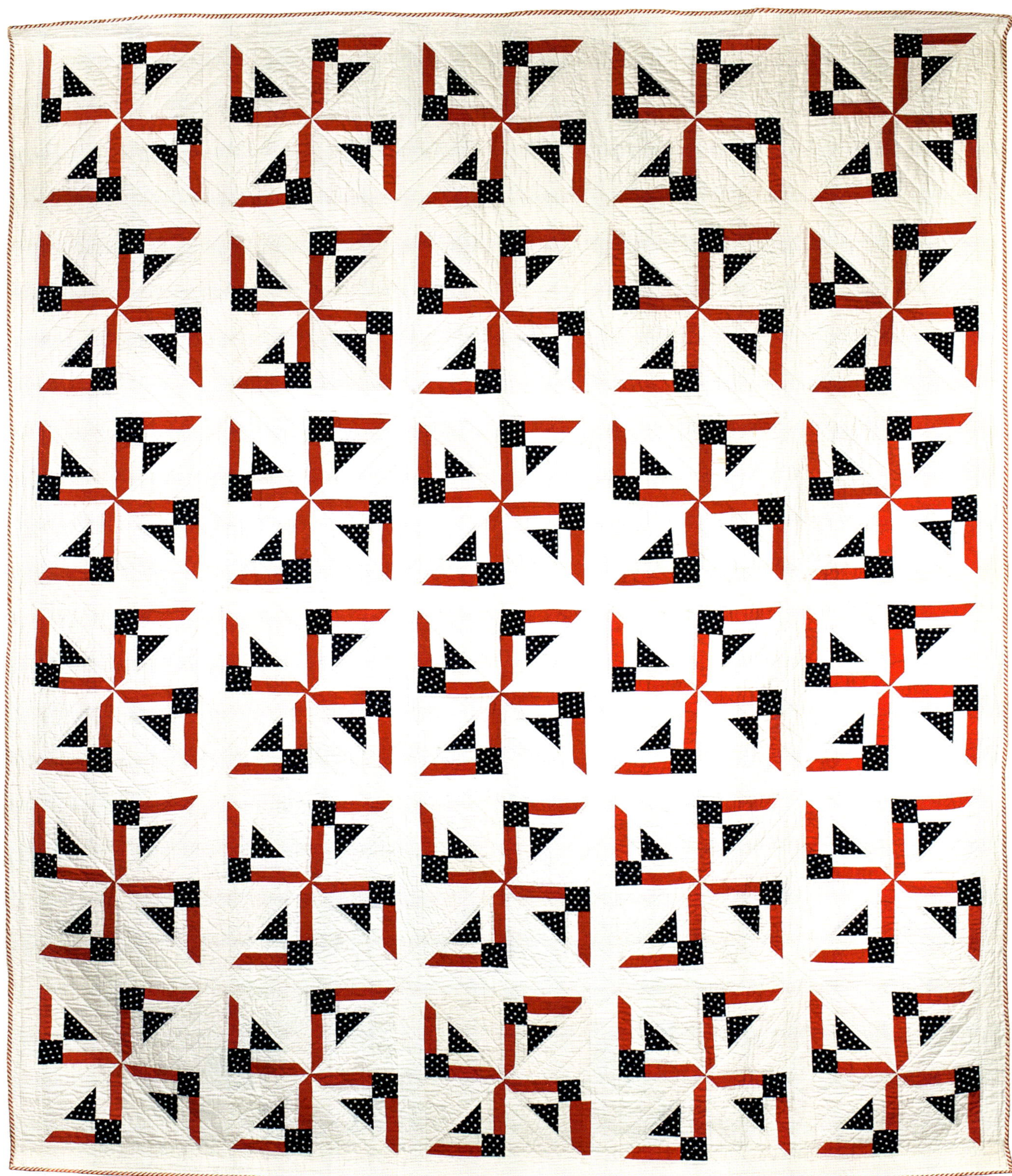

Courtesy of the National Archives and Records Administration, Dwight D. Eisenhower Presidential Library, Abilene, Kansas

Bertha Smith, *Windmill Variation* (1950s), 94 × 78.5 in.

for the president as a person but also as a symbol of the country. Patriotic quilts donated to Gerald R. Ford take us to the Bicentennial, the subject of a later chapter.

The word "patriotism" usually evokes national fervor, and a related concept of loyalty and commitment applies to residents of villages, towns, cities, and states. Patriotism can be expressed in numerous ways, even in protests stemming from concern about issues and actions conflicting, or seeming to conflict, with America's ideals.

NATIVE AMERICANS AND BICENTENNIAL AMBIVALENCE

During the last quarter of the nineteenth century, missionaries taught members of the Lakota, part of the Sioux nation, how to make quilts. Some makers incorporated narrative imagery, while most makers preferred the eight-pointed star as their pattern, a motif similar to the Morning Star in their cosmology. Sometime between 1900 and 1910, Rebecca Blackhorse created a quilt depicting a year in the activities of her Sioux tribe. This celebratory pictorial work can be "read" via the lines of images that wrap around from upper left to lower right. Several of the images are repeated, representing ritual and the rhythm of life. Blackhorse evidently suggested the passage of time by a bird looking at its nest of eggs at the beginning, ending with the same bird beside its nestlings. The maker's visual celebration of her tribal activities speaks of pride at the local level.[12] A tightly knit sense of community contributes to the solidarity of members of First Nations in the US, reflecting patriotic attitudes toward their own sovereignty.

In 1934, Congress passed the Indian Reorganization Act, reducing federal control of reservations and encouraging tribal autonomy. This legislation also specifically recognized Native Americans as US citizens. Fifteen Oglala Lakota women created individual blocks assembled into the *Remembrance*

Collection of Teresa Barkley

"Win with Ike" campaign handkerchief

Collection of Teresa Barkley

John F. Kennedy memorial fabric, 1966, made in Liberia

International Quilt Museum, University of Nebraska-Lincoln, 2008.041.0038E

Hortense Beck (Topeka, Kansas), 1990–1991 copy of Rebecca Blackhorse, *Sioux Indian Life* quilt, 79 × 68 in.

Remembrance Quilt, 1934, 63 × 63 in., Pine Ridge Indian Reservation, South Dakota

Volckening Collection, Portland, Oregon

Lakota Sioux "Bicentennial" Quilt, ca. 1976, 70 × 74 in.

Quilt, in which they embroidered their names and the date April 11, 1934, on their blocks. Because men dominated the tribal governance, women from the community gathering to create such a political quilt was a memorable action. This quilt commemorates the start of the Pine Ridge Indian Reservation in South Dakota as a self-governing body. Larry Belitz, curator of the Wounded Knee Museum at the time of the 1973 Wounded Knee Occupation, salvaged this important cultural document after the fire that occurred then.[13]

Native Americans have expressed patriotism for the US itself, fighting in our wars and joining veterans' organizations. Star quilts gifted to those who served have recognized and honored that service, often in the flag colors of red, white, and blue. While some of those Native American quilts from the 1970s have been categorized by collectors as Bicentennial quilts, they might simply be quilts of honor for veterans and their families, for whom our flag colors would be appropriate.[14] Ambivalence toward celebrating America's Bicentennial pervaded the First Nations. As reported by the *San Francisco Chronicle* concerning Oregon, "The state's Indians are divided over support of the Bicentennial. Some support the celebration and are preparing to add their contribution to local observances. Others say support of the country's 200th anniversary indicates approving what they see as the destruction of Indian life, and the taking of Indian land."[15] For tribes participating in the Bicentennial programming, we might expect to see Bicentennial quilts. But unless we have evidence directly from the maker(s) that this is the case, we need to be careful with such categorizations.

WOMEN WAVING THEIR FLAG

We might not think of suffragists as taking time for needlework, but they did indeed, especially for purposes of fundraising. Supporters of women's suffrage at the grassroots level realized the value of quilts to raise money, as documented by a Kansas newspaper: "Bazaars are no new feature to feminine annals. Mrs. Grinstead held one recently at Liberal for campaign expenses. She cleared $10. One object of special interest was a quilt pieced for the suffrage cause by Grandmother Patrick, who is nearly 92 years old."[16] The fundraiser was Minnie Johnson Grinstead, a teacher, lecturer for the Women's Christian Temperance Union, politician, and dedicated advocate of women's suffrage. In 1918, she won on the Republican ticket to become the first woman to serve in the Kansas legislature (women had the right to vote in Kansas as of 1912). By 1976, women were becoming a powerful presence in American politics, and hundreds of women, as individuals and in groups, embraced quilt making as a quintessential women's art for their commemorative quilts.

The Museum of Fine Arts in Boston owns a quilt called the *Hoosier Suffrage Quilt* that evidently was completed in Indiana during the early twentieth century, prior to the 1920 passing of the Nineteenth Amendment. Pieced in red-and-white vertical stripes with white stars appliquéd on blue, this quilt referencing the US flag contains more than three hundred embroidered names assumed to indicate supporters of women's suffrage. Susan B. Anthony's name is among them. While the flag-like colors and format of this quilt do suggest a statement concerning government policies, much more research needs to be done to determine whether the quilt truly was associated with women's suffrage. We do know that many of the embroidered names are those of families residing in Indiana at the time. But the quilt might also be a Temperance quilt. Many people, Susan B. Anthony among them, were involved in both the suffrage movement and the various temperance organizations.

Suffrage leaders did pause to stitch ceremonial "ratification stars" to their tricolor white, purple, and gold suffrage flag in recognition of each state as it ratified the Nineteenth Amendment. After Congress passed the amendment in June 1919, three-fourths of the states finally ratified the amendment, which took until August 1920. We might assume that women who had worked for much of their lives to have the vote for all women at the national level could have celebrated their victory by making quilts. But such quilts have proved to be exceedingly rare, and that may have been caused by another event coinciding with the Nineteenth Amendment's passage—the flu pandemic that began in 1918 and lasted for more than a year. Many people were simply too sick or too consumed with caring for others to have leisure time for quilt making. Even though nurses and doctors worked ceaselessly, there were too few medical personnel and too many seriously ill patients. Also, family quilts were used to pad boards for makeshift stretchers and to wrap the bodies of loved ones for burial, which may have resulted in the loss of quilts commemorating women's suffrage as well as of patriotic quilts made during World War I.

WORLD WAR I

The US Civil War prompted an outpouring of patriotism on both sides of the conflict in the form of fundraising quilts and quilts for soldiers, and a similar impetus produced quilts in a united national effort as the Spanish-American War raged for eight months in 1898, with Theodore Roosevelt as a heroic figure. The Relief Corps raised funds for the war effort through quilt sales and auctions, with one of those quilts reappearing for auction during World War I relief efforts, as reported in Kansas: "The quilt was made by the ladies of the Relief Corps twenty years ago, during the Spanish-American war. It has a large American flag in the center and a Cuban flag in each corner. The states of the Union, outlined, form the blocks in the quilt. The quilt sold for $15.00 and has been returned for sale this week. So if you want that patriotic quilt come prepared to bid high Saturday."[17] Stitching outlines of the states in a quilt would become a favorite way for quilters to celebrate the Bicentennial.

World War I began in Europe in 1914, continuing until 1918. After Germany increased submarine attacks in the Atlantic and sank the ocean liner *Lusitania*, killing some 120 Americans aboard, outrage surged throughout the US to support Allied forces. Between April 1917 and November 1918, our country sent more than one million soldiers to the European battle front, while women worked in the war effort and joined the American Red Cross, founded in 1881 by Clara Barton. During wartime, Red Cross volunteerism was closely aligned with patriotic sentiment, providing ambulance drivers, nurses, and medical supplies. As in other philanthropic causes, quilts helped raise money for the Red Cross during World War I, such as a 1918 repeat auction in Kansas just after the war ended that raised nearly $300 from the quilt being sold repeatedly at auction and the sale of tickets to the event (that amount being worth a little more than $6,000 in today's money).[18]

In addition to auctioning and raffling quilts for the Red Cross, quilters raised money during World War I and shortly afterward with signature quilts, which worked in several ways. Individuals would contribute a fixed amount of money to have their names on the quilt in a piece of fabric, either signed or embroidered, with gold stars indicating mothers who had lost a son or sons. Alternatively, some quilts featured the names of soldiers who were fighting or had fought in the war, with gold stars next to the names of those who had been killed in action.[19]

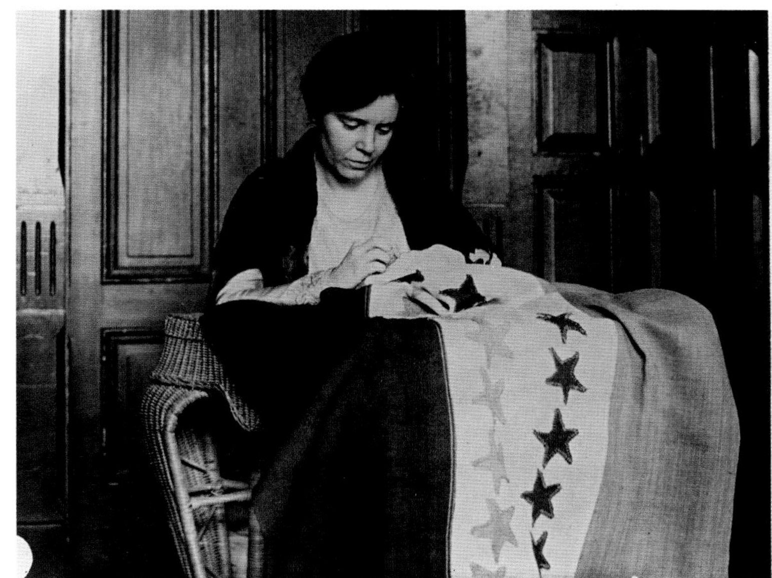

Library of Congress Prints and Photographs Division

Alice Paul stitching star on ratification flag

Quilts helped raise funds to send to US soldiers fighting in Europe, with commercial establishments publicizing the sales, such as in the display window of a dry-goods store in Leavenworth, Kansas: "The most noticeable feature of the display is a patriotic quilt which is . . . the work of Mrs. Swoboda of Kansas City, Mo. The center of the quilt is made of squares of red delane on which are outlined the insignias of all branches of the army service, navy and marine corps, also all of the different branches connected with the war camp community services. . . . Figures of President Wilson and Uncle Sam are also designed. . . . The quilt took second prize at the Sedalia, Missouri[,] state fair." Proceeds of the quilt sale were sent to a machine-gun company in France where some of the local men were serving.[20] Military insignia would later be incorporated into some of the Bicentennial quilts.

Quilts featuring poppies memorialized the wartime dead, prompted by the famous 1915 poem by Lieutenant Colonel John McCrae:

In Flanders fields the poppies blow
Between the crosses, row on row
That mark our place, and in the sky
The larks, still bravely singing, fly
Scarce heard amid the guns below.

As pointed out by Sue Reich, "The VFW (Veterans of Foreign Wars) adopted the poppy as its official flower in 1922. In 1924, a poppy factory was built in Pittsburgh, providing another source for the commemorative flower Even today, wearing the poppy signifies honor for those who lost their lives in the 'Great War.'"[21] Veterans and auxiliaries sell paper poppies each year to commemorate Memorial Day. Patterns for appliquéd and pieced poppy quilts were advertised in magazines and newspapers. American Legion women's auxiliaries created poppy quilts as fundraisers, as did Red Cross auxiliaries that advertised their events: "One of the attractions of the bazaar is the poppy quilt, which was made and donated by Mrs. Hammer of the Valrico Red Cross auxiliary."[22]

For many years after the armistice, the poppy symbol was a major focus of World War I commemoration, such as in an annual poster contest for schoolchildren documented by *The Tennessean*, "now showing in the American Legion room of the War Memorial building [in Nashville]. The arrangement of the posters this year is excellent, each wall of the room being centered by a portrait or group of photographs of World War heroes and scenes, with the posters hung on either side."[23] Similar poppy poster contests were held in other states, with the posters of local winners sent to statewide competitions. Quilters across the country would have had memorial poppies in mind due to all the press publicity and fundraising quilts exhibited. During the Bicentennial, schoolchildren throughout the country participated in creating group quilts to celebrate 1976, engaged in our history like the children in these poster contests.

WORLD WAR II

After Japan's surprise attack on US ships in Pearl Harbor on December 7, 1941, our country joined the Allied forces and began to mobilize against Japan, Germany, and Italy. The war ended in September 1945 with the surrender of Japan. With eleven million American women and men serving in the military during those four years, our supplies of various fabrics for home sewing began to dwindle. Wool was allocated for uniforms, and silk, previously supplied by Japan, had virtually disappeared. With silk factories in Italy and other European sources shuttered by the war, and Great Britain needing the cloth produced in India, quilt makers in the US had to rely on readily available textiles,

▶ *Hoosier Suffrage Quilt*, before 1920, 73.5 × 74.5 in., probably made in Indiana

International Quilt Museum, University of Nebraska–Lincoln, 2021.013.0027

Liberty Star Quilt, ca. 1941, 95.5 × 80.5 in.

International Quilt Museum, University of Nebraska–Lincoln, 2021.108.0074, Sue Reich Collection

Airplane Quilt, ca. 1941–1945, 79 × 71 in.

Museum of Fine Arts, Boston, Frank B. Bemis Fund, with funds donated anonymously, 2012.170; photograph Ó 2026, Museum of Fine Arts, Boston

International Quilt Museum, University of Nebraska–Lincoln, 2011.013.0001

The Dorcas Sunday School Class (Iowa), *Red Cross Quilt*, 1917, 82.5 × 76 in.

such as feed sacks, flour sacks, and small pieces of fabric from worn-out clothing, curtains, etc. Newspapers, magazines, and quilting companies such as Mountain Mist encouraged quilters to create scrap quilts: "Like Joseph's Coat which gave it its name, this scrap quilt is done in multicolored materials. It's such an easy one, for it takes but two pattern pieces to make it. Why not have a regular old-time quilting bee?"[24]

Quilts with patriotic themes, of course, were ubiquitous, often described in local newspapers: "Mrs. Roxie Amsberry of Oshkosh . . . has completed a patriotic quilt that is unique and attractive. In the center are an American flag in red, white, and blue, a liberty bell, and the inscriptions 'God Bless America' and 'In Union There Is Strength.' Fourteen Douglas bomber planes, the world's largest in 1941, make up the main body of the quilt."[25] The Great Seal of the United States appeared in wartime quilts, as it later would in 1976: "Mrs. Chase Warner is making a patriotic quilt that is especially appropriate now. In various blocks she has worked historical designs, each with the date. Such events as the trip of Columbus in 1492, Betsey Ross making the flag, George Washington commanding the Revolutionary army, Lincoln making an address are shown in various blocks. Each alternate block is the seal of the United States. While the quilt is not completed, enough has been done to show what a beautiful piece of work it will be when finished."[26]

International Quilt Museum, University of Nebraska–Lincoln, 2021.108.0004, Sue Reich Collection

Victory Quilt (Kentucky?), ca. 1945, 80 × 78 in.

A quilter in Nebraska, Mrs. Ernest Sukraw, created a chronological pictorial history of the US interpreted through the blocks on her quilt, with the last block bearing the inscription "Remember Pearl Harbor, December 7th, 1941." This quilt may have been touring parts of the state, since the quilter lived in Maxwell and the quilt was being admired at a Kiwanis Club meeting in North Platte: "Each block on the quilt is separated from the others by a wide red and white band, with white stars on a blue field in the corners of each. All designs and work on the quilt were free hand drawn and worked, and members said it was one of the finest pieces of hand work they had ever seen."[27]

As they did during World War I, quilters donated their work to the Red Cross to raise money for the war effort of World War II: "The patriotic quilt made by Mrs. Sam Cox in Cherokee, Oklahoma, and presented to the Red Cross brought $63.00 when sold during the July 4th Observance Monday, by the Cherokee War Dads."[28] In some instances, purchasers bought war bonds, not the actual quilt itself, also in Oklahoma: "Mrs. Ira

Dallas Museum of Art, anonymous gift, 1998.212

Pictorial Sampler Quilt, ca. 1940–1945, 76 × 81 in.

International Quilt Museum, University of Nebraska–Lincoln, 2021.108.0021, Sue Reich Collection

Patriotic Yo-Yo Quilt, ca. 1940–1945, 101.5 × 85.5 in.

Goodwin, Hinton, Okla. . . . boosted bond sales during the third war loan drive by a substantial sum. Mrs. Goodwin made a patriotic quilt which she donated to the drive and the purchaser bought $2,650 worth of war bonds to get the quilt."[29] During 1976, the Bicentennial Committees in numerous towns created a pictorial quilt that was raffled for a fundraising event.

After Winston Churchill first raised two fingers to indicate a "V" for victory, the BBC began wartime broadcasts with three dots and a dash, Morse code for the letter "V." While the "V" stood for different words in different European languages, in the US it meant victory, and Victory quilts. Sue Reich informs us that "the symbol and slogans for Victory V's were fully established when the United States formally declared war in December 1941. Defense factory workers flashed the Victory V symbol as they passed one another at shift changes. There were V letters, Victory boats, Victory gardens, V bonds and V mail."[30] Colors of Victory quilts almost always were red, white, and blue, usually red and blue against a white background to create a graphically dynamic surface. Like other types of quilts during the war, Victory quilts made excellent fundraisers, such as in this Nebraska repeat auction: "A 'Victory' quilt in a beautiful red, white, and blue star pattern, made by the Sunflower Club, was sold at auction at the Anderson sale barn last Thursday. This club is comprised of a group of farm women living just across the line in Kansas and has helped the Red Cross in many ways. Only recently they decided on the quilt idea, and it certainly was well worth their time and efforts. Andy Anderson resold the quilt over and over until the nice sum of $170.00 was reached."[31]

Motifs of flowers and other plants, continually popular in quilt designs, assumed an aspect of national significance during the war because of Victory gardens. Patterns appeared for Victory Garden quilts with blocks depicting appliquéd fruits and vegetables, and with blocks embroidering floral motifs in the shape of a "V." Approximately half of American households that included a decent-sized yard cultivated Victory Gardens—nearly 20 million acres of land. Growing one's own food was considered part of an American's patriotic duty, and wartime quilts reflected that aspect of our battle. Floral imagery popularizing the state flowers would reappear in Bicentennial quilt projects offered by magazines.

International Quilt Museum, University of Nebraska–Lincoln, 2021.108.0043, Sue Reich Collection

Victory Garden Quilt, ca. 1941–1945, 100 × 76 in.

PATRIOTIC QUILTS AFTER THE WORLD WARS

From the summer of 1950 until the summer of 1953, the US was directly involved in the Korean War, supporting South Korea against invading troops from North Korea. In this bloody conflict, some 37,000 Americans died and more than 92,000 were wounded. The Red Cross expanded its services and volunteer program to aid the war effort, resulting in fundraisers across the country. As in previous wars, quilts served as fundraising vehicles for the Red Cross and other causes, including the ongoing support of veterans. Although quilt historians write about the "lull" in US quilt making during the 1950s and early 1960s, the evidence in newspaper reports and published quilt patterns suggests a slightly different narrative. Here are a few examples of patriotic quilts alone:

1951, at the Oklahoma State Fair, Handicrafts exhibit, reported on the Society ("Soc") page of a Muskogee newspaper: "Also on exhibit were quilts in many patterns, including three quilts featuring as the design the 48 states and the state flower of each. One of these patriotic quilts took first place in the division."[32] Some of the Bicentennial quilt kits combined outlines of state shapes that surrounded state flowers.

1954, in Minnesota: "Red, white, and blue are the predominant colors in the patriotic quilt fashioned by members of the Woman's club of Minnesota Lake. Proceeds from sale of the bedspread-size patchwork will go for restoration of Independence Hall, Philadelphia, Pa. The club, along with others belonging to the General Federation of Women's Clubs, has the renovation for a project this year."[33] This quilt was on display at the federation's national conference.

1958, in West Virginia: "The sale of poppies on Veterans Day was reported a success. A patriotic quilt with 168 names was sold and proceeds from this project will be sent to the district treasurer and local auxiliary fund."[34]

1961, at the Amarillo Tri-State Fair: "One extra-patriotic quilt creator produced a red, white, and blue quilt from some of the brightest colored material she could find—[cloth] pork sausage wrappers. 'I just like the colors. I don't want to advertise the brand of pork sausage.'"[35] What we are witnessing here is a continuum of patriotic imagery in American quilts, like an underground current that would surge into a powerful river by 1976.

1962, at the Ohio State Fair's Arts and Crafts Show (more than three hundred words describing a single quilt titled *The Pride of Ohio*, by a quilter who won the grand prize in 1952 and 1955 in the quilt division): "Mrs. Mary Borkowski of Dayton spent three years working on the quilt, which is adorned with a map and many symbols emblematic of the State of Ohio."[36] The writer went on to itemize each component, including imagery celebrating John Glenn, and eight state seals honoring the US presidents associated with Ohio. Such comprehensive examples of state pride abounded in Bicentennial quilts.

1963, at the Kansas State Fair: "Irene Koeneke, widow of Dr. A. E. Hertzler of Halstead and a noted physician herself, was awarded the sweepstakes for a patriotic quilt she entered. The quilt had scenes of early America, sown [*sic*] on a background of blue and white stars, with red, white and blue edging. The backside is deep red."[37]

PREPARING FOR 1976

Plans for America's 1976 Bicentennial began ten years earlier, with Congress establishing the American Revolution Bicentennial Commission "to provide for the observation and commemoration of this anniversary and these events through local, State, National, and international activities planned, encouraged, developed, and coordinated by a national commission."[38] The Bicentennial was assigned three themes—Heritage '76 (the past), Festival USA (the present), and Horizons '76 (the future). All three were gathered under the rubric Festival of Freedom. Initially, the cities of Boston, Miami, Philadelphia, and Washington, DC, were the top contenders to anchor the festivities, with the commission settling on a world's fair in Philadelphia and a whopping budget of $1.25 billion (more than $10 billion today) to establish a Bicentennial Park in each state. Eventually these grandiose plans were canceled, since the commission proclaimed a multicity exposition, with "no commercially oriented world's fair in the traditional sense anywhere in the nation during the Bicentennial era."[39]

Other major cities, such as Houston and San Francisco, were invited to join the party. San Francisco's preparations attempted to fold the city's own bicentennial into the national celebration, dubbed the Twin Centennial, including an exhibition of antique and vintage quilts planned for the San Francisco Art Institute from Mary Strickland Quilts in San Rafael. While that 1976 quilt exhibition eventually would draw a large, appreciative audience and garner numerous positive press reviews, several other events did not go well during their planning stages, such as the Freedom Train. This private venture, charging admission to view historical documents in railcars, would have paid a salary of $85,000 to a Wall Street commodities broker in charge of the event. For this and other planned events, critics wanted to know how they were relevant for minorities—a question that concerned many Bicentennial committees across the nation. By June 1975, the *San Francisco Examiner* reported, "the Twin Bicentennial organization had not only run out of leaders but of money. There was not enough to run its nine-person office through the fiscal year."[40] While San Franciscans may have privately celebrated their city's anniversary while cheering the US Bicentennial parades and regattas in 1976, official commemorations modestly rode the coattails of the national observation—such as a 1976 postmark stamped by San Francisco post offices featuring the "twin bells" of the Liberty Bell and a mission bell.

★

The three themes of the celebration were Heritage '76 (the past), Festival USA (the present), and Horizons '76 (the future).

★

The momentous decision to create numerous celebrations across the country potentially helped free up more funding for state and local participation, with the commission urging all Americans to find for themselves the meaning of life, liberty, and the pursuit of happiness, encouraging patriotism at the

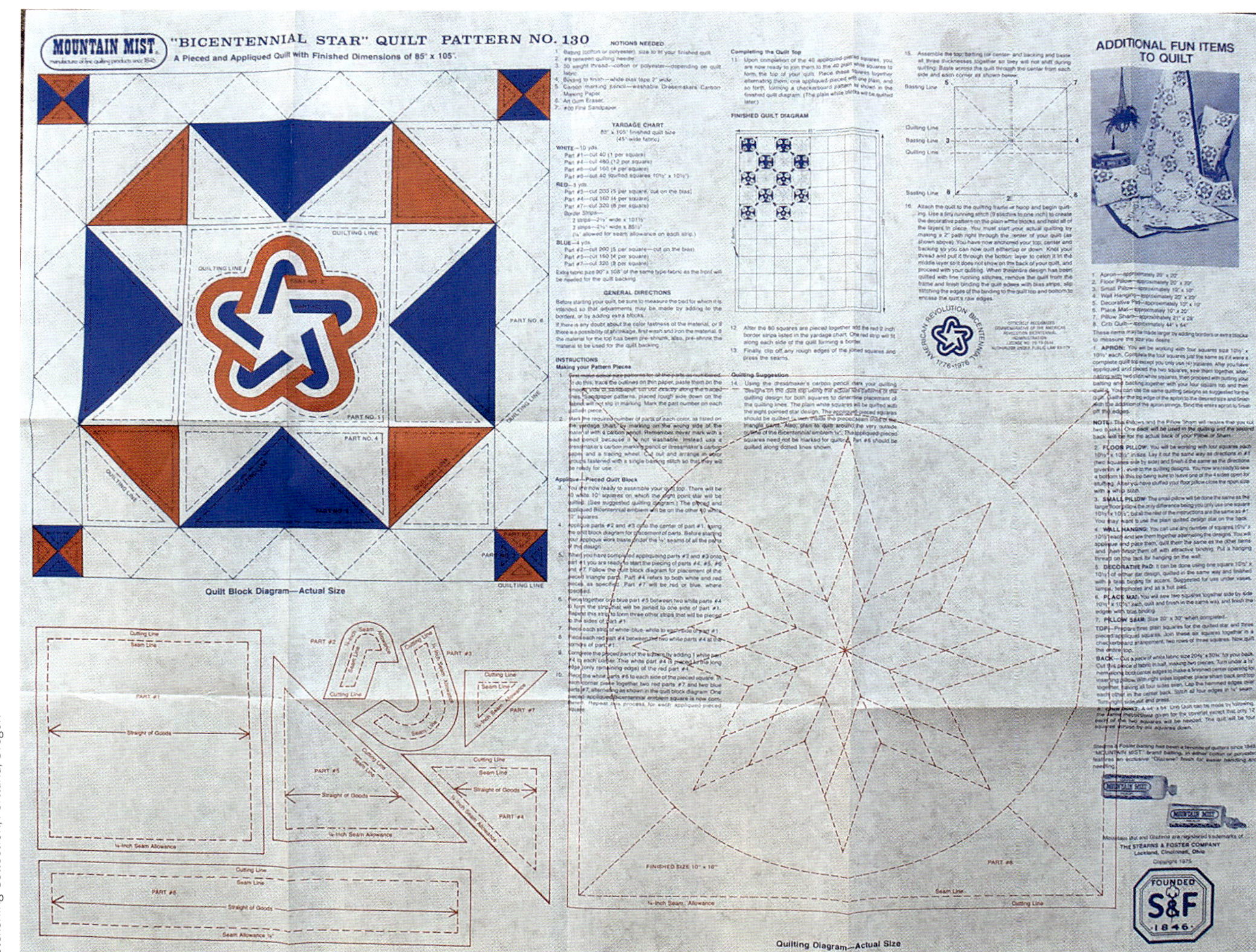

Volckening Collection, Portland, Oregon

Mountain Mist, *Bicentennial Star Quilt* instructions, ca. 1976

grassroots level while relieving commission members of engaging with controversial issues at the national level. The commission, emphasizing that the universal language of art is one of the most effective means of communication, recommended Arts on Parade as an important aspect of Festival USA: "The Commission invites American artists and craftsmen of all ages, backgrounds, and talents and all communities to step forward and join the Arts on Parade."[41] Many quilt makers did just that, as we shall see, individually as well as communally.

By 1972, allegations of budgetary mismanagement and involvement of private-interest groups, especially big business, in the commission resulted in its disbanding. The Senate Subcommittee on Federal Charters, Holidays and Celebrations had held a series of hearings to air complaints from women's organizations such as Women's Concern, the American Indian Movement (AIM), the Afro-American Bicentennial Corporation (ABC), and several state commissions. Tammy Gordon's research noted, "The 1976 observance . . .

revealed that historical memory played a key part in the major social, cultural, and political changes taking place in the middle of the 1970s. It was the first national observance in which Americans previously disenfranchised by more traditional historical narrative—African Americans, women, American Indians, workers, young people—armed themselves with the information presented by the new social history and demanded a voice and representation in the federal body responsible for guiding the observance."[42] These groups argued that their own activities, carried out in the spirit of the American Revolution, deserved recognition and approbation, if not federal funding. *Ms.* magazine became very involved in Bicentennial planning, publishing an ongoing calendar notifying readers of bicentennial-related events connected to women's issues.[43] These events for America's two hundredth birthday would include conferences on women in urban environments, on Black women and the Bicentennial, and various exhibitions. *Ms.* magazine promoted a Bicentennial Quilt Contest in Warren, Michigan, described in chapter 6, along with other events.

In December 1973, the American Revolution Bicentennial Administration (ARBA), the name we see on the Bicentennial logo, replaced the commission while eventually accomplishing some of its objectives. Celebrations in 1976 began with the Tournament of Roses Parade in Pasadena, California, on New Year's Day, televised across the country. The floats included what looked like a sea of US flags, the Liberty Bell and a gigantic birthday cake in flowers, a covered wagon, a stagecoach, and salutes to our military. These iconic symbols of American history would appear in 1976 with the Bicentennial logo on soda cans, liquor flasks (one shaped like the Liberty Bell that played our national anthem when being poured), paper plates, kites, underwear, and countless other products commercializing the Bicentennial for businesses that paid licensing fees to the federal government. One of those businesses was Mountain Mist, which had been a leader in the quilting industry for more than a century. Their *Bicentennial Star Quilt* in red, white, and blue included a pattern and kit, also a pillow kit, with white fabric blocks printed to indicate positioning of the logo motifs in appliqué. We can find the completed quilts scattered in collections across the country, along with hundreds of other Bicentennial quilts. Let's now explore that treasure trove.

CHAPTER 6

Happy Birthday, America

In its *Index of Bicentennial Activities*, the American Revolution Bicentennial Administration (ARBA) listed more than two thousand official events taking place between March 1975 and December 1976.[1] More than 150 of these events involved quilt exhibitions and contests, and apparently the ARBA approved additional events after the list was published. I have found quilt-related activities publicized in local newspapers not mentioned in the *Index*, even though they are designated as approved by local Bicentennial committees, such as the National Bicentennial Quilt Contest in Warren, Michigan; promoted by *Ms.* magazine; and sponsored by the Warren Historical Commission and the Women's Association of Macomb County Community College in the summer of 1976.[2] Mary Schafer, quilt historian and collector in addition to being known as an avidly creative quilter, won a third prize for one quilt in the competition and honorable mentions for others.

Robert Shaw has pointed out, "Interest in quilts broadened and deepened in the years leading up to the Bicentennial, as people around the country looked back to their long-neglected roots and began to realize how much could be found in the humble domestic quilt."[3] Quilt contests composed a popular division of Grange events and state fairs, such as in "Revolution—Then & Now," the theme of the 1976 Alaska State Fair in Fairbanks, where the Bicentennial Quilt Contest offered a first prize ("premium") of $5.00. Categories for entries included group projects and individual work, divided into traditional patterns and original Bicentennial designs. Exhibitors were asked to include a brief written explanation with their entry.[4]

Collection of Sandra Sider

Alaska State Fair booklet, 1976

Collection of Sandra Sider

Ohio Grange Cook Book, 1976

As in 1876 with the *National Cookery Book*, Bicentennial recipe books in 1976 complemented American democratic tradition in that the recipes were submitted by individuals within the books' various communities in open calls for submissions.[5] The *Crazy Quilt of Good Eating*, assembled by employees of the Signode Steel Strapping Company, visually linked the American tradition of quilt making with its "sampler" of recipes in 1976. A *Bicentennial Cook Book* issued in 1976 by the Illinois State Fair, the Freedom Fair 76, featured our flag's red and white stripes in its cover art. In recognition of the historic occasion of 1976, the flyleaf described the recipes as "What Our Nation Was Eating On Its 200th Birthday." Several of the recipes nod to American history, such as Bicentennial Apple Lassie Cake, Chocolate Lincoln Log, and Cherry Tree Cake.

Album[6] quilts and other grid-like quilt constructions can be seen as prime examples of patching together numerous units to form a whole, and in some Bicentennial cookbooks, the cover art illustrates a quilt as symbolic of building the book. The twenty-seventh edition of the *Ohio State Grange Cook Book*, published in July 1976, had the subtitle *Commemorative of Our Nation's Bicentennial*. Its title on the front cover is situated within a rectangle surrounded by crazy-quilt patches edged with printed cross-stitch. According to a message to the "Homemaker," the first edition "was printed in 1938, [and] over two hundred thousand have been printed. A small profit is realized on each book and is added to the Student Loan Fund."[7] With its grassroots membership of farming families, the National Grange takes "pride in being citizens of such a great Nation . . . [looking forward] to the future of our country with strength and enthusiasm."[8]

The *Quilter's Cookbook: Calaveras County Bicentennial Quilt* incorporated images from this commemorative album quilt to structure the book. Eighteen pictorial rectangles from the finished quilt by the Independence Hall Quilters in White Pines / Arnold, California, function as divider pages between sections of the recipes. The editor explained the book's purpose: "Within these pages you will find the culinary secrets of scores of Mother Lode homemakers and friends who have shared their kitchen skills in order to support their Community Center."[9] As we shall see below, a keen sense of community prompted numerous Bicentennial quilts, mostly in pictorial album style, the individual blocks having been created by community members, assembled by one of their members, and then often quilted by a group gathered together around the quilt.

While "community" usually means people living near each other, the term can also describe a group of people, in a broader sense, communing for a common purpose. Bicentennial quilts celebrating a state, region, or city fulfilled this goal. In several instances, quilts served dual purposes—to commemorate the US Bicentennial while also marking a major anniversary specific to a particular community.

ALBUM QUILTS IN GROUP PROJECTS

For the *Calaveras County Bicentennial Quilt*, more than fifty mountain women in the Ebbetts Pass area of the Sierra Nevada range gathered in 1975 to honor their Calaveras County heritage by creating a pictorial album quilt. That group in 1976

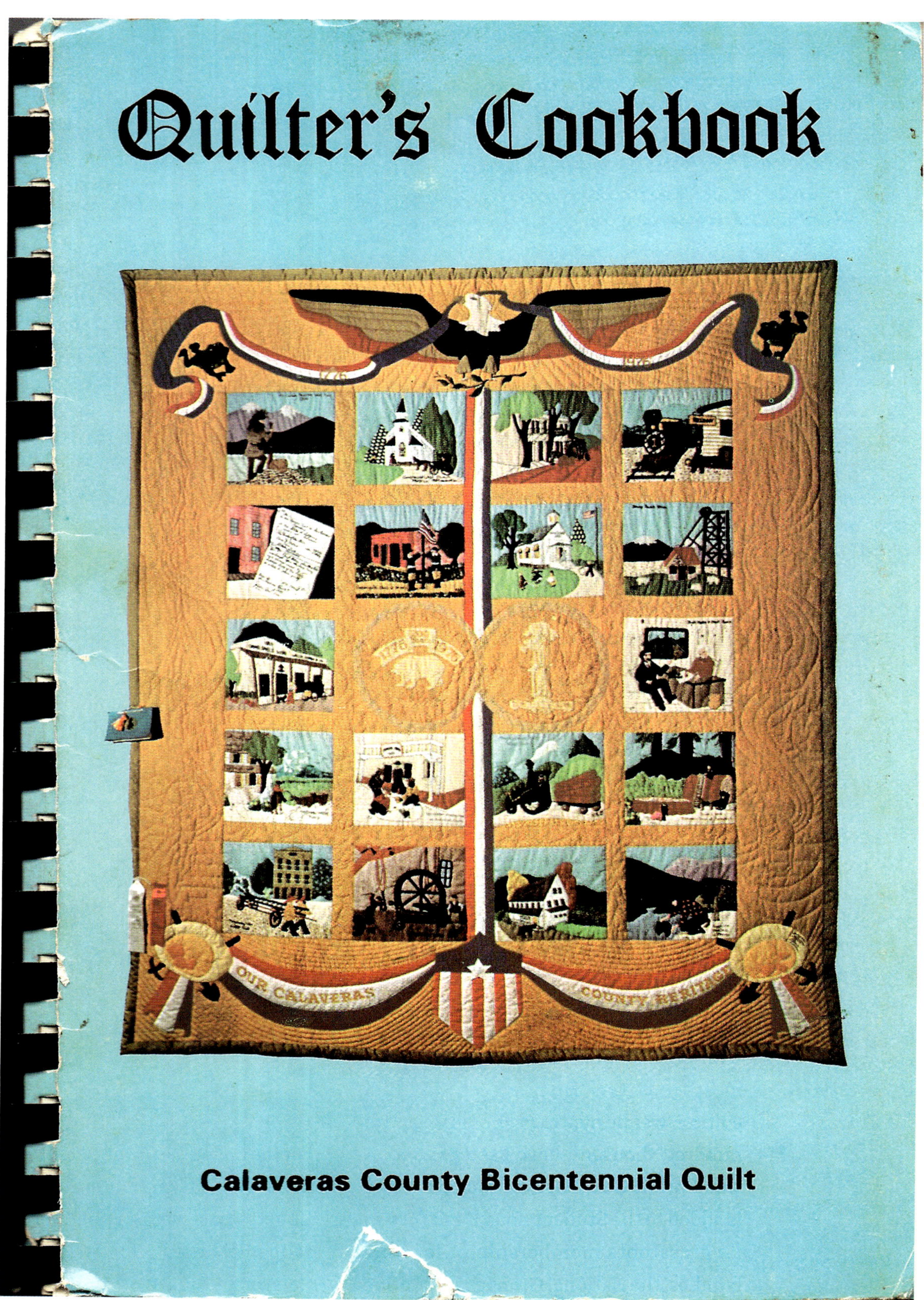
Quilter's Cookbook
OUR CALAVERAS
COUNTY HERITAGE
Calaveras County Bicentennial Quilt

◀ *Calaveras County Bicentennial Quilt* on cookbook cover, 1976

became the powerhouse organization known as Independence Hall Quilters. They host the annual Mountain Heirloom Quilt Faire and donate dozens of comfort quilts to worthy causes, among other initiatives. For their initial project in 1975, the group chose to recognize the nineteenth-century architecture and vibrant history of gold-rush country. Two local watercolorists, Bobby Comer and Mary Lou Humber, designed the scenes. Each of the eighteen blocks tells a story, such as about Murphy's Hotel, where the guest book was signed by Ulysses S. Grant, Mark Twain, and other notable visitors. As an official Bicentennial project, this quilt proudly bears the seal of the California Bicentennial stitched near the center.

While some of the Bicentennial group quilts focused on images of the past, many others documented towns and activities as they were in the mid-1970s, preserving fabric snapshots of buildings and scenery. The *Exeter Bicentennial Quilt*, created by the Women's Alliance of the First Unitarian Society at Exeter (New Hampshire), alternates eighteen appliquéd and solid-red squares within a tied structure. Like many of the Bicentennial town quilts, this one was raffled as a fundraiser, at a Christmas fair in 1975. The family owning it took good care of their piece of history, eventually donating it to the Exeter Historical Society, where the quilt resides today.

Gladys C. Boalt, designer, *Putnam County Bicentennial Quilt*, 1976, 108 × 86 in.

The *Putnam County Bicentennial Quilt* celebrated the bicentennials both of Putnam County in New York and the US. Completed in 1976, the quilt later took first prize in its division at the Houston Quilt Festival and was selected to be published among the one hundred pieces in *The Twentieth Century's Best American Quilts*. Glady Boalt, textile designer and needlework expert, organized this quilt at the request of local women who wanted to commemorate the dual bicentennials. A total of nineteen women met weekly with Boalt, who taught them how to make a quilt.[10] For her design inspiration, Boalt interviewed knowledgeable people in Putnam County about historical details, imbuing the quilt with authenticity and historical accuracy. Unlike most album quilts, assembled in a grid, the *Putnam County Bicentennial Quilt* appears like a series of artful vignettes without obvious borders surrounding the blocks, with dense contour quilting that emphasizes each scene. The concept of an album block being contributed for each county in a state also applied elsewhere, such as in the *North Dakota Centennial Quilt, 1889–1989*.[11]

In Portland, Oregon, a group of fifteen Black women activists led by Jeannette McPherson Gates began work in 1974 on *The Afro-American Heritage Bicentennial Commemorative Quilt*. Its thirty album-style squares honor the heritage and contributions of the Black community in US history. Gates's daughter, Dr. Sylvia Gates Carlisle, is the only surviving participant in the project. While a student at Stanford, she made the square illustrating a Black Power fist. She recalls, "The ladies were intentional about memorializing Black excellence in the face of Oregon's institutional racism. . . . The Bicentennial was a big deal, but folks acted like we were a footnote to American history."[12] Honorees in the quilt include poet Phyllis Wheatley, abolitionist Frederick Douglass, suffragist Mary Church Terrell, musician Louis Armstrong, singer Marian Anderson, activist Martin Luther King Jr., and baseball icon Hank Aaron. The quilt toured to Harvard University, the US Department of State, and other venues. Much later, while on display in the Oregon Historical Society, the quilt itself became part of American history on October 11, 2020, the "Day of Rage" for Indigenous peoples protesting Columbus Day. The mob broke into the museum, spattered red paint, and otherwise vandalized the site and its objects, taking the quilt when they left. Although damaged, the quilt was found the next day, then professionally restored and kept as a memento of this episode in the American narrative.

Only a few community album quilts created for the Bicentennial were accompanied by a book elucidating local history for the quilt images, crediting the maker(s) of each of the blocks. *The Bicentennial Quilt of Springfield, Vermont*, a notable exception, was made by the Home Efficiency Club

Jeannette McPherson Gates and friends (Portland, Oregon), *The Afro-American Heritage Bicentennial Commemorative Quilt*, 1976, 87 × 73.5 in.

Springfield Art & Historical Society

Home Efficiency Club, *The Bicentennial Quilt of Springfield, Vermont*, 1976, 94 × 79 in.

Springfield Art & Historical Society

Detail, *The Bicentennial Quilt of Springfield, Vermont*

Oregon Historical Society 77-571, courtesy of Portland Textile Month, photo by Caleb Sayan

25 FULL SIZE PATTERNS
No. 4 • $1.25 • IND • 35168
a LOPEZ publication
Lady's Circle
PATCHWORK QUILTS
Our Choice Of
THE BEST OF
BICENTENNIAL QUILTS
A Trip To
America's Biggest
Quilt Auction
Applique' From
Indian Designs
Table Settings,
Aprons,
Bedspreads
NORTH
DAKOTA
0
70989 35168

Lady's Circle Patchwork Quilts front cover, 1976

sponsored by the Vermont Extension Service. This quilt, while completed for the US Bicentennial, also celebrated more than two hundred years for Springfield, which received its charter in 1761 and was organized by 1764, developing into a machine-manufacturing center thanks to plentiful power from the Black River, which flows through town. Defined along its eastern border by the much-larger Connecticut River, Springfield had efficient access to water transport for the town's manufactured products. An embroidered map in the center vertical row of the quilt recognizes the role of these rivers in the town's history. Narratives for the squares encapsulate aspects of Americana, such as a wooden covered bridge—"One dollar fine to drive faster than a walk across this bridge"—the Joel Ellis Doll (highly desirable today among collectors), the Little School House, and the Bandstand.

Magazines and newspapers helped popularize album quilts as expressions of community spirit, often categorizing them as friendship quilts, which also follow the album format. A 1976 issue of *Lady's Circle Patchwork Quilts* publicized the fifty state winners of the Mountain Mist State Flowers Friendship Quilt Contest, 1975 (pictured here on the front cover). This category of pictorial album quilts created for the Bicentennial featured state birds, state trees, occasionally state mammals or insects, and outlines of the state maps, with numerous kits marketed to quilters who needed a little help with their designs. The images to embroider were usually preprinted on fabric or offered as heat-transfer patterns. Those interested in creating album quilts depicting local historic sites and images associated with the various states could find plenty of inspiration in periodical publications during the Bicentennial era. In today's polarized society, it can be challenging to imagine how so many people could have been fired up toward a common goal, but the Bicentennial managed to popularize the idea of an American identity unified in its diversity and individualism, if only for a brief period. As Jimmy Carter said in 1976, when accepting his party's nomination for president, "Nineteen seventy-six will not be a year of politics as usual. It can be a year of inspiration and hope, and it will be a year of concern, of quiet and sober reassessment of our nation's character and purpose."

ALBUM QUILTS FROM INDIVIDUAL MAKERS

The album quilt format inspired many individual quilters who preferred to work in a nonnarrative, pictorial style. Martha Lipsanen, a charter member in 1978 of the Pajaro Valley Quilt Association, had a career working for the Red Cross, acknowledged in the badge and blue stars from her uniform appliquéd onto her *Bicentennial Quilt*. Executed in embroidery and appliqué, the album squares document events in America history and popular culture, ending with an astronaut walking on the moon. The banner along the top is filled with embroidered imagery of a more personal nature, such as the masks of tragedy and comedy for Lipsanen, who acted in local theater productions. The center top of the quilt depicts an eagle holding up a swag inscribed with "We the People"—not the usual patriotic eagle but, rather, a bird that looks somewhat like the Native American thunderbird.

In 1990, Eugenia Mitchell, a prolific quilter, founded the Rocky Mountain Quilt Museum

Rocky Mountain Quilt Museum, PQ.1991.001.048

Eugenia Mitchell, *Colorado Centennial Quilt*, 1976, 78 × 76 in.

in Golden, Colorado. One of the quilts she donated to the museum was her 1976 *Colorado Centennial Quilt*, celebrating Colorado's statehood in 1876 along with that of the US Bicentennial. Her medallion album quilt alternates embroidered and appliquéd imagery on white with solid-red squares, most of them quilted with outlines of the blue columbine, the state flower. Others contain embroidered text significant for American history. Her pictorial squares feature several depicting the blue columbine, a lark bunting (Colorado's state bird), a blue spruce (the state tree), a bighorn sheep (the state mammal), and symbols such as Betsy Ross sewing the US flag.[13] Silhouettes of the thirteen original colonies fill a horizontal band near the top, emphasizing the Centennial State's shared anniversary with America.

Teresa Barkley's *Bicentennial Bride's Quilt* celebrated the wedding of a friend that took place in January 1976. While much of the imagery in this album quilt personally celebrates the bride and her groom, several aspects celebrate the Bicentennial, notably the Bicentennial eagle on a handkerchief in the center block along with woven Bicentennial memorabilia. An embroidered quotation from Benjamin Franklin inscribed beneath the sun's rays at the top of the quilt was made when our Constitution was completed in 1787: "But now at length I have the happiness to know that it is a rising and not a setting sun," referring to an image decorating the arms of George Washington's chair during the sessions of the Constitutional Convention.

The *Bicentennial Bride's Quilt* was the Delaware state winner in the Great Quilt Contest of 1977–1978 (see chapter 7). The fifty-one winning quilts toured the US from 1979 to 1981 with the Smithsonian Institution Traveling Exhibition Service, in an exhibition titled *Quintessential Quilts: The Great American Quilt Contest*. Barkley's quilt also won first place in the Bicentennial category at the National Quilting Association (NQA) Quilt Show in Washington, DC, in 1977. This group, founded in 1970, disbanded in 2016 and spun off the National Association of Certified Quilt Judges, which offers a formal certification program. Organized in Washington, DC, during the germination of Bicentennial projects, the NQA's contribution to increased interest in quilting paralleled and may have added to the Bicentennial fervor. Partially thanks to efforts from the NQA to professionalize the judging of quilt contests, more quilt entries began to be submitted during the 1970s to these contests, such as those at state and county fairs and at quilt symposia.

American History and Americana as Seen on Quilts

Nonpictorial Bicentennial fabrics and quilts favored patriotic colorways with letters and

Volckening Collection, Portland, Oregon

Bicentennial Quilt, 1976, detail of eagle hatching, painted from an Artex Hobby Products kit numbers celebrating "USA" and "1776–1976" or simply stripes, dots, and other shapes in red, white, and blue. Textile manufacturers also offered designs in dress-weight fabric, perfect for quilt making, hearkening back to American historical moments and the "simpler times" of colonial America. Images included the Liberty Bell, Revolutionary War soldiers with fifes and drums, Paul Revere on horseback, sailing ships, flintlock rifles, the eagle with a shield, and household furnishings such as spinning wheels and old-fashioned clocks.

Artex Hobby Products, headquartered in Lima, Ohio, capitalized on this theme by marketing kits containing roll-on paint tubes with ballpoints that could be applied directly to fabric, along with transfer paper and linen fabrics on which Bicentennial designs were printed. These featured the ever-popular Liberty Bell, Betsy Ross stitching the flag, the US map styled as an American flag, and much more. Extremely popular, Artex products involved more than 20,000 individual instructors who demonstrated and sold the paints and accessories through hostesses and groups from ten to twenty people.[14] Like Tupperware parties of the 1950s and 1960s, friends and neighbors attending these parties were expected to purchase something. The astonishingly high number of instructors might explain the quantity of Artex Bicentennial quilts, which keep turning up in online marketplaces today. Under the aegis of "Enterprise '76," Artex advertised its paint products in newspapers as fun family activities, and the sales parties enabled many hostesses to earn income and acquire Artex products for their own family projects at a discount.

Della May Morris, an avid Kansas quilter, commemorated Revolutionary War events in her *Sons of Liberty Bicentennial Quilt*, which won third prize in the National Grange Bicentennial Quilt Contest. She made the quilt for her ten-year-old grandson. Events in the quilt include writing the Declaration of Independence, the Boston Tea Party, winter at Valley Forge, and surrender of the British; figures include Paul Revere, Betsy Ross, Patrick Henry, John Paul Jones, and a Native American with buffalo. A decade before the Revolutionary War began in 1775, an activist group called the Sons of Liberty was protesting British rule of the thirteen colonies and legislation such as the Stamp Act. Their members included Samuel Adams, who became a delegate to the Continental Congress, and John Hancock, president of the Congress.

The *Bicentennial Heritage Quilt* by Mary Pemble Barton was awarded a first prize in the Textiles division at the 1976 Iowa State Fair and was selected to be published in *The Twentieth Century's Best American Quilts*. The appliquéd imagery, which includes heirloom fabrics from her collection for the figures' clothing, traces Barton's own family's migration westward—a personal view of Americana. She depicted buildings, such as churches near the central eagle and rows of houses; female figures accompanied by different miniature quilt blocks; male figures with tools; and covered wagons along three borders. Her imagery suggests the self-sufficiency demanded of America's early pioneers, when you brought your tools with you and did handwork on textile home furnishings along the way.

Bicentennial quilts celebrating towns across America often juxtaposed events pertaining to national and local history. The

▸ Teresa Barkley, *The Bicentennial Bride's Quilt*, 1977, 107.5 × 75 in.

Private collection, photo by Peter Gillespie, 426 Photography

Volckening Collection, Portland, Oregon

◀ *Bicentennial Quilt*, 1976, 94 × 66 in., painted from an Artex Hobby Products kit

Ulster County Bicentennial Quilt, made by forty-two Ulster women, each creating an appliquéd block, is on permanent display in the library of Ulster County Community College. One of the ten original counties of New York state, the region saw its share of Revolutionary War history. The quilt depicts George Washington standing beside his white horse, other figures from the Revolutionary era, several local waterways, a spinning wheel, historic Ulster buildings, and various old-timey activities. Hopewell, New Jersey, has a significant Revolutionary War heritage involving local establishments, reflected in the *Hopewell Bicentennial Quilt*, that also celebrates the town's historical monuments. As we move farther west, away from the original colonies, American history is commemorated in Bicentennial quilts representing towns and cities by images of Native Americans, soldiers, landmarks that guided pioneers, founding figures and foundation legends, and the establishment of local industries such as ranching, mining, and lumber.

Several Bicentennial quilts showcased specific events, such as the 1976 Applegate Wagon Train, meant to re-create the original 1846 Applegate Trail journey through Oregon. As a southern alternative to the arduous Oregon Trail, this new route led some three thousand settlers into the valleys of southwestern Oregon during the nineteenth century. The *Bicentennial Applegate Trail / Applegate Wagon Train Quilt* commemorated the wagon train leader, George McUne, as well as the trek across Oregon. He founded the Pioneer Village in Jacksonville, Oregon, depicted at the top of the quilt. A map at the bottom shows the route of the trail. Designed by Evelyn Williams, with needlework by Dora Scheidecker and Kay Reding, the piece was quilted by the Jacksonville Museum Quilters, founded in 1976 by Scheidecker. The hand quilting here follows the quilt's theme, with outlines of Conestoga wagons stitched into the design. Each year the quilters created a new quilt with a local history theme: the Chinese, Hawaiians, Native Americans, the Oregon Trail, the Applegate Trail, and the arrival of the railroad (see chapter 8 for the *Ashland Railroad Centennial* quilt). A large wagon wheel divides the center of the Applegate Trail quilt by eight spokes, each section containing an image representing an aspect of the journey (we see wagon wheels in other commemorative quilts made in the western states). One of the wagon spokes honors Chief [Edward] Chiloquin mounted on his horse. He became internationally famous in 1974, when he refused to accept $273,000 from the federal government as payment for terminating his tribe and letting the federal government take over their extensive pine forest and the headwaters of the Klamath River named after the tribe. The Applegate Trail, passing directly through the Klamath Basin, impinged on the daily lives of the tribe.

Quilts honoring the US presidents were a special category of patriotic Bicentennial project, using signatures, silhouettes, and quasi-realistic depictions of faces. *McCall's* offered a "presidents' gallery" quilt pattern of thirty-six silhouetted profiles against a gridded background that had been designed earlier, updated by adding a Ford pillow.[15] Ohio quilter Mary Borkowski, a prize winner in several state fairs (see chapter 5), created more than one such quilt in her original designs during the Bicentennial era. "Her

The Henry Ford Museum, Object ID 77261

Della May Morris (Arcadia, Kansas), *Sons of Liberty Bicentennial Quilt*, 1976, 105 × 87 in.

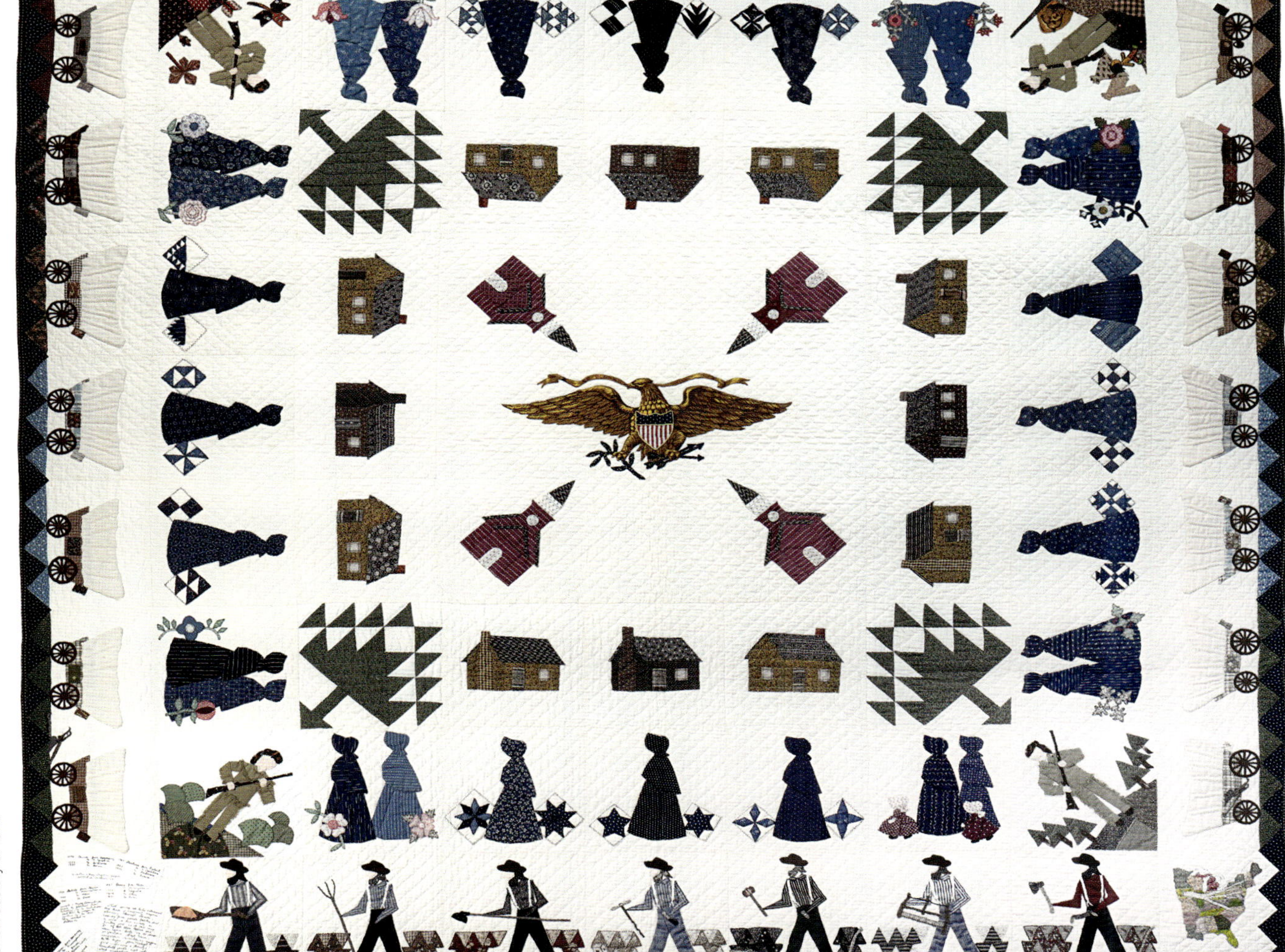

State Historical Society of Iowa

Mary Pemble Barton (Iowa), *Bicentennial Heritage Quilt*, 1976, 101 × 98.5 in.

Courtesy of the Rogue Valley Genealogical Society, Inc., of Medford, Oregon

◀ Evelyn Williams, designer; Dora Scheidecker and Kay Reding, needlework; quilting by the Jacksonville Museum Quilters, *Bicentennial Applegate Trail / Applegate Wagon Train Quilt*, 1976, 86.5 × 63.5 in.

presidential quilt includes 36 likenesses of U.S. presidents, sewn in ovals and squares with the addition of President Ford added in a small oval with President Nixon. It was shown on television newsreel."[16] Borkowski, an early proponent of thread painting among quilt artists, also created a 1976 *White House Birthday* quilt, embroidering over the facsimiles of presidential signatures.

PRESIDENTIAL BICENTENNIAL QUILTS

After Richard Nixon resigned as president in August 1974, following the shocking Watergate episode in American politics, Gerald Ford became the first president never to have been elected to a national office, after having served only one year as Nixon's vice president. But he stepped in and did his best to officiate during the Bicentennial, from one end of America to the other, even joining up with the Bicentennial Wagon Train Pilgrimage when it reached Valley Forge, Pennsylvania—America's only participatory nationwide event for 1975–1976, consisting of more than three hundred covered wagons, at least one from each state, plus individual groups with their own wagons and some five thousand riders on horseback. The Wagon Train groups followed traditional migration routes such as the Oregon, California, and Santa Fe Trails; the Great Platte River and Mormon Roads; the Santa Fe, Old Spanish, and Natchez Traces, and more, traveling eastward instead of westward. They celebrated July 4, 1976, at Valley Forge.[17]

The Gerald R. Ford Presidential Museum owns an impressive collection of items commemorating our two hundredth birthday, including quilts gifted to the White House in 1976. These include quilts made around the country by schoolchildren, the Girl Scouts, nursing-home residents, and quilt guilds—a true sampling of the grassroots aspect of the Bicentennial. As might be expected, some of these works celebrate the presidents themselves, such as an album quilt of forty squares made by the fifth- and sixth-grade classes of Bloomingdale Elementary School in Fort Wayne, Indiana. The students stitched names of all thirty-eight presidents and their years of serving in the office in the individual squares, filling the two extra squares with an eagle and the Liberty Bell. The school's principal presented the quilt to President Ford during his visit to Indiana. Cub Scout Pack 66, Den 3, of Princeton, New Jersey, made a Bicentennial quilt, presented to a member of President Ford's staff in 1976 in the White House Rose Garden. The scouts stitched fifty squares, each containing the silhouette of a state, with its date of statehood indicated. They marked the thirteen original colonies with

Courtesy of the Rogue Valley Genealogical Society, Inc., of Medford, Oregon

Detail, *Bicentennial Applegate Trail / Applegate Wagon Train Quilt* red stars, emphasized by red sashing unifying the quilt. In addition to state flowers and birds, silhouetted maps of the states and of the entire US were ubiquitous in Bicentennial quilts, as were the eagle and Liberty Bell. When Betty Ford visited Houston in 1976, she was gifted with a Liberty Bell quilt by the Golden Age Manor Ladies. Thirteen red stars circling the dark-blue bell on a white ground represent the original colonies within this patriotic palette.

THE RED, WHITE, AND BLUE

Among the hundreds of American quilts completed between the early and latter 1970s, many featured the patriotic colors of our flag, and some of them—not surprisingly—reproduced the flag itself, while others used the colors in geometric and abstract designs. In several instances, red, white, and blue were used ironically in political protests, exercising our First Amendment right to raise objections about policy and procedure, notably concerns about the Vietnam War as well as discrimination against Black voters.

Quilts in the red, white, and blue color scheme proliferated in craft magazines during 1976, with a patriotic sampler quilt featured among the images on the cover of *McCall's Bicentennial Quilt Book* filled with patterns celebrating two hundred years of American quilting. That cover quilt was a king-sized sampler quilt consisting of nine huge blocks, each 30 inches square. The Stearns & Foster company joined the Bicentennial quilt bandwagon by offering Mountain Mist pattern 130, the *Bicentennial Star* featuring the US Bicentennial logo in appliqué, designed by Betty Alfers, a company employee. Thanks to publicity from the company's hometown newspaper, this pattern came to be known (unofficially) as the "official U.S. Bicentennial quilt." Stearns & Foster had been placing quilt patterns inside their wrappers since around 1929, later offering the patterns themselves via mail order.

▸ Cub Scout Pack 66, Den 3 (Princeton, New Jersey), *Bicentennial Quilt*, 1976, 91 × 68 in., featuring US states and their capitals

President Ford ringing replica of the Liberty Bell on ship during Operation Sail in New York Harbor, 1976

Library of Congress Prints and Photographs Division

President Ford in Michigan Bicentennial wagon train, 1976

Library of Congress Prints and Photographs Division

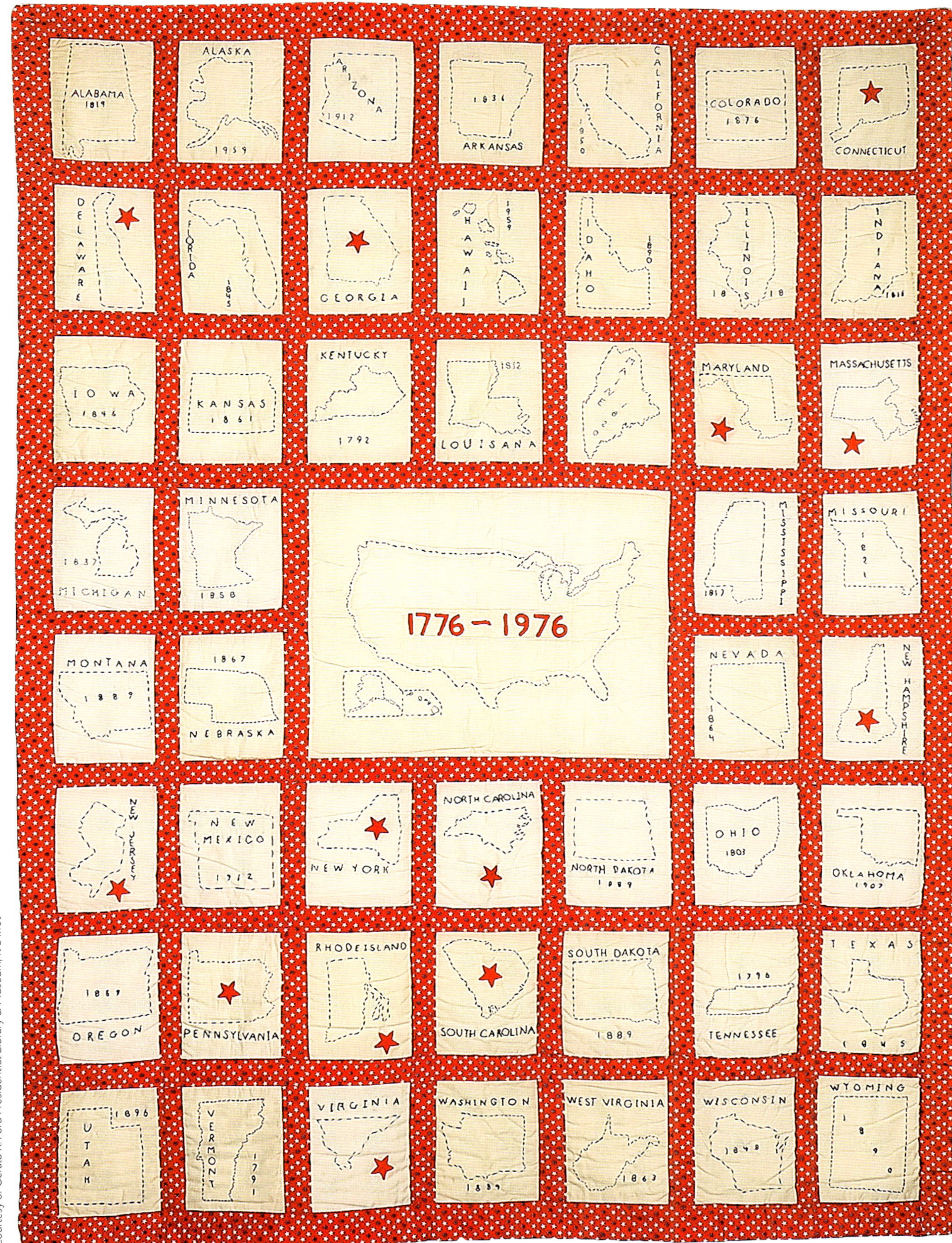

Courtesy of Gerald R. Ford Presidential Library & Museum, 1984.109

McCALL'S NEEDLEWORK & CRAFTS

BICENTENNIAL QUILT BOOK

$1.25
14050

1776-1976

200 years of America's quilts!

Complete how-to's for 34 designs antique and new

W/7501

McCall's *Bicentennial Quilt Book*, front cover (*sampler quilt at bottom center*)

Courtesy of the Rogue Valley Genealogical Society, Inc., of Medford, Oregon

Courtesy of Gerald R. Ford Presidential Library & Museum, 1982.139

Bloomingdale Elementary School (Fort Wayne, Indiana), *Bicentennial Quilt*, 1976, 80.5 × 52.5 in.

One of the more striking *Bicentennial Flag* quilts, by Barbara McKie, recalls the international flavor of some of the Centennial bandanas containing our flag at the center, surrounded by smaller flags of many nations. McKie began incorporating her photographs into quilt art after her retirement in 1970, making her more than ready to jump into quilt making during the Bicentennial era. In her 1976 quilt, the US flag fills her map of the country, with the stripes unifying east and west. She pieced sections of flags representing various foreign countries to create a sense of perspective that seems to elevate the US map out of her picture plane toward the viewer.

Dolores Miller, known today for her *Galaxy* series of art quilts, was inspired by Bicentennial quilt making. She explains: "The very first quilt I made was in 1976, from a pattern in *McCall's Quilting Magazine*. Though I'd sewn since childhood, it was that cover image that inspired me to try making a quilt. It's on my bed right now, exposed knots, cotton/poly fabric, and all! I quickly discovered I didn't like just red, white, and blue, so pink, yellow, maroon, and brown fabrics were incorporated into the design, an early sign of my becoming a textile artist."[18] Miller's combination of solid colors with floral prints in the Log Cabin barn-raising setting resulted in a lively surface. Fiber artist Colleen Ansbaugh recalls that the first quilt on which she worked was ca. 1976, a patriotic *1000 Pyramids*, collaborating with her mother, Gladys Larson Kendall. Wool clothing materials in the quilt were personally associated with the family. Blue was cut from a coat that Gladys wore in high school, red from a coat worn by Colleen in high school, and white from a coat worn by Gladys's mother. Ansbaugh's mother cut out the triangles, and

Courtesy of Gerald R. Ford Presidential Library & Museum, 1984.83

Golden Age Manor Ladies (Houston, Texas), *Bicentennial Quilt*, 1976, 98 × 80 in.

Barbara McKie, *Bicentennial Flag Quilt*, 1976, 61 × 73 in.

Volckening Collection, Portland, Oregon

her daughter laid them out on a table for placement before piecing.[19] The pattern for this quilt is similar to that of all-over designs of Centennial quilts repeating small units in geometric shapes, sometimes with a souvenir textile in the center.

Donna Bister became interested in making quilts during the 1970s, splurging on a trip to Ithaca, New York, to attend the *Finger Lakes Bicentennial Quilt Exhibit*. There she attended classes by Jo Diggs, Beth and Jeffrey Gutcheon, and Jean Ray Laury. Commissioned to reproduce an antique blue-and-white star quilt for a California King bed, she pieced, appliquéd, and quilted for months. Her studio work included smaller quilts for the wall, some of which were displayed in exhibitions. Bister's 1976 quilt illustrated here, as she tells us, "was an experiment for my own pleasure—piecing blocks, then cutting them in half and rearranging them until I liked the design."[20] She does not remember it as being specifically a Bicentennial quilt, just that there was so much red, white, and blue fabric available to use in 1976. In that same year, the Vermont Quilt Festival premiered as a Bicentennial activity, with Bister hired four years later to organize classes for the event.

The Bicentennial also produced an abundance of red, white, and blue yarn and thread. California artist Katherine Westphal stitched an embroidered art quilt depicting three *Bicentennial Angels* in a patriotic palette. She described her freewheeling creative process: "I let the textile grow, never knowing where it is going or when it will be finished . . . until my intuitive and visual senses tell me it is finished and the message complete."[21] With two light and one dark angel dominating the composition, this artist may have been exploring concepts of polarity during 1976.

Signature quilts became popular during the Bicentennial era, usually with the signatures in squares of fabric that had been mailed to the signers. In some examples, the quilter(s) hand-embroidered over the signatures to ensure their longevity. Illinois quilter Mina K. Kuthe created an original composition for her Bicentennial quilt, sending the recipients white cotton fabric in the shape of diamonds turned horizontally for signing, which she embroidered using dark-blue thread and pieced together with fabrics in solid red and blue, calling her work *The All American Signature Quilt*. The borders feature white stars on a blue field, each stitched with the name of a state, circling the quilt in the order of their admission to the US. In a newspaper article, Kuthe explained that she was inspired by the Bicentennial and by a 1972 article in *Life* magazine about a quilt signed by Abraham Lincoln. She mailed more than two hundred

▸ Dolores Miller, *Bicentennial Log Cabin* detail, 1976

fabric diamonds with her handwritten letter, receiving 154 signatures for her quilt. President Nixon's and his family's signatures were in Kuthe's mail the morning he resigned, followed the next day by signatures from President Ford and family. Kuthe remarked, "I thought it was very thoughtful of them to sign my swatches, with everything else they had to do just then."[22] Other signers included Hank Aaron, Phyllis Diller, Jackie Gleason, Angela Lansbury, Peggy Lee, Liberace, and numerous politicians.

Another red, white, and blue signature quilt was made in 1973 in reaction against the 1972 American bombing that obliterated Bach Mai Hospital, one of the largest

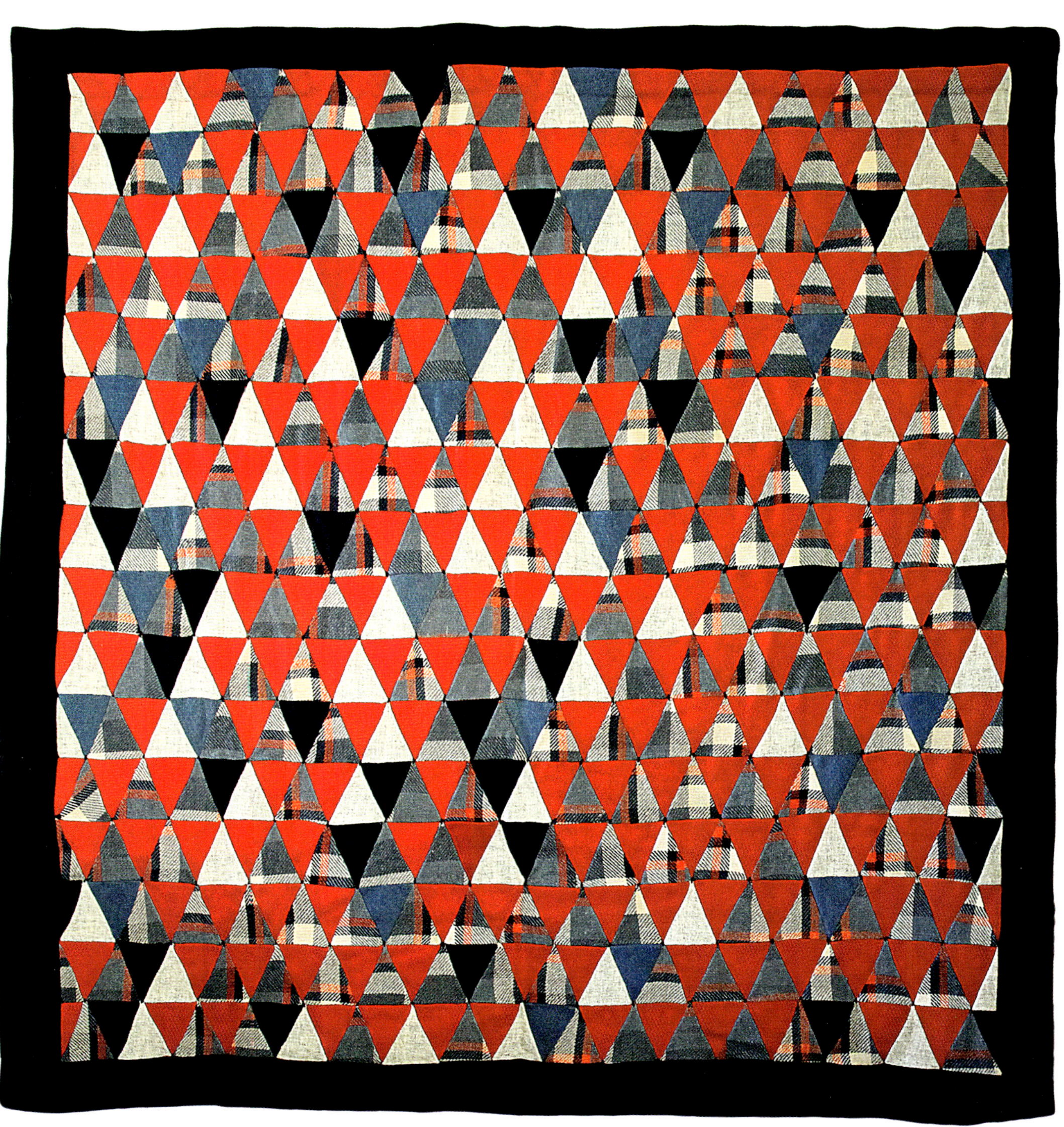

Gladys (Larson) Kendall and Colleen (Kendall) Ansbaugh, *1000 Pyramids Bicentennial Quilt*, 1976, 75 × 68 in.

hospitals in Hanoi, killing twenty-eight staff members and numerous patients. Various peace groups in the US rallied to protest the bombing. California quilt artist and political cartoonist Genevieve Guracar (known as "bulbul" in her cartoon art), decided to organize a signature quilt in album format by mailing white squares to Americans sympathetic to the peace efforts. Those who sent signed squares back to the artist included Bella Abzug, Shirley Chisholm, Judy Collins, Dick Gregory, William Kunstler, Eugene McCarthy, Kate Millett, Pete Seeger, and Benjamin Spock. Connie Young Yu, a scholar of Chinese American history, took charge of assembling the quilt with a group of peace activists in Palo Alto, California, who alternated the signed squares with blue and red squares. The young man who won the quilt when it was auctioned planned to ride his motorcycle across the US, displaying the quilt as part of the peace movement. After being persuaded that the quilt could be damaged during his journey, he donated it back to the peace union, and eventually the *Vietnam Era Quilt* made its way to the International Quilt Museum at the University of Nebraska.

Black quilters were making red, white, and blue quilts referencing decades of discrimination against their voting rights and personal freedoms, such as Irene Williams's ca. 1975 *Vote, Housetop Variation* in the Museum of Fine Arts, Boston. As a member of the Gee's Bend community of Black quilters, Williams had experienced their bitter struggles to vote during the 1960s. She made several quilts incorporating a cotton print covered with the word "vote" alternating with stars in patriotic colors. Georgia quilter Jesse Telfair created three versions in the 1970s of her famous *Freedom* quilt, all now in museum collections. One of these quilts traveled in the *Missing Pieces: Georgia Folk Art 1770–1976* exhibition. All three quilts appear similar, with large blue letters spelling the word "FREEDOM" on a red background in six horizontal rows, interspersed with white and red strips. During the 1960s, Telfair registered to vote in Georgia and helped register Black voters. For these actions, she was fired from her job working in the cafeteria of an elementary school. Her *Freedom* quilts memorialize her experience and affirm every American's freedom to vote.

Faith Ringgold, known for her story quilts and painting, also created performance pieces, beginning with *The Wake and Resurrection of the Bicentennial Negro*, first performed in 1976 as Ringgold's response to the Bicentennial, interpreted in the *Chicago Tribune* as giving "visual form to the growing gulf between the white American dream and the black American reality."[23] Like many African Americans

Courtesy of browngrotta arts, photo by Tom Grotta

Katherine Westphal (Berkeley, California), *Bicentennial Angels*, 1976, 26 × 32 in.

in 1876, the artist found nothing to celebrate in American "independence" that condoned slavery and racial injustice. Her narrative focused on the destructive forces of drugs, racism, and poverty within the Black experience.[24] For five years, Ringgold toured the US, involving college students in her multimedia performances of this piece. For the staged background, she mounted painted fabric works from her quilt-like series *Window of the Wedding,* influenced by Tibetan Buddhist thangkas and Congolese Kuba cloth. Not surprisingly, there was no combination of red, white, and blue in these wall hangings.

THE PEOPLE'S BICENTENNIAL QUILT

The People's Bicentennial Committee (PBC) founder Jeremy Rifkin was exasperated with what he saw as the commercialization and lack of taste penetrating the Bicentennial.[25] Being a political activist, Rifkin obviously took an extreme position. But the money brought in from licensing fees and other marketing helped fund one-third of the Bicentennial events, providing millions of federal dollars for local projects. Among the many projects associated with the PBC was *The People's BiCentennial Quilt*.[26]

This quilt's forty-five album squares feature a different take on American history from the textbook versions illustrated in some of the quilts previously described. Images in the quilt's squares refer to America's concentration camps imprisoning Japanese American citizens, Shays' Rebellion of 1786 (when farmers protested against foreclosure of their land), the Native American Trail of Tears, child labor in factories, union busters, the struggle for women's suffrage, lynching of African Americans, school integration, and student protests against the US military in Southeast Asia.

The forty-four women who created the squares included African Americans from East Palo Alto, California, addressing aspects of racial injustice. Along them was Bea Keesey, a great-granddaughter of the famous abolitionist John Brown. Genevieve Guracar organized the project, while Connie Yu researched and wrote the book accompanying the quilt.[27] As we look toward America's semiquincentennial in 2026, her comments in the book's foreword bear repeating: "All our lives we've been fed history in which minority people's struggles have been omitted or negated, in which women have been degraded, and in which imperialist conquest, monopoly and militarism have been viewed as heroic. We wanted to portray the *people* as making history: the nameless, countless members of movements and

▸ Donna Bister, *Red, White, and Blue Quilt*, 1976, 57 × 57 in.

Collection of Sandra Sider

Connie Young Yu, *The People's BiCentennial Quilt: A Patchwork History* (East Palo Alto, CA: Up Press, 1976), front cover

Volckening Collection, Portland, Oregon

struggles that have affected the soul and character of America. We felt there was much in American history that could unite us in a cynical time."

THE BICENTENNIAL BOOST FOR QUILTS

Much has been written to document the fact that the Bicentennial prompted many people to begin making quilts, or at least to try their hand at quilt making, especially through the craft and home magazines: "Here at *Lady's Circle* we have received letters, pictures, and notices and rumors about the fun everyone is having with their quilt shows and auctions and we've wished we could get to every one of them. Even more we've wished we could bring them all to you in pictures but there's no way to touch more than a very small sample."[28] That excitement blossomed from Bicentennial fabrics, quilt contests, exhibitions, television programs, books, and magazines—several of which produced special issues covering Bicentennial topics, including craft magazines featuring quilt patterns.

In July 1976, George Gallup reported the results of his nationwide Bicentennial poll, in which only 11 percent of Americans said that they planned to travel for the Bicentennial. Instead, they were staying home, with "making Bicentennial quilts" on their list of activities, along with fireworks, beauty contests, tree planting, and painting fire hydrants in patriotic colors.[29] Testimony from today's quilt makers confirms their Bicentennial commitment to quilt making and subsequent involvement in the craft; for example, from Diane Knoblauch, fiber artist: "I started quilting in 1978 after seeing the McCall's (I believe they put on the contest) article with their Bicentennial contest winners. I had been sewing for about 8 or 9 years at that point. I joined my first guild in Arkansas in 1983, and in 1986 I moved to California for four years, where I studied with dozens of national teachers, eager to become a teacher myself. It was there that I got to meet Jinny Beyer, who won that contest as well as other notables [such] as Michael James, Joan Schulze, Jan Myers-Newberry, and so many more."[30]

Ann Baldwin May shared her quilting journey: "In the years leading up to the Bicentennial, I remember an emphasis on renewing American crafts. In 1974, I took my first quilting class at a neighborhood fabric store. We learned to make a sampler [using] 6 different quilting techniques. We made yoyos for one, not my favorite. However, that was the beginning of a lifetime of making quilts. I stopped counting my traditional bed quilts at 300. About 2010, I . . . switched to art quilts. In 2016, I opened a small studio in the Santa Cruz Art Center [in California]. I participate annually in the juried Open Studios Art Tour in Santa Cruz County. Quilting has been a lifetime passion of mine."[31] For many makers, quilt making stuck, evolving into a rewarding aspect of their lives and even a new career path for those creating quilts in their homes and studios, sometimes becoming teachers, authors, and fabric designers for quilt makers. Bicentennial commemorations also encouraged individual makers as well as groups to create quilts celebrating or protesting other anniversaries as time progressed.

▸ Mina K. Kuthe (Maywood, Illinois), *The All American Signature Quilt*, 1974–1975, 99 × 67 in.

International Quilt Museum, University of Nebraska–Lincoln, 2006.022.001

International Quilt Museum, University of Nebraska–Lincoln, 2007.008.0001

Genevieve Guracar (Mountain View, California), *Vietnam Era Quilt*, 1973, 80 × 63.5 in.

Irene Williams (Gee's Bend, Alabama), *Vote, Housetop Variation,* 1975, 89 × 81 in.

CHAPTER 7

Quilts in Vogue

The first stage in becoming a quilt artist during the decade leading up to the Bicentennial and during the following decade was, for many people, learning how to make a quilt. This skill was accomplished with publications, workshops and other classes, and knowledge from family members or friends, and individually by trial and error. A few makers working in the quilt medium, such as Charles and Rubynelle Counts and Ed Larson, never learned how to quilt but instead hired others to quilt their designs. Although they did not handle a needle and thread for their artwork, these individuals created compositions in which the stitching was considered the final element of design as they collaborated with quilters.[1]

HOW-TO PUBLICATIONS: BOOKS

Most useful for beginners were books that included patterns, measurements, quilting instructions, and photographs of completed quilts.[2] Among the most popular books during the 1960s was *101 Patchwork Patterns* (1931, numerous later printings) by Ruby McKim. The Dover reprint of this book in 1962 joined the publisher's list of thirteen other books on patchwork. McKim wrote her book in a direct, relaxed style, assuring the reader that anyone could make a quilt. The introduction notes that many quilt makers were young women with "unspoiled imaginings"—implying that modern young women could also participate "in the game of quilt making" (p. 3).[3] *101 Patchwork Patterns* was an important book for many quilt artists, including Joan Schulze, especially when she first began to teach quilt making.

Another very successful Dover reprint was *The Standard Book of Quilt Making and Collecting* (1949; Dover, 1959) by Marguerite Ickis. Although this book focused on designated patterns, the chapter "The Quilt's Design and Its Parts" includes a paragraph on "Making Your Own Design." Her text closes with a word of encouragement for those contemplating original designs: "There is no limit to design sources, if you have ideas and imagination" (p. 25).[4] This sort of encouragement was invaluable during the 1960s, when quilt makers had few resources for original designs. Donna Renshaw has been mentioned as an influence, including her publications on quilting, such as *Quilting, a Revived Art: Cultivate the Art of Making*

Something with Your Own Hands,[5] published ca. 1975, riding the Bicentennial buzz. Her chapter 1 begins "Quilt making is an art. It follows close to painting, spinning, weaving, mosaics and all types of arts and crafts." Renshaw viewed quilt making as a woman's art, situating it firmly in women's history and targeting her book toward women in the home. Although her book is a step-by-step manual, the text focuses on process and not on patterns. She encouraged originality in design: "One nice thing about quilt making, you can use your own imagination and do anything you wish to do, along with bringing out your creativity, or the nonconformity you've always had a longing for."[6] Women who worked as homemakers were encouraged by such comments to pursue quilt making as a creative outlet, to relieve the presumed boredom of their daily lives.

The editors of Sunset Books issued a useful series of books on quilt making, such as *Quilting and Patchwork*, first published in 1973, with six printings by the end of 1974.[7] Paula Nadelstern, for example, learned how to quilt from a Sunset book, as did Carolyn Mazloomi.[8] Although *Quilting and Patchwork* offered mostly preconceived projects, a few of the works illustrated were avant-garde—such as the quilts designed by Charles and Rubynelle Counts and Joan Lintault. "How to Create an Unusual Quilt" (p. 58) must have piqued the curiosity of many readers with its list of "eighteen capsule ideas . . . using a variety of techniques" in printing, freehand (e.g., painting and batik), and needlecraft (e.g., collage and lettering).

Michael James found the books by Averil Colby, among others, to be very helpful when he was learning to make quilts. Colby's book

Collection of Sandra Sider (all books illustrated in this chapter)

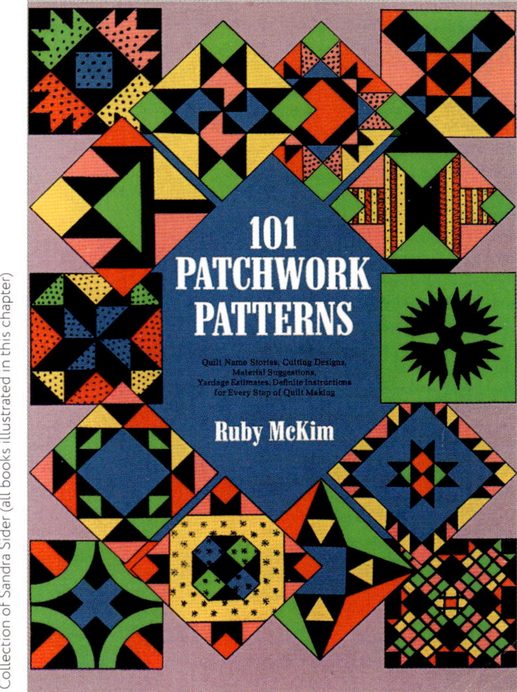

Ruby Short McKim, *One Hundred and One Patchwork Patterns* (New York: Dover, 1962), front cover

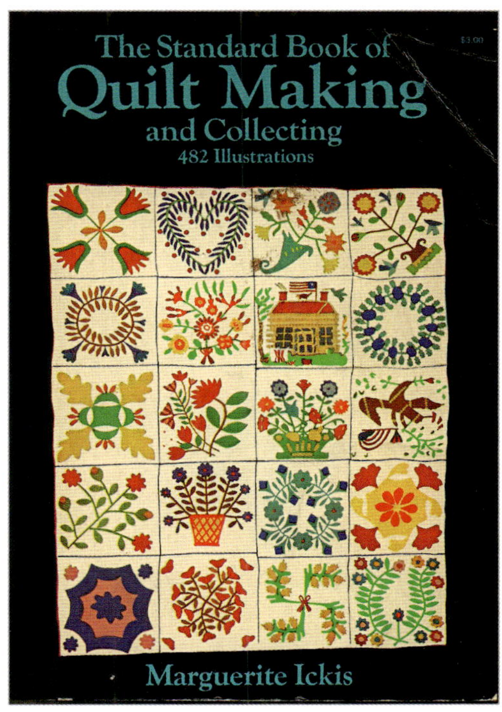

Marguerite Ickis, *The Standard Book of Quilt Making and Collecting* (New York: Dover, 1959), front cover

titled simply *Patchwork* (first published in 1958) is filled with precise instructions for every stage of quilt making, with occasional aesthetic comments accompanying the practical information. For those just learning how to quilt, even the most basic steps could present a problem. Caryl Bryer Fallert Gentry was among those who began making quilts by leaving ⅝-inch seams (normal for clothing construction), quickly realizing that this amassed too much fabric on the back of the quilt.[9]

Condé Nast Publications joined the quilt bandwagon, with books such as their *Vogue Guide to Patchwork and Quilting*.[10] This 1973 book included not only patterns, but also illustrations of entire rooms (including a lampshade) busily decorated in patchwork designs, as well as a frontispiece of trend-setter Gloria Vanderbilt "the painter, photographed in her beautiful all patchwork bedroom . . . [showing] how patchwork can be really dazzling for interior decoration" (caption, p. 5). On the same page, the editor encouraged readers to make quilts from new fabric because "this means that a modern patchwork can be designed from start to finish."[11] This how-to book included brief discussions of basic shapes for patchwork, with useful design information: "By using contrasting tones and very simple shapes it is quite easy to achieve some extraordinary optical illusions . . . by changing the layout of the triangles, but still using dark and light fabrics, you can get a fractured effect" (p. 20). This "fractured" approach would be one of the techniques by which several contemporary quilt artists, such as Marie Lyman and Molly Upton, made the leap from quilter to quilt artist.

Beth Gutcheon, *The Perfect Patchwork Primer* (Baltimore: Penguin Books, 1974) [originally published in 1973], front cover

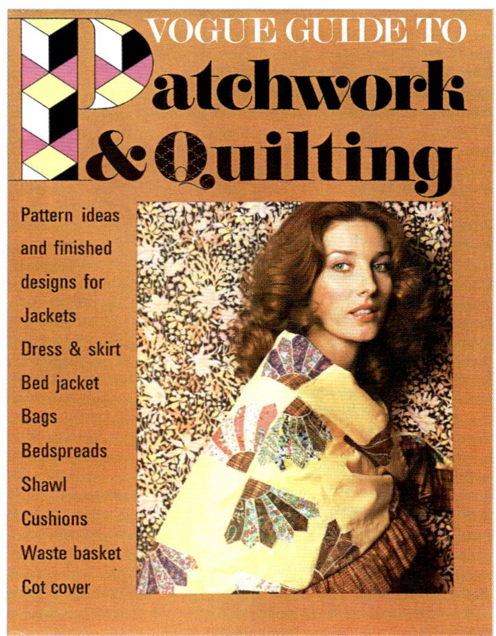

Vogue Guide to Patchwork and Quilting (New York: Condé Nast, 1973), front cover

HOW-TO PUBLICATIONS: PERIODICALS

Magazines marketed to women, the *Progressive Farmer*,[12] various newspapers, and other periodical publications featured quilt projects, usually a pattern or patterns that readers were expected to copy faithfully. A few new magazines in the 1960s and 1970s were created specifically for quilt makers, such as *Quilters' Journal*, published between 1977 and 1987, edited by Joyce Gross.[13] The articles discussed technique as well as quilt history. One of the most popular magazines created for quilt makers, *Quilter's Newsletter Magazine*, began its publication in 1969 (as *Quilter's Newsletter*), edited by Bonnie Leman.[14] Before the magazine went out of business in 2016, its circulation had reached more than 200,000 people.

Lady's Circle Patchwork Quilts, a magazine coedited by Carter Houck and Janet Chill, gave potential quilt artists a balanced presentation of original designs and patterns. Issue no. 14 (1979), for example, published an article by Beth Gutcheon on "The Quilts of Molly Upton as Works of Art" (pp. 6–11, 71), which included illustrations in color. The editors were careful to distinguish between original designs and patterns, explaining, "When patterns are not included, it is due to the fact that these are personalized designs and belong to the makers of the quilt" (p. 3).

McCall's was among the women's publishers dominating the field of quilting and patchwork, issuing several books and magazines in which garments were emphasized as much as quilts to support the McCall Pattern Company. Interestingly, the surface designs for garments often were rather avant-garde, while most of the quilt patterns remained relatively traditional. The editors of McCall's Needlework & Crafts published a series of books titled *Quilt It!*, with the second book issued in 1972 and reprinted in 1973 and 1974. *McCall's Contemporary Quilting* (1963, with eight new editions through 1975) featured dynamic original quilts by such artists as Barbara McKie and Virginia Avery, but with the expectation that readers would copy their designs.

HOW-TO WORKSHOPS, CLASSES, AND LECTURES

Neophyte quilt makers could learn the basics in workshops and classes if they happened to live near a facility where such instruction was offered,[15] or could afford to travel.[16] A few educational institutions included fiber as part of their art or crafts curriculum, such as the Cranbrook Academy of Art (Bloomfield Hills, Michigan) and the Oregon School of Arts and Crafts (Portland),[17] but not all of them offered quilting per se. Marie Lyman was among those teaching quilt making at the Oregon School of Arts and Crafts in the latter 1970s,[18] but Cranbrook never had a formal class in quilting or quilt making in the 1960s or 1970s. Gerhardt Knodel, director of Cranbrook from 1970 until 1996, clarified: "Because the nature of the graduate program is to support individual courses of study determined by each student, there were some students who used the conceptual framework of quilt making and its techniques in their work. Most of that experimental work was useful in enhancing appreciation of the legacy of quilt making, and in stimulating ideas about the potential for integrating aspects of the practice into new innovative forms of expression."[19]

Quilt art pioneer Alma Lesch taught textile arts at the Louisville School of Art (Kentucky) beginning in 1961. Like Lyman and a few other quilting teachers during the 1960s and early 1970s, Lesch traveled and presented workshops. Betsy Cannon, a quilt artist since 1968 known for her embellished pictorial quilts, remembers the interesting experience of studying quilt making with Lesch in the mid-1970s at the Arrowmont School of Arts and Crafts (Gatlinburg, Tennessee). Lesch also taught at the Haystack Mountain School of Crafts (Maine), a facility mentioned as influential for several artists during their early years of making quilts or learning other crafts involving textiles. The Penland School of Crafts in western North Carolina provided instruction in fiber that included quilt making; Terrie Hancock Mangat is among the contemporary quilt artists who profited from workshops taken there.

Jeanne Williamson has a 1978 BFA in fibers and crafts from the Philadelphia College of Art, where she began by majoring in jewelry, weaving wire for her pieces and taking elective courses in the Fibers Department. She took a class in quilting, in which the students used templates for cutting patterns and learned fine hand quilting, not being permitted to make any knots in the thread. Williamson stresses that "the quilt making we did then was *very* traditional, with no creativity except for the colors we paired together."[20] She found a more appealing way to work with fabric in stitched collage. In some schools, quilting was offered under the rubric of needlework. Studio classes in fiber art could be found cross-listed with the fledgling women's studies program of the 1970s,[21] a result of the feminist movement.

Several artists have mentioned the early workshops of Jinny Beyer (sometimes given in her home) as a formative influence on their quilt-making skills, especially in the technique of drafting patterns. Jane Hall, for example, studied compass drafting in one of her classes. Beyer's 1979 book, *Patchwork Patterns*, which defines geometric patterns by categories on the basis of a grid system, was rather traditional in its approach. But the final chapter of Beyer's book, "Original Design," voices ideas presented in her classes that were useful for students attempting to create their own designs, such as not planning the entire quilt at once but instead working with the fabrics, turning the blocks different ways, and appreciating that a "whole new dimension" can result in the interplay of fabrics (p. 177).[22]

In 1971, Beth Gutcheon began offering quilting workshops in New York City and, according to Robert Shaw, "quickly became the most prominent teacher on the East Coast."[23] She and her musician-husband Jeffrey Gutcheon created original quilts based on unique variations of vintage blocks, displaying them in their loft at 510 Broadway, where she conducted workshops and sold fabric. By the spring of 1972, Gutcheon had numerous students and was becoming well known, partly thanks to press coverage such as an illustrated article by Rita Reif in the *New York Times*.[24]

CREATING ORIGINAL QUILT DESIGNS: BOOKS

The earliest book on contemporary quilt art viewed as an important source for artists whom I contacted is Jean Ray Laury's groundbreaking *Quilts & Coverlets: A*

lsa Brown, *Creative Quilting* (New York: Watson-Guptill, 1975), front cover

Ann-Sargent Wooster, *Quiltmaking: The Modern Approach to a Traditional Craft* (New York: Drake, 1972), front cover

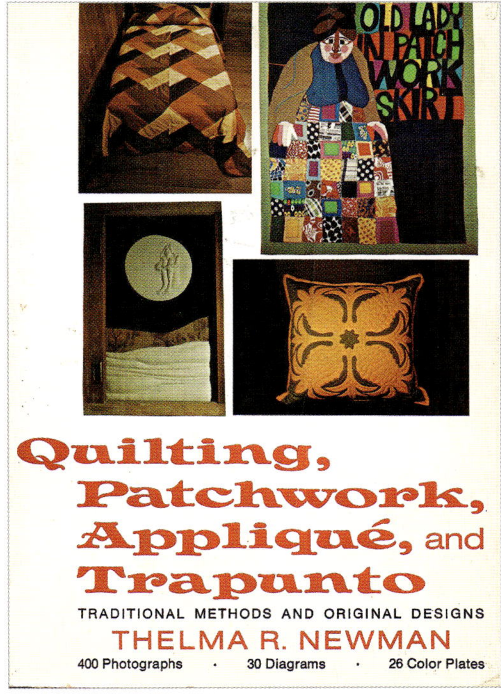

Thelma R. Newman, *Quilting, Patchwork, Appliqué, and Trapunto: Traditional Methods and Original Designs* (New York: Crown, 1974), front cover

Michael James, *The Second Quiltmaker's Handbook: A Guide to Design and Construction* (Mountain View, CA: Leone, 1993) [originally published in 1978], front cover

Contemporary Approach (1970). This 128-page publication promotes contemporary quilts, such as a Tracey Emin–like construction with lettering and text by Stephanie Cyr (p. 46), several modernist quilts in color by Charles Counts and the Rising Fawn Quilters (pp. 60–61 and 63), and Joan Lintault's famous conceptual piece *La Chola en la Colcha*, in which a stuffed figure in a pieced "garment" appears to be swelling out from under the quilt (p. 64).

Many of the images in Elsa Brown's book *Creative Quilting* (1975) resonate with contemporary and near-contemporary works in the world of what was then called "fine art," beginning with Romare Bearden's collaged painting *Patchwork Quilt* (ca. 1972),[25] in which he incorporated scraps of fabric. Other provocative works were a fantasy landscape by Helen Bitar (p. 65), a piece by Kathryn McCardle Lipke featuring knotted rope reminiscent of the art of Eva Hesse (p. 80), and *Man Pyramid* by Lenore Davis (p. 122), which quivers with the energy of a Keith Haring drawing. Brown's introduction informed the reader: "Fabric has become an important sculptural medium for relief as well as three-dimensional forms. Many artists who formerly worked with more traditional materials have turned to cloth to create imaginative wall hangings, dolls, sculptural objects, and body coverings" (p. 10) [fig. 9].

Quilt Making: The Modern Approach to a Traditional Craft (1972) was a how-to book by painter and sculptor Ann-Sargent Wooster, whose credentials included classes at Parsons School of Design and the School of Visual Arts in New York. Her introduction stated, "Recently, many painters, sculptors, and designers have been turning to soft materials to create their designs."[26] The images of avant-garde quilts and fabric sculptures included Nell Booker Sonnemann's 6-foot-high *Woman Clothed with the Sun* (p. 158); she described her three-dimensional forms as "appliqué . . . moving into open space" (p. 157).[27]

Thelma R. Newman's purpose in writing *Quilting, Patchwork, Appliqué, and Trapunto* (1974) focused on "one's own ability to create original and personal forms."[28] Along with illustrations of original artwork by contemporary artists in the US, she featured ethnic textiles from Africa, India, and Panama—all important design sources for some quilt artists during the 1970s. The contemporary quilt art in this book was extraordinary, including *The Point*, a semiabstract fabric collage by Bets Ramsey (facing p. 25), and

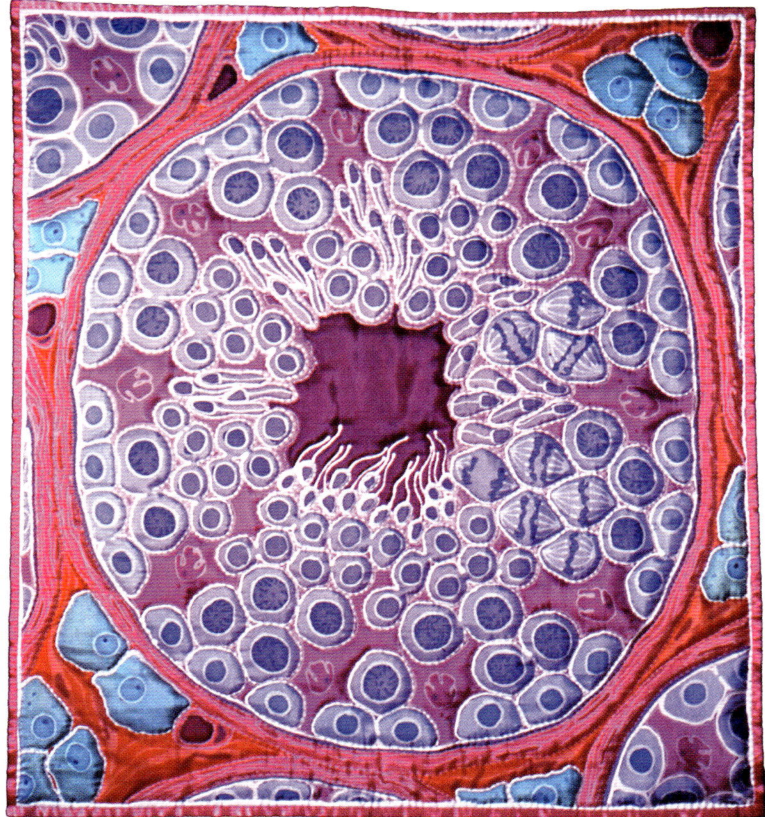

Sue Benner, *Semiferous Tubulae: mature*, 1980, 24 × 21 in.

Margaret Cusack's Warhol-like fabric portrait of Aldous Huxley (fourth page of color figures following p. 24). Many of these works were innovations on the part of the artists—their newest pieces, some never before published. Bets Ramsey remarked concerning *The Point,* "I was trying some new ideas and they seemed to work."[29]

The Complete Guide to Quilting (1974) by Audrey Heard and Beverly Pryor also promoted quilt making as contemporary art, cautioning readers to learn basic techniques (which were included) before venturing into original designs. The authors explained their purpose in writing the book: "It gives us great pleasure to see quilts hung on walls, serving as decorative focal points in the manner of paintings. Excitement of color and harmony of design should be the goal of every person who puts needle to cloth."[30] The illustrations juxtaposed traditional pieced and appliquéd quilts, along with others in pictorial folk-art style, with several modernist works, such as quilts in op art style by Barbara McKie (p. 191) and Sharon McKain (p. 205).

Quilt artists who were active in the 1970s have cited several other books as instrumental in their creative development. Near the top of the list of all these books would be *The Perfect Patchwork Primer* (1973) by Beth Gutcheon, *The Quilt Design Workbook* (1976) by Beth and Jeffrey Gutcheon, *The Quilt Makers Handbook: A Guide to Design and Construction* (1978) by Michael James, and *The Second Quilt Makers Handbook: Creative Approaches to Contemporary Quilt Designs* (1981), also by James.[31] Not only did these books encourage originality, but they also provided basic patterns that readers could expand and alter. Moreover, the Gutcheons and Michael James offered workshops conducted in a relaxed yet involved attitude, with the teachers carefully explaining the lessons in their books. Katie Pasquini Masopust says, "Michael James transformed my high school art knowledge to art quilts."

Because Beth Gutcheon's book appeared relatively early, and in the popular Penguin Handbook series, and possibly because of her positive exposure in the press, this publication was extremely influential. *The Perfect Patchwork Primer* was, in fact, one of the first how-to books on quilt making used by Michael James in the mid-1970s. Most importantly, it was written from the point of view of a quilt maker who viewed the craft as having the potential of an art form, who assumed that the satisfaction of creating quilt art "lies in the realm of esthetics and self-expression . . . to push the tradition a step forward, to say something new about ourselves, and about quilt making."[32] In addition to depicting quilts by the Gutcheons, *The Quilt Design Workbook* included images of several innovative abstract quilts by Susan Hoffman and Molly Upton—inspirations to anyone beginning to work with quilts as art.

The Quilt Maker's Handbook (1978) by Michael James gave readers a clear, detailed appendix titled "On Color in Quilts," which was based on his experience as a painter and referring to the color theories of Josef Albers; the twenty-one color plates illustrated some of these concepts. Like the Gutcheons, James wrote a book that could be used in workshops. The author praised quilt making from a philosophical point of view, as a "tangible means to reaffirm our individualities and creative capabilities" in a highly automated world.[33] The introduction

Courtesy of the artist

Michael James, *Razzle-Dazzle*, 1975, 96 × 84 in.

also affirmed quilts as art: "In our general recognition of quilt making as an *art* form, we have come to acknowledge its rightful place as one of many sophisticated modes of visual expression" (p. 2). Artists of the 1970s who simply ignored the futile "art versus craft" controversy experienced how "new technical challenges imposed by different design considerations create . . . a vital interchange between craft and art" (p. 3). Instructions in James's book, written by a recognized virtuoso of the genre, allowed students to balance precision with spontaneity. *The Quilt Maker's Handbook* appeared at a fortuitous moment in American quilt history, in that numerous potential quilt makers (mostly women) had been inspired by the Bicentennial celebrations in 1975–1976, which included quilt exhibitions and publications.[34] They were eager for more information.

Almost all the helpful books published before the early 1980s were how-to books, which makes sense because people were trying to learn how to deal with quilts as an artistic medium within the limitations of structural fabric. But in 1978, a remarkable publication by Pattie Chase and Mimi Dolbier, definitely not a how-to, caught the attention of virtually everyone working with quilts as art. Sue Benner and Robin Schwalb, for example, cite this book as being of tremendous influence on their early work. Titled *The Contemporary Quilt: New American Quilts and Fabric Art*, it brought quilt art into the limelight, exploding on the scene with a monumental eye surmounting a flamboyant pyramid in a 1976 quilt by Sas Colby on the front cover, and Jody Klein's fantastical, three-dimensional interpretation of stars and stripes in *Bumpy Quilt* (1973) on the back. The former featured photo transfer; for the latter, the artist used hand-dyed fabric. Susan Hoffman's architectural tour de force *Spires, Coutances Cathedral* (1975) graced the half title, and Molly Upton's majestic *Torrid Dwelling* (1975) served as the frontispiece. Every work in the book was illustrated in color, highlighting the significance of quilts as art.

One other how-to book concerning quilting was an interesting source for several artists: Pauline Chatterton's *Patchwork & Appliqué* (1977). A British fiber artist, Chatterton had previously published two books on crochet, and the innovative aspect of her latest publication was that not only did she explain how to make quilts, but she also explored how the designs of quilts could be translated into knitting, crochet, and bargello needlework. The chapter titled "Inspiration for Appliqué" included abstract quilts by Michiko Sato (p. 47), Sas Colby's quasi-psychedelic figural quilt inspired by a Beatles' song and created partially with photographic printing (p. 48),[35] and abstract Mylar quilts by Patricia Malarcher (pp. 49–50). This book helped stimulate quilt artists to experiment with new materials, techniques, and processes.

Embellishing a quilt surface usually was referred to as "stitchery" during the 1960s and 1970s, with several books on this topic inspiring artists to learn embroidery and other types of freehand needlework. Three books evidently were especially useful to quilt makers. The goal of *Adventures in Stitches: A New Art of Embroidery* (1949) by Mariska Karasz was to instruct the reader how to "develop into a painter in thread."[36] The author, who had solo exhibitions in

New York City, was also known as a clothing designer. The linear embroidery of Karasz inspired B. J. Adams, early in her career as a quilt artist. David van Dommelen also used the word "art" in the title of his 1962 book, *Decorative Wall Hangings: Art with Fabric*.[37] Known chiefly as a designer, the author had this to say about his work: "My field of concentration in wall hangings contributes as much to the Fine Arts as does contemporary painting. . . . To me, the stitch . . . has as much message as the stroke of a brush. I find myself in a medium that is completely unexplored, ready to be discovered and opened to the world" (p. 178). Artists with fiber art illustrated in this book include Alice Adams, Jean Arp, Mariska Karasz, Jean Ray Laury, Marilyn Pappas, and Frances Robinson.

By far the most influential book of stitchery for quilt artists of the 1960s and 1970s was Jean Ray Laury's *Applique Stitchery* (1966), with many of the images showing quilted appliqué, all in examples made by the author herself. More importantly, Laury stressed idea and design much more than technique, assuring readers that simple techniques executed with basic equipment could express interesting concepts. Laury said that stitchery "means much the same as needlework, but avoids the connotation of stamped patterns, directions, and limitations."[38] She advised readers to begin by becoming involved with an idea and an attitude, "The idea or intellectual content will give a work its validity; the attitude or emotional content gives it its strength; the act or physical involvement gives it its form. This is true in all media."[39]

Finally, "soft art" was becoming a popular alternative art form during the 1970s, with *Stitched and Stuffed Art: Contemporary Designs for Quilts, Toys, Pillows, Soft Sculpture and Wall Hangings* (1974) by Carolyn Vosburg Hall epitomizing the diverse aspects of this genre.[40] Some of the contemporary quilts and quilt-like structures were by Alma Lesch, Bonnie Gisel (four-patch squares wired together, with the piecing seams turned outward), and Gwendolyn Hogue (tie-dyed silk quilted to burlap). The author, who had been an art critic for ten years, had an MFA from the Cranbrook Academy of Art. The book quickly became known, possibly because the noted crafts critic Lisa Hammel gave it a positive review in the *New York Times*.[41] The back flap of the dust jacket mentions that "the author has helped to dispel the artificial distinction between arts and crafts."

Embellishing a quilt surface usually was referred to as "stitchery" during the 1960s and 1970s.

CREATING ORIGINAL QUILT DESIGNS: PERIODICALS

While books might reach an audience of a few thousand readers, many periodicals had circulations into the tens of thousands and even more. In addition to her books, Jean Ray Laury influenced new quilt artists through her articles and images of her quilts published in periodicals. Yvonne Porcella was among the numerous artists struck by this work—Laury's writing as well as her quilts—in *Family Circle* magazine and other publications. Laury's quilts were featured on several covers of *Family Circle* during the 1970s, and a brilliant red comforter by Laury appeared in an issue of *Cosmopolitan*, covering a presumably nude couple involved in lovemaking, with the caption "Quilt a Sensuous Quilt"—a surprisingly hip, new image for quilts.[42] Laury's first published article, and the one she considers most important,[43] appeared in a 1960 issue of *House Beautiful*, discussed below. In 1979, *Quilt World* published an image of Laury quilting on its cover, with a feature article titled "A Heart to Heart Talk with . . . Jean Ray Laury."[44] The article summarized her success as an author and quilt artist, indicating the various means by which Laury had achieved her current status. This text and others like it provided those attempting to be quilt artists with successful role models.

Nancy Halpern, *Crow Quilt*, 1976, 96 × 84 in.

As mentioned above, *Lady's Circle Patchwork Quilts* published an article by Beth Gutcheon titled "The Quilts of Molly Upton as Works of Art" in 1979 that included illustrations in color. Although other periodicals had mentioned, or even featured, quilts as contemporary art, few readers had seen anything like the extraordinary graphic quilts by Upton and Susan Hoffman—especially not in a *Lady's Circle* publication. The influence of these images was far-reaching. Valerie Hearder shared this memory from South Africa: "In 1972, I was 20 and living in South Africa when I taught myself to make quilts based on English paper piecing. . . . There was no established history of quilt making in South Africa so batting or quilt fabrics were unheard of. I used indigo print fabrics from the African marketplaces. When I saw Upton's quilts in [the magazine] I was profoundly moved. There was such strength in her quilts that were non-traditional back in the early '70s. That was exciting to me and informed my resolve to make my own designs."[45] This sort of testimony is similar to that of others concerning newspapers and magazines of the 1970s and early 1980s illustrating the quilt art of Rhoda Cohen, Nancy Crow, Gayle Fraas and Duncan Slade, Nancy Halpern, Michael James, Carolyn Mazloomi, Ruth McDowell, Yvonne Porcella, and other artists.

Quilter's Newsletter Magazine began publishing avant-garde quilts in 1971, with a black-and-white image of Mary Borkowski's

Outer Space created for the Ohio Historical Society.[46] In 1974 the magazine announced that Diane Leone had won Best of Show in an art exhibition at the Triton Museum in Santa Clara, California. Leone was quoted as saying, "When a revived home art competing with all the other media gets that kind of recognition, you have to admit that quilt making is definitely an art form."[47] During the mid-1970s, with the excitement of the Bicentennial, *QNM* set up a Quiltmobile that the editor's husband drove around parts of the country, showing old and new quilts and looking for interesting quilts to publish in the magazine. By then the publication was publishing works in color, illustrating such brilliant fiber art as the silkscreened quilts of Cindy Miracle, at that time a graduate student in art at Claremont College.[48] Increasingly, *QNM* added articles on surface design processes, with the cover of an issue in 1976 featuring Jeanie Spears's batik quilt *Red, White, and Woman*, a tribute to both the Bicentennial and International Woman's Year (1975).[49] In the following year, art-related issues were emphasized as Michael James began a series of articles designed to help in using color in quilts. The illustrations included contemporary quilts by Radka Donnell and Nancy Halpern.[50]

Craft Horizons began publication in 1941, with the title changed to *American Craft* in 1979.[51] This journal was significant, partly because it included announcements and reviews of most of the major quilt shows, regional as well as national, at the very beginning of the studio quilt movement. New materials, techniques, and processes were reported in its pages,[52] along with essays and transcribed panel discussions and interviews dealing with pedagogical and theoretical aspects of craft. Contemporary quilt art was featured in several nearly full-page images, such as a white-and-beige work by Rubynelle Counts,[53] an abstract quilted banner by Canadian artist Caroline Wickham,[54] and a conceptual quilt by Jody Klein.[55] Trude Guermonprez, an influential weaver, had a political piece in color on the cover of the June 1976 *Craft Horizons*.[56] Having trained in Europe at schools that practiced Bauhaus aesthetics, in 1947 she taught Anni Albers's classes at Black Mountain College. Later she taught at the California School of Fine Arts (San Francisco), and then at the California College of Arts and Crafts (Oakland), continuing the Bauhaus influence. Numerous fiber artists, some of whom became quilt artists, took her workshops.[57] California eventually began to rival New England and Ohio as a hotbed of contemporary quilt art.[58]

Even though the images were in black and white, the studio quilts, quilted objects, collaged fabric, and tapestries and other wall hangings illustrated in the "Exhibitions" section of *American Craft* were inspirational. The 1980 issue alone featured work by Nancy Crow and Marie Lyman,[59] Lucas Samaras and Patricia Malarcher,[60] Jody Klein and Risë Nagin,[61] and Helen Bitar (in color) and Tafi Brown (who won an award with her quilt *Rockingham Raising V*).[62] That same issue included a large image of one of Anne Kingsbury's cape-like quilted wall hangings.[63] Thus, artists were exposed to the vital new medium of studio quilts, and in an open environment in which the work of Marie Lyman was mentioned on the same page as the art of Bruce Nauman, Peter Reginato, and Robert Rauschenberg (who "demonstrated

▸ Helen Bitar, *Mountain in the Morning*, 1976, 106 × 83 in.

Photo by Michael Gordon

Tafi Brown, *The American Wing VIII*, 1976, 86 × 59 in.

that he has opened up many new territories hitherto taboo in sculpture," with materials that included string, lace, and "chintzy cloth").[64]

Fiberarts magazine was first published in 1975, with antique quilts described as art fairly early, in the May/June 1976 issue.[65] Initially, *Fiberarts* focused on weaving and other textiles[66] but occasionally offered profiles of artists working in the quilt medium, often described as "wall hangings" or "fabric constructions." One example is the work of Virginia Jacobs, for which both terms were used: "She uses the skills of hand and machine sewing, quilting and appliqué, in conventional and inventive ways, creating new techniques as needed to carry out her designs."[67] The highly ornamental, personal nature of these designs, handsomely illustrated, suggested new avenues to those working in the quilt medium. By the end of the 1970s, *Fiberarts* was featuring articles on workshops and schools with instruction in fiber art and textile design, such as the San Francisco School of Fabric Art.

Joan Schulze, *California*, 1976, 104 × 96 in.

CREATING ORIGINAL QUILT DESIGNS: HOW-TO WORKSHOPS, CLASSES, AND LECTURES

In the artists' surveys conducted for this book, the workshops and lectures of Jean Ray Laury were praised more often than those of any other teacher, not only for the practical information they contained, but also for her sense of humor, which kept the presentations interesting. Caryl Bryer Fallert Gentry happened upon a lecture by Laury in 1982. Having run out of thread for the quilt project she had brought with her on a trip, Fallert went to a local fabric shop and heard about a lecture that evening titled "Quilting or the Breakfast Dishes"[68] sponsored by the local quilting guild. Her reaction to the lecture was a typical Laury revelation, the room being filled with enthusiastic, laughing women and the speaker her usual witty and articulate self—and doubly impressive because she had an MA in art from Stanford. Fallert Gentry began designing her first original quilt as soon as she returned home.

Guilds of quilt artists as such had not yet formed before the 1980s.[69] While a multitude of traditional, large quilt guilds peppered the country by the 1970s, quilt artists[70]—who did not yet use that appellation—gathered in smaller, more-informal groups. Numerous organized groups did focus on "stitchery" and textiles, which sometimes included original quilted work, and whose guest lecturers and workshop directors shared technical and design information that could be applied to quilts. During the 1960s, the Textile Arts Guild (Athens, Ohio), for example, numbered future quilt artist Virginia Randles among its members; at that time, she was concentrating on weaving. Joan Schulze was a member of the Peninsula Stitchery Guild[71] as of the later 1960s, one of the first groups of its kind in US, which often had workshops and critiques. In the early 1970s, Schulze took a motivating weeklong workshop in San Francisco with the British needlework expert Constance Howard, who became her mentor. The workshop was very open ended, as students experimented with several techniques, especially variations of embroidery. Schulze recalls that she was struggling to use imagery and words in the mid-1970s, finding appliqué in embroidery an interesting way to do that. B. J. Adams also benefited from her contact with Constance Howard. Joy Saville happened to attend meetings of the Peninsula Stitchery Guild in 1975 while on sabbatical in the Bay Area, with the classes taught by Evie Landes very helpful for her work at the time. Later in the 1970s, Saville learned from guild lectures by Walter Nottingham.

Nonsewing workshops in which students learned new techniques and processes also contributed to the studio quilt movement. The American Craft Council sponsored several of these workshops. Tafi Brown took part in a 1973 American Craft Council photography workshop, about which she says, "What I learned there meshed with my values and lifestyle and with what was available to me . . . at that time with a synergy that propelled me into my art quilt career. The workshop and the resulting influence on me were totally unplanned and unexpected."[72] This experience led to Brown's serendipitous creation of cyanotype studio quilts, a medium in which she has excelled for more than three decades.

Linda MacDonald, *Blues*, 1976, 90 × 80 in.

Ed Larson contributed a nonsewing aspect to the pictorial quilt workshops that he taught during the 1970s from Maine to California. The images were very self-referential,[73] with Larson sketching the imagery that each student wished to incorporate into a quilt. He then taped pieces of brown paper together to reproduce the images to scale, so that the students could have patterns for cutting out pieces of fabric.

These narrative projects often were quite personal. Michael James taught his workshop students to train their eyes, at the same time giving practical advice about streamlining the fabric-piecing process, with the result that several of today's quilt artists credit James's classes and books as formative influences on their studio practice. Linda MacDonald, for example, recalls that his first book "was invaluable because he showed how to stack all the pinned pieces up and sew them in long 'flags' through the sewing machine. His work was important too because it was contemporary."[74] James taught quilt making throughout southeastern New England during the mid-1970s, helping to make that area of the US a nexus of quilt art, albeit on a smaller scale than that of Ohio, or of the hotbed of fiber art that included studio quilts in the Bay Area.[75]

As reported in *Quilter's Newsletter Magazine*, "By 1980 a substantial group of professional quilt lecturers and workshop leaders was available to the many quilt guilds seeking programs for their monthly meetings or for larger symposiums and conferences. Jeff Gutcheon taught his 'diamond patchwork' concept at the West Coast Quilter's Conference in Spokane, Washington, and Chris Edmonds was teaching pictorial appliqué classes. Jinny Beyer's medallion classes were extremely popular, and Yvonne Porcella's workshops based on her new book *Pieced Clothing* were very well received, especially after Houston's 2nd Quilt Market debuted the Concord/Fairfield Processing Fashion Show—an event that was repeated every year."[76] In addition, a few new programs were founded that focused exclusively on textiles, notably the Fiberworks Center for the Textile Arts in Berkeley, California (1973–1987). Equally influential, and in some instances amazingly so, were the exhibitions of fiber, textile, and quilt art of the 1960s and 1970s.

QUILTS ON VIEW AS WORKS OF ART

The 1960s saw various small exhibitions of contemporary quilt art across the country, often with the quilts shown alongside other types of craft objects, or in faculty shows.[77] The First Annual Western Craft Competition, exhibited at the Seattle Center in 1964, featured quilt art by Helen Bitar and Katherine Westphal. The Northeast regional section of *Craftsmen USA '66*, shown at the Delaware Art Center and the Museum of Contemporary Crafts, included an appliqué quilt by Sophia Adler. A few solo shows featured quilt work, such as Nik Krevitsky's 1966 exhibition in San Francisco at Temple Emanu-El, which displayed twenty padded, quilted works titled *Paintings in Thread*, described in *Craft Horizons* as having "the imposition of opaque and transparent yarn structures making use of both surface and pictorial space in the best way."[78]

In 1971, the Whitney Museum of American Art (New York) mounted the first comprehensive exhibition of quilts to be seen in a major museum whose mission focused on contemporary art, with an emphasis not on the historicity of the works, but rather on quilts as visual objects: the now-famous *Abstract Design in American Quilts*. Joan Lintault says, "It was a wonderful experience to see such an exhibition at a prestigious museum." The sixty quilts in the show were from the collection of Gail van der Hoof and Jonathan Holstein, both of whom had backgrounds in contemporary art and who developed an appreciation of quilts during the later 1960s. In 1973 and 1974, twenty-one venues in the US exhibited parts of the collection that had been shown at the Whitney, plus thirty additional quilts (forty-five in each of the two parts), in a tour directed by the Smithsonian Institution Traveling Exhibition Service (SITES).[79] Some of the quilts also traveled to Europe; Sylvia Einstein, for example, saw them in Switzerland. Numerous artists interviewed for this book saw one or more of the installations.

In his 1971 catalog essay, Holstein stated, "Quilt makers did in effect paint with fabrics, laying on colors and textures, borrowing, and trading here and there or purchasing particular colors or patterns of materials they needed to complete their designs."[80] For their collection, Van der Hoof and Holstein made a point of purchasing quilts that worked for them as paintings, "creations in which the maker had posed and successfully solved interesting aesthetic propositions."[81] The 1971 exhibition caused young people working in diverse media to value the quilt as an art form. Paula Nadelstern and Robin Schwalb were among them. Michael Cummings not only viewed the quilts as art but also began considering Rothko paintings within a similar aesthetic framework. He recalls, "There was a historic moment when the definition of craft and art were put aside." Beth Gutcheon viewed the Whitney show as "most important to me." Reviews of *Abstract Design in American Quilts* revealed a deep appreciation of quilts as art, evidently to the surprise of some of the reviewers.[82]

The first few years of the 1970s saw sporadic, local exhibitions of contemporary quilt art in several parts of the country, such as those organized by Joyce Gross in Mill Valley, California. Then, in 1975, three exciting museum and gallery shows were mounted in the Northeast. Susan Hoffman and Molly Upton exhibited quilts together in the Kornblee Gallery (New York) in *Quilted Tapestries*, showing pairs of quilts inspired by various themes; Hoffman, Upton, and Radka Donnell had a group show of mostly abstract quilts at the Carpenter Center for the Arts, Harvard University; and the DeCordova Museum in Lincoln, Massachusetts, organized *Bed and Board*, exhibiting original contemporary quilts along with contemporary woodwork.[83] The quilt artists in *Bed and Board* included Elsa Brown, Sas Colby, Lenore Davis, Beth and Jeffrey Gutcheon, and Michael James (who at the time was teaching quilt making at the DeCordova Museum). Nancy Halpern describes the exhibition: "More selective and determinedly nontraditional, this work was elegantly set off by white museum walls and proper lighting."[84]

Preparations for the US Bicentennial in 1976 prompted several significant quilt-related events, including *Quilts '76*, organized by the Boston Center for the Arts (at the mammoth Cyclorama building); the Great Quilt Contest, with its subsequent touring exhibition; and *The New American Quilt*, exhibited at the Museum of Contemporary Crafts (New York) in 1976.[85]

The Boston show, which was not juried, had 173 quilts, mixing traditional and contemporary work. It was a glorious hodgepodge, seen by thousands of visitors. Sylvia Einstein's first quilt, executed in appliqué, was in the exhibition. Nancy Halpern, who had a quilt in the show, recalls that the event was organized into "crazy categories."[86] Discussing both *Bed and Board* and the Boston exhibition,

Therese May, *Therese*, 1969, 90 × 72 in.

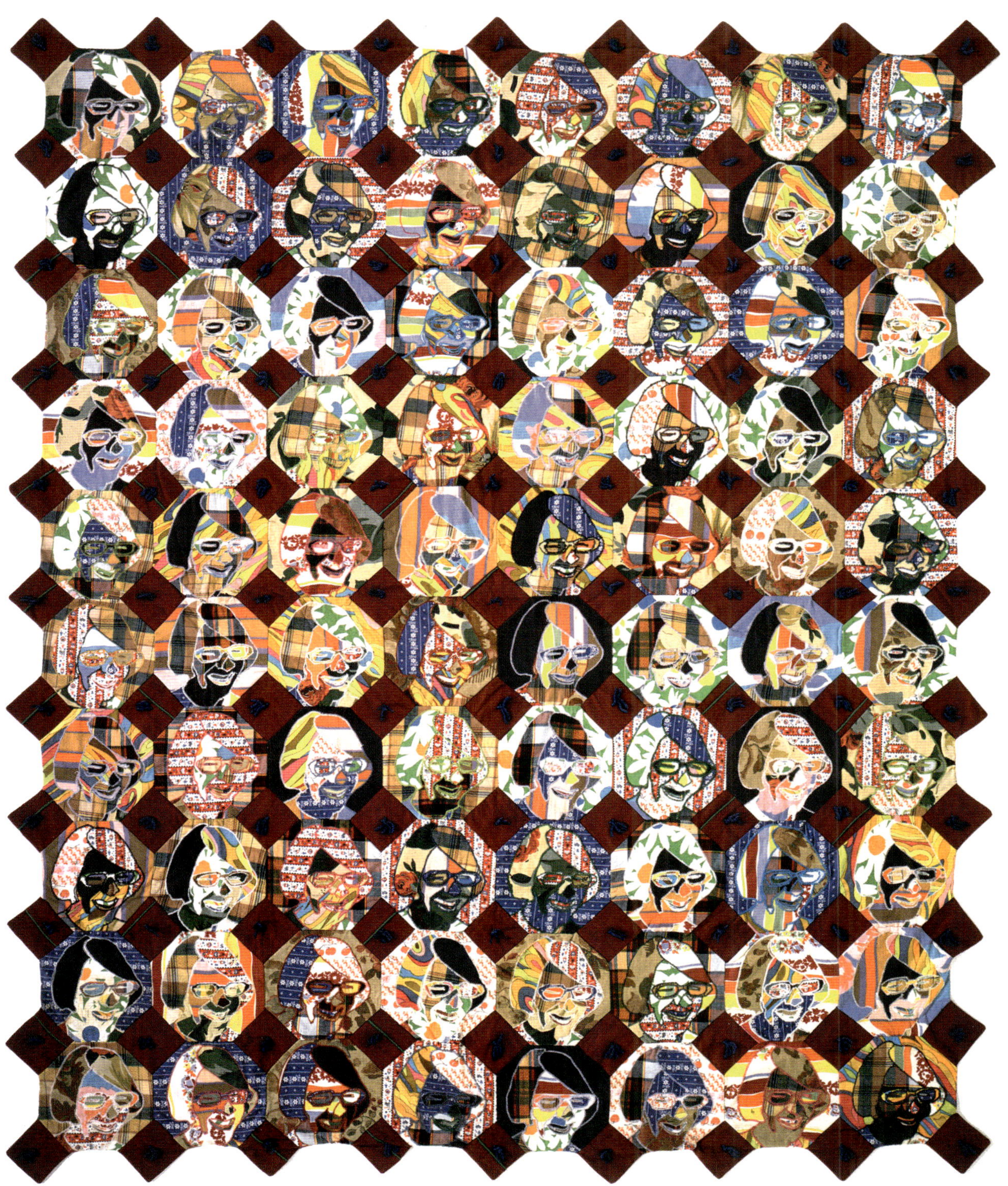

Halpern has remarked, "The most impressive feature of *both* shows was undoubtedly the variety of quilts displayed. Design ideas had been gathered from every corner of the map and from individual consciousness, and the resulting quilts were intrepid and vital. Although there was concern for good workmanship, these shows were less noteworthy as exhibitions of great stitching than as displays of great imagination."[87]

The Great Quilt Contest, sponsored by the U.S. Historical Society (a private organization) and the Museum of American Folk Art, was advertised via *Good Housekeeping*. The call for images resulted in some ten thousand entries, from which fifty-one quilts were selected, the most outstanding[88] examples from the US plus the District of Columbia. The national winner, announced in 1978, was a quilt pieced by Jinny Beyer; this recognition catapulted her to a position of prominence among quilt artists. Nancy Erickson says that she first realized the possibilities of quilts as art after she saw this exhibition, a "wow" experience that prompted her to move from fabric sculpture to "flatties."

In *Erica Wilson's Quilts of America* (1979), Wilson documented quilts in the exhibition, adding works by several of the runners-up. Although some of the quilts are traditional in concept, the contestants having utilized templates in a pattern for piecing or appliqué, others are entirely original, such as several pictorial quilts and abstract compositions. Most of the illustrations are in color. The artists who made some of the strikingly original quilts include Teresa Barkley, Lisa Courtney, Chris Wolf Edmonds, Ed Larson, Martha Mood, Susan Murphy, Karee Scarsten, and Joan Schulze.

Born in England, Erica Wilson graduated from the Royal School of Needlework, bringing her embroidery talents to New York, where she lectured in museums and opened a shop on Madison Avenue. Invited to host one of the first craft programs for the Public Broadcasting Service (PBS), Wilson created *Erica*, her popular how-to television series of the 1970s that included quilt making within the art of embroidery. An article in *Uncoverings* analyzed her success: "Beyond an interest in technique, she also investigated—with all the zeal of the

The Great Quilt Contest received some ten thousand entries, from which fifty-one quilts were selected in 1978, representing each state and the District of Columbia.

Bicentennial—some of the history (and, unwittingly, the myths) behind patchwork, applique and whitework. One of the factors that made Wilson so popular and so influential was that while she was keenly interested in the past, she did not present quilts or needlework as old-fashioned or stodgy."[89] This open-minded approach to quilt design, enriched by her love of history during the Bicentennial era, significantly encouraged quilt making among her viewers and readers.

The New American Quilt exhibition (1976) was the first quilt show in a major museum to feature contemporary, nontraditional work exclusively, and the show traveled. Lisa Hammel's review for the *New York Times* informed readers across the country about this astonishing show, which featured thirty-eight quilts by twenty-four artists, including Teresa Barkley, Helen Bitar, Elsa Brown, Lenore Davis, Radka Donnell, Gayle Fraas and Duncan Slade, Susan Hoffman, Joan Lintault, Molly Upton, Wenda von Weise, and Katherine Westphal. Hammel described how quilt artists "have been stretching the limits of the folk idiom through new processes and new techniques, new images and new ideas, until they have come out at the other end with something totally individual—the quilt transcendent."[90] The *Craft Horizons* review presented readers with graphic evidence of the originality and significance of these quilts, with Westphal's luminous *Puzzle of the Floating World* reproduced in color on the cover of the journal. As the review made clear, "the new-directions quilters are having their day . . . with a brilliant showing of contemporary quilts."[91] Several quilt artists that I interviewed were impressed by this exhibition, and others had quilts in the show.

Momentum for contemporary quilt art continued to build during the second half of the 1970s, prompted by the Bicentennial quilt exhibitions (mostly of traditional work), craft and design competitions, workshops, new books and magazines, and easier processes for applying color and imagery to fabric. Art schools were beginning to recognize quilt art. In 1976, for example, three students at Pratt Institute (New York) exhibited quilt art projects at the school. Kathleen Caraccio, Gertrude Sappin, and Deborah Hallam printed, painted, stamped, and stitched fabric works that were then completed by Amish quilters in Ohio.[92]

Penny McMorris organized *Ohio Patchwork 76*, viewed by Gayle Pritchard as "the point of confluence for Ohio artists already exploring quilt making as an art form in the 1970s."[93] Traditional quilts were shown along with more innovative works in this juried traveling show; the only requirements were that the quilts had to have been made in Ohio within the past three years. Original quilts by Nancy Crow, Françoise Barnes, Wenda von Weise, and Judi Warren Blaydon were included. Directors of art centers, galleries, and museums in Ohio had an early and enthusiastic appreciation of contemporary quilt art, partly due to the efforts of McMorris. Also in 1976, the first event that can be considered, in retrospect, as a national quilt conference was held in Ithaca, New York, in conjunction with the Finger Lakes Bicentennial Quilt Exhibit. The presenters included Beth Gutcheon and Jean Ray Laury, who by that time were well known as a result of their books and workshops. Virginia Avery was among the many artists who either attended or heard about the events from others. She referred to the conference as a turning point for her career. In Houston, Quilt Fair '76, the forerunner of the popular annual festival, was organized by Karey Bresenhan. The Houston festival first exhibited studio quilts in 1984.[94]

In 1977, Hofstra University's Emily Lowe Gallery (on Long Island) exhibited twenty quilts by fourteen "contemporary craftsmen," more than half of whom were male. This show caught the attention of the press and was reviewed in the *New York Times* by David L. Shirey (who later became chair of the Fine Arts Department at the School of Visual Arts, New York). Like Holstein and van der Hoof, he preferred graphically abstract quilts, such as *Razzle Dazzle* by Michael James (see image, page 184), "an extraordinary

Photo by Michael Gordon

Judith Content, *Sweltering Sky Kimono*, 1982, 61 × 52 in.

combination of poetic design and fresh color combinations."[95]

The American Craft Council (ACC) sponsored a *Young Americans* exhibition in 1977. *Fiber/Wood/Plastic/Leather*, the first series in this competition, opened at the Southeastern Center for Contemporary Art (Winston-Salem, North Carolina) in conjunction with the ACC'S conference. Selected works toured to several major US cities across the country. Glen Kaufman reviewed the *Fiber* component for *Craft Horizons*, remarking on the strong presence of quilts and quilt-like objects among the seventy-one works by fifty-eight artists: "The influence of the Museum of Contemporary Crafts' *'The New American Quilt'* exhibition and the exhibitions sponsored by the newly formed Surface Design Association seem evident."[96]

QUILT NATIONAL, 1979

Although the fifty-six quilts in the first *Quilt National* exhibition[97] were displayed in a partially renovated dairy barn, attendees were undeterred by the surroundings. Nearly one-quarter of the forty-five artists selected by the three jurors were from Ohio—not surprising, given the preponderance of quilt artists in the state. Beth Gutcheon reviewed *Quilt National* for *Fiberarts* magazine, with significant coverage that included four quilts illustrated in color: by Nancy Crow (one of the show's organizers), Radka Donnell, Nancy Halpern, and Wenda von Weise, plus black-and-white images of quilts by Françoise Barnes, Tafi Brown, Rhoda Cohen, Virginia Randles, and Maria McCormick Snyder. Interestingly, Gutcheon dismissed *The New American Quilt* exhibition as disappointing, while remarking that *Quilt National '79* "has turned out to be the stimulating and all-encompassing show one hoped for."[98] Gutcheon pointed out that "the entries were limited to original designs (no traditional work or work done under supervision)."[99]

The first *Quilt National* was a watershed event for contemporary quilt art, comments Pritchard: "Like the Whitney show in the 1970s, Quilt National serves as the dividing line between what came before and what was to follow."[100] The 1979 exhibition helped encourage several artists—for example, Tafi Brown, Terrie Hancock Mangat, and Katie Pasquini Masopust—to embrace the quilt medium. *Quilt National* enhanced the reputations of every artist who had the good fortune to be included. Several had solo shows or other major exposure shortly after the 1979 exhibition. Radka Donnell, for example, had a solo show of fifteen quilts in 1980, at the Art Colloquium Gallery in Salem, Massachusetts. The review of Donnell's exhibition in *Fiberarts* magazine by Pattie Chase illustrated five quilts in color, with an appreciation of "the sense of movement in the quilts, the rhythm of line and angle playing against the color and form to create an object of beauty and function that is simultaneously intended as a serious work of art."[101] With *Quilt National*, the American quilt as an art form definitely had arrived, only three years after the US Bicentennial had helped springboard quilt making to national attention.

CHAPTER 8

Time After Time

History has taught us that communities around the globe have celebrated centennials, sesquicentennials, and other major anniversaries for centuries. These events became an American phenomenon of the late nineteenth century, with many US states, towns, and cities commemorating their anniversaries.[1] Being a relatively large country originating from an assortment of cultures in the various colonies and territories, the US needed to formulate a national identity to claim its place in the global political and economic scene. That process initially resulted in the 1876 Centennial, which in turn prompted subsequent celebrations, especially after American industry and tourist bureaus realized the commercial possibilities of such events.

Even into the twenty-first century, the US Centennial continued to fascinate quilters and collectors. *The 1876 Centennial Quilt*, purchased in 1997 at an estate sale by Barbara Menasian of Manchester, Connecticut, became the subject of a quilt challenge in 2015, when Menasian posted a photo of the quilt on Facebook.[2] By that date, the internet was enabling quilt makers to communicate and share images worldwide. She hoped to unlock information about the quilt's origins, to no avail. Quilt historian Karen B. Alexander, intrigued by the quilt, asked the collector if Alexander's quilt group on Lopez Island in the Pacific Northwest might have her permission for their members to replicate the quilt. Menasian not only agreed but also joined the group remotely to work on her own quilt challenge as a new quilter. Anne Dawson, an avid quilter and specialist in quilt restoration, drafted the patterns for seventy-four blocks, with the quilters adding their original interpretations of colors and fabric styles, inserting their own initials. The quilts resulting from this homage to an unidentified maker celebrating a singular moment in American history went on display at the Houston International Quilt Festival in 2018.[3]

In chapter 4, we discussed world's fairs and international expositions commemorating special anniversaries, most of which included quilts on view and exhibitions of interest to makers of American quilts. The last half century has witnessed many more events marking significant spans of time, from one end of the country to the other, with quilts often interpreting and documenting the occasion. Those described below,

1876 Centennial Quilt, 1876, 93 × 91 in.

Collection of Barbara F. Menasian, photo by Robert S. Harrison Photography

sampled from a longer list involving quilts, are included in my book because the topics intrigued me, the selections represent geographic diversity, and publishable images could be obtained for most of these quilts in time for my deadline.

1986: STATUE OF LIBERTY CENTENNIAL

During the 1960s, especially in connection with the New York World's Fair in 1964, images of the Statue of Liberty appeared on souvenir plates, statuettes, key chains, shirts, scarves, pocketknives, spoons, decals, postage stamps, and posters for New York City tourism. United Air Lines printed her image on their travel poster, and the Mets included her on one of their felt pennants. California fiber artist and textile designer Katherine Westphal, inspired by a historic painting to create a quilt celebrating this famous symbol of freedom, designed her 1964 *Unveiling of the Statue of Liberty*.[4] American artist Edward Moran, residing in New York when the statue was installed in 1886, had painted Lady Liberty majestically rising out of the fog and clouds with American flags waving from the harbor.[5]

In 1986, the centennial of the Statue of Liberty was commemorated by the Great American Quilt Festival, sponsored by the 3M corporation in association with the Museum of American Folk Art, with most of the events at Pier 92 in New York City. A survey by the magazine *Better Homes and Gardens* had revealed interest in quilt making by several million people, resulting in the sponsorship, which required purchase of a 3M product to enter the contest. Contemporary quilters vied for the first prize of $20,000 and second prize of $7,500. According to the contest rules, judges of the quilts looked for "fine design, expert craftsmanship, and adherence to the contest theme—'Liberty, Freedom and American Heritage in honor of the Statue of Liberty Centennial celebration.'"[6] Each quilt entered also had to be 72 by 72 inches, an awkward size for using on a bed when the quilts were returned to their makers. Each had to be the work of a single quilter—which was not how many women worked on quilting at that time—and each had to be made completely by hand. As pointed out by Jane Przybysz, who interviewed a few of the state winners, they were perturbed about what to do with their quilts when the exhibition tour ended, and that the exhibition labels failed to mention their statements about each quilt.[7] The festival included an exhibition of "patriotic" antique quilts; demonstrations by Amish, Hmong, and Seminole makers; and lectures by artists, collectors, curators, and historians—although the actual show winners evidently had little opportunity to participate. Editors of quilting magazines and newspapers made sure that the events were reported to their readers, as analyzed by Tammy Gordon: "The celebration of the 100th birthday of the Statue of Liberty in 1986 provides an interesting comparison to 1976. . . . Because it was a major landmark visible from water and proximate to Ellis Island, the famous immigration processing station, it quickly became a symbol of immigrant hopes and American dreams."[8]

Exhibitions during the festival included commercial installations sponsored by the textile industry, such as Laura Ashley's contest titled "My State." Children aged six to ten submitted drawings, from which designs were made into quilts by groups in

▸ Marianne Fons (Iowa), *The Lady Liberty Medallion Quilt*, 1986, 72 × 72 in., Iowa state winner in the Great American Quilt Contest, celebrating one hundred years of the Statue of Liberty

State Historical Society of Iowa

Courtesy of the Rogue Valley Genealogical Society, Inc., of Medford, Oregon

Sue Waldron (Oregon), designer, quilting by the Jacksonville Museum Quilters, *Ashland Railroad Centennial Quilt*, 1986, 75 × 68 in.

the participating states of California, Illinois, Missouri, New York, Ohio, Pennsylvania, Texas, and Washington (see below). Laura Ashley displayed the quilts in their booth.

1986: ASHLAND, OREGON, RAILROAD CENTENNIAL

During the nineteenth century, the railroads geographically linked the US, but at a high cost, especially for the Chinese workers who lost their lives in hazardous areas while boring tunnels and erecting trestles through mountainous terrain. The *Ashland Railroad Centennial* quilt, completed in 1986, includes a topographic map of the Siskiyou Mountains, the treacherous route that had to be laid to connect the last miles of track opening that region of Oregon to Northern California. By depicting buildings and other structures completed by the Oregon & California Railroad, this album quilt's eleven pictorial blocks testify to three years of intense planning and labor beginning around 1884, when the first train pulled into Ashland, a lumber mill town eager to receive timber from Northern California once the final stage of the route could be completed. Railroad Park in Ashland, like the quilt, pays homage to a memorable episode in the town's history.

Courtesy of the Rogue Valley Genealogical Society, Inc., of Medford, Oregon

Detail, *Ashland Railroad Centennial Quilt*

1988: POTWIN PLACE, KANSAS, CENTENNIAL QUILT

Jeanne Hirschberg, known for her needlework as much as for her quilting, organized work on the *Potwin Place Centennial Quilt* in collaboration with several neighbors.[9] They resided in the Potwin Place Historical District, a neighborhood since 1899 within the city of Topeka, famous for its classically charming houses in Queen Anne and Victorian styles, with the blocks framed by brick-surfaced streets (some of which remain today). Large traffic circles landscaped with grass and trees also have been kept intact, helping to maintain the historical atmosphere of the neighborhood.

In 1869, an Ohio banker named Charles Potwin purchased 70 acres from a Shawnee Native American, subdividing the land into lots for a housing development that was founded as Potwin in 1888. As Potwin's centennial approached, Hirschberg and her group approached the residents of each home, giving them packets of materials in appropriate colors to re-create their particular site, to scale, for the quilt. For residents unable to participate, Hirschberg's group created their home for the composition. She herself assembled the block for the local school, adding her two children in the scene. The group spent several months quilting the monumental top in Hirschberg's basement,

Kansas State Historical Society

enjoying the camaraderie of a quilting bee. All those who helped stitch the quilt together are credited by name in a panel.

1988: WILMINGTON, DELAWARE, CELEBRATES 350 YEARS

By the time this book is published, numerous towns and cities in the US will have celebrated their tricentennial anniversaries. During the twentieth century, only a few locales could claim continuous growth for three hundred years, but Wilmington, Delaware, claimed 350, their sesquarcentennial (halfway between three hundred and four hundred years). In 1638, Swedish colonists "purchased" the land that today is Wilmington from Chief Mattahorn of the Lenape, whose band had been residing there for a large part of each year. As the Swedes were followed by the Dutch and eventually British colonists in the 1660s, the Native population was pushed out of the area. Wilmington's first commemorative US postage stamp appeared in 1938, a three-cent stamp for the tricentennial engraved with an image of the Swedes and Finns landing and meeting the Lenape.

Quilt artist Teresa Barkley's family moved from Nebraska to a suburb of Wilmington when she was four, and her husband's family is from Wilmington. She explains that both her mother-in-law and father-in-law worked tirelessly to improve the city, and they

Teresa Barkley (Maplewood, New Jersey), *The Wilmington Stamp*, 1987, 64.5 × 64.5 in.

Jeanne Hirschberg (Topeka, Kansas), *Potwin Place Centennial Quilt*, 1988, 8 × 13.5 feet, with the artist

inspired her to want to celebrate its 350th anniversary with a quilt. Barkley has a lifelong fascination with postage stamps. In fact, she says that much of what she has learned about history has been as a result of her curiosity about people and events depicted on commemorative textiles or postage stamps.[10] She designs many of her quilts as oversized "stamps," styled in borders of scalloped fabric suggesting the serrated edges of antique stamps. Her 1988 quilt *The Wilmington Stamp* celebrates the city's history and landmarks, such as the Wanamaker store and Old Swedes Church (1698). Wilmington played a crucial role in resisting the British during the American Revolution.

1989: THE WASHINGTON STATE CENTENNIAL

In 1985, the Wednesday Friendship Quilters of Edmonds, Washington, completed their *Laura Ashley Washington State Pictorial* to celebrate the state's centennial coming up in 1989. Today the quilt resides in the Washington State Historical Society.[11] Like the other quilts submitted for Laura Ashley's "My State" contest for the Statue of Liberty centennial in New York, children around the state created images for the project that the quilt group interpreted via appliquéd fabrics and quilting. In this piece, the quilting depicts an outline of the torch of Liberty above both of the bottom corners. At least one Laura Ashley fabric had to be used in the composition. As we saw earlier, several aspects of the 1986 festivities were heavily commercialized. By the 1980s, the quilting industry was capitalizing on quilt challenges.

The Washington quilt became part of an exhibition touring the state in 1989–1990, *Women and Their Quilts: A Washington State Centennial Tribute,* accompanied by a fully illustrated catalog with the same title, officially supported by the 1989 Washington State Centennial Commission. As happened in other parts of the US, the 1976 Bicentennial may have prompted individual states to make commitments for commemorating their statehood anniversaries. The catalog honors not only the women who created the quilts, but also their history, including portraits, along with a section about women collectors.[12] The earliest dated quilt was completed in 1833 for her wedding by Eliza Kay Brown in a *broderie perse* medallion design with triple borders known simply as *Eliza's Quilt,* passed down from one Eliza to the next until her great-great-granddaughter Eliza shared her family quilt for the exhibition and book. In impeccable condition, this quilt was never used for sleeping, instead being displayed on a bed when a special guest was visiting, then removed to protect it for future generations.[13] The respect and admiration for quilters and their quilts infuse the book with a love of history as expressed through women's work.

Wednesday Friendship Quilters (Edmonds, Washington), *Laura Ashley Washington State Pictorial Quilt*, 1985, 72 × 72 in.

1992: CHRISTOPHER COLUMBUS QUINCENTENNIAL JUBILEE

Christopher Columbus's five hundredth anniversary in the US was in trouble years before its commemorative date of 1992 arrived. The website of the US Government Accountability Office (GAO) documents that the thirty members of the Christopher Columbus Quincentennial Jubilee Commission had raised less than $890,000 of their goal of more than $3 million between 1986 and 1990, most of the money having been contributed by the members themselves. Their cash balance at the end of 1990 amounted to only $43,000, and they had failed to acquire corporate sponsorships. The GAO determined that Congress needed to increase the amount of funding and provide adequate oversight of the commission. Even so, and with $2 million in seed money from the federal government, the quincentenary was met with hostility by several groups. In Berkeley, California, for example, the first Indigenous Peoples' Day was held on what would have been Columbus Day in 1992, protesting the explorer's treatment of Indigenous Caribbean people.

While the second Monday in October continues to be celebrated as the federal holiday known as Columbus Day, in many towns and states the holiday officially is now

Washington State Historical Society, 2020.12.1

Collection of Teresa Barkley

Columbian Quincentennial bandana, 1992

Debby Kratovil (Fairfax, Virginia), *Columbus Quilt*, 1994, 36 × 36 in.

Castine Historical Society, 1996.75.1

Castine Community Bicentennial Quilt (Castine, Maine) detail, 1996. See pages 212–213.

called Indigenous Peoples' Day. The 1992 Columbus Jubilee marked the beginning of his downfall as an iconic national figure, especially when compared with the extravagant 1893 celebrations honoring him in Chicago (see chapter 4). Nevertheless, textile mills and souvenir shops jumped at the chance to market the jubilee, and the federal government minted special Columbus coins to help fund events such as a flotilla of tall ships in New York and parades in our major cities. Nearly two dozen cities and towns bearing the name "Columbus" hosted festivities, with the Columbus Metropolitan Quilters in Ohio's capital making a large pictorial album quilt depicting landmarks and aspects of city history, a registered project of the jubilee.

Jinny Beyer, a prize-winning quilter, fabric designer, teacher, and author, designed a 1992 "Discovery" fabric line in cotton for RJR Fashion Fabrics, marketed to quilters. Beyer wrote an illustrated booklet to accompany her commemorative collection, full of suggestions for how to use the motifs in a quilt, plus three patterns for complete quilts. She informed readers, "I felt that the 500-year quincentenary of the discovery of the Americas was a fitting time to produce a line of fabrics to acknowledge this event." While we now acknowledge that "discovery" does not adequately describe what happened in 1492, her fabric was beautifully produced, some of the colorways designed as monochromatic prints on off-white backgrounds like antique toile, and quilters purchased the yardage. Debby Kratovil, a prolific quilt maker, used the fabric in her 1992 *Columbus Quilt*, creating three squares that feature sailing ships along with a compass motif from one of the prints.

Castine Community Bicentennial Quilt (Castine, Maine), 1996, 24 ft. wide

1996: BICENTENNIAL OF CASTINE, MAINE

The town of Castine, located in Penobscot Bay, was founded in 1796. For its bicentennial in 1996, sixty members of the community appliquéd and pieced a monumental quilt, 24 feet long. The town displays it for several months each year as a quilted mural in a historic school maintained through the Castine Historical Society. This visual history lesson represented in seven large narrative squares, read from left to right, is joined together by eight panels depicting flora and fauna of the Maine coast. Images of the river and bay flowing along the bottom unify the entire composition, witnessing significance of these waterways to all inhabitants of the site through two centuries, from Native American canoes to the Maine Maritime Academy's training ship. Several flags along the top document governing entities during the town's timeline. The first square depicts the quilters' interpretation of the original Abenaki inhabitants, "People of the Dawn," with a sunburst flag at the top. Square 2 shows the British defeating colonial forces in 1779 during the Penobscot Expedition, a strategic blow to the colonies during the Revolutionary War, since their supplies from the northeast were cut off, and the colonial ships were scuttled in Penobscot Bay. Because Castine was part of the Massachusetts Bay Colony at the time, that colony's militia, including Paul Revere, participated in the fighting.

2000: SESQUICENTENNIAL OF THE STATE OF CALIFORNIA

In 1850, California became our thirty-first state. As the California Sesquicentennial Commission anticipated the 150th anniversary of statehood, its members asked the California Heritage Quilt Project (CHQP) to create a pictorial quilt presenting a historical overview of the state's fifty-eight counties. Sixty-seven participants from around the state created fabric vignettes assigned by quilt artists Ellen Heck and Zena Thorpe, then the quilt traveled around Northern California, where it was hand-quilted by volunteers aged ten to eighty-five. More than 250 people worked on this masterpiece. Helen Powell, coordinator of the project, presented Governor Pete Wilson with the quilt as a gift for the people of California. Between 1998 and 2000, it toured throughout California and was seen by four million people. Today the *California Sesquincentennial Quilt* resides in its custom display case in the California History Museum in Sacramento.

Imagery in the quilt plays with time, overlapping various eras and events, with the borders at top and bottom depicting California's agricultural products. This quilt has been used as inspiration to teach elementary schoolchildren facts about the state's landscape and history though a Timeline game and map of California. An interactive website provides additional educational information and activities, where we learn that many of those involved with the quilt came from families who had contributed to the state's history: https://www.californiaheritagequiltproject.com.

California State Archives, 2001-09-06

As an example of how the quilt artists creating individual vignettes approached the project, we can access the website and click on any of the vignettes. When assigned the Spanish dancers, Margarete Heinisch contacted William Estrada, curator of El Pueblo de Los Angeles Historical Monument on Olivera Street, the historic heart of the city. Consulting the archives, he shared with her images of clothing from the *Dances of Mexico* book. Each vignette artist, as much as possible, tried to make sure that the imagery conformed to the facts of history.

◀ California Heritage Quilt Project, *California Sesquicentennial Quilt*, 1998, ca. 10 × 10 ft.

2012: THE ARIZONA STATE CENTENNIAL

President Taft signed Arizona into statehood in 1912 as the forty-eighth member of the US, finalizing the number of stars on our flag for nearly half a century until Alaska and Hawaii joined. In 2009, several quilt groups in Arizona coordinated efforts for the Arizona Centennial Quilt Project, completing the double-sided *Arizona Centennial Commemorative Quilt* in 2011. This spectacular quilt toured the state in the Arizona Centennial Celebration Quilt Exhibit, *100 Years—100 Quilts*. Designated as an official Centennial Commission Legacy Project, the commemoration received funding from the State of Arizona as well as from numerous other sources, facilitating the publication of a catalog illustrating each quilt, accompanied by its maker's statement.[14]

Shannon Quigley, youngest member of the California Heritage Quilt Project, in front of the *California Sesquicentennial Quilt*, 1998. She helped in the quilting with her mother.

Some of the quilts resembled tourist postcards, and images of pictorial postcards were interspersed throughout the book. Other quilts in the exhibition paid homage to the Native American cultures of Arizona, the rancheros by reproducing cattle branding symbols, historic architecture, desert vistas, animals, and the Southwestern palette of colors. In many of the quilts, not only the pieced and appliquéd fabrics but also the stitchery referenced Arizona, as in the quilt by Mary Fay Patrick, who said, "I tried to convey the spirit of Arizona in my quilting by using desert animals and rock formations. Colors were based on the Arizona copper mines and mountain ranges. I also used decorative stitches that reminded me of barbed wire and cactus needles."[15]

Planning for the *Arizona Centennial Commemorative Quilt* began in 2009, when Wanda Seale, a member of the Arizona Quilters Hall of Fame, organized a group of women to design the quilt. When their call went out statewide for volunteers to work on segments of the quilt, seventy-five people responded. The makers each received packets containing their assigned pattern, hand-dyed fabric, water-soluble stabilizer, and instructions. By the time the quilt was finished, some eighty-eight Arizona quilters had contributed to the project, producing a double-sided work of art, actually two quilts

Arizona Historical Society, TS 2011.351

Arizona Centennial Quilt Project, quilting of front by Gina Perkes, *Arizona Centennial Commemorative Quilt*, 2011, 79 × 80.5 in.

conjoined. The verso includes the state flag, names, and various images, while the front features a state map filled with landmarks and other images, a riotous cluster of state flowers at the left, and animal habitats along the right side. Yellow and red sunburst rays of the state flag anchor the bottom edge.

2013: GRAND CENTRAL TERMINAL CENTENNIAL

City Quilter partnered with *American Patchwork & Quilting* magazine to sponsor a quilt challenge honoring the one hundredth anniversary of Grand Central Terminal, one of the Beaux-Arts icons in New York City. The centennial event coincided with the twentieth anniversary of the magazine. City Quilter, which closed permanently three years later when the owners retired, was the premier quilt shop and exhibition gallery for quilt artists in New York. The owners also designed fabric lines for quilters, including fabrics celebrating the train station's centennial, at least one of which had to appear in the quilts being considered for the competition. Of the entries submitted from twenty-five states, thirty quilts were selected for the exhibition, held in 2014 at the New York Transit Museum at Grand Central Terminal, with the exhibition booklet explaining the event's purpose: "The art of quilting and the architecture of one of America's most famous buildings combine to create a platform for a challenge that celebrates the life and times of an [*sic*] historic structure."[16] While most of the contestants interpreted the theme pictorially, a few artists abstracted their thoughts. Beth Carney, awarded second prize, created a quilt using color and line to suggest the star-studded ceiling as well as the tunnel's cement walls, patterned by a century of rivulets.

Beth Carney (New York), *Chasms 16: Under the Stars*, 2014, 34.5 × 24 in.

2014: SESQUICENTENNIAL OF THE EMANCIPATION PROCLAMATION

The year 2013 marked the 150th anniversary of Abraham Lincoln's Emancipation Proclamation, freeing all enslaved persons in the Confederacy, with 2014 becoming the sesquicentennial year of the Senate passing the Thirteenth Amendment to the US Constitution, extending that freedom nationally, and the House of Representatives finalizing the amendment in 1865. In 2014, Dr. Joan M. E. Gaither, fiber artist and civil rights activist, organized the *1864 Maryland Sesquicentennial Slave Emancipation*

Photo by Archival Arts

◀ Dr. Joan M. E. Gaither (Maryland), *1864 Maryland Sesquicentennial Slave Emancipation Proclamation Quilt* (2014), 10 ft., 4 in. × 10 ft., 4 in.

Proclamation Quilt, a mixed-media documentary story quilt in conjunction with the Maryland Commission on African-American History and Culture. She worked with 426 individuals within twenty-four organizations to complete this monumental quilt, measuring 10 feet, 4 inches on each side. The pictorial quilt features a block from each of Maryland's twenty-three counties, plus one representing the city of Baltimore, Gaither's hometown. She has been touring the quilt throughout Maryland for ten years, with the goal of exhibiting it in every county and the city of Baltimore.

The year 1864 in the title commemorates the outlawing of slavery on November 1 in Maryland, a state not included in Lincoln's document, since Maryland never joined the Confederacy. Numbers in all but two of the blocks reflect the numbers of votes in each county for and against slavery, graphically relating the history of emancipation in Maryland. Among all the community-based quilts created after the US Bicentennial, Gaither's project has to be one of the most ambitious—in scale as well as in the sheer number of participants. Firmly situated within the vibrant tradition of African American storytelling quilts, the *1864 Maryland Sesquicentennial Slave Emancipation Proclamation Quilt* brilliantly speaks its message of freedom.

Peg Pennell (Ashland, Nebraska), *Mount Rushmore National Memorial,* 2015, 36 × 24 in.

2016: NATIONAL PARKS CENTENNIAL

More than four hundred sites fall under the jurisdiction of the National Park Service (NPS), established in 1916 by President Wilson. Between 1929 and 1933, President Herbert Hoover expanded the land designated for national parks by 40 percent. In 2016, the Herbert Hoover Historic Site in West Branch, Iowa, exhibited the *Birthplace Centennial Quilt,* a community project overseen by Tami Urmie and Tara Langley of Cotton Creek Mill Quilt Shoppe. They designed fifty square blocks, one for each state, pieced by local quilters who chose their own fabrics to represent their assigned national park.

In addition to the nature preserves covered by previous acts, in 1933 President Roosevelt

FIND YOUR
PARK
WEST BRANCH, IOWA
NATIONAL PARK SERVICE

◀ Tami L. Urmie and Tara Langley (Iowa), designers, *Birthplace Centennial Quilt*, 2016

signed an executive order soon after his inauguration that transferred dozens of monuments and military sites to the NPS, including the area known as Mount Rushmore. Today, it would seem unlikely that the funding for a monument like Mount Rushmore would be easily approved, given its location on land sacred to the Lakota Sioux, who call the mountain Six Grandfathers. Political activists during the 1970s climbed the mountain above the sculpted faces to unfurl banners voicing their opposition to the monument's location and message.

When Nebraska prize-winning quilt artist Peg Pennell mulled over possible subjects for her art quilt to be submitted for the touring exhibition celebrating the NPS centennial, she thought of Mount Rushmore, impelled by "the grandeur of the sculpture itself. Reading the history of how the artwork was created was fascinating. The sheer enormity of the project and the vision to carry it out was an incredible feat. The huge sculpture superimposed against the natural setting is an inspiring and enduring monument to the founders of democracy."[18] A quilter since the 1970s, Pennell began her quilting journey during the Bicentennial era. Her first appliquéd quilt was created as a Bicentennial quilt.

2015: ANCHORAGE, ALASKA, CENTENNIAL QUILT

Although Alaska became a state only in 1959, the city of Anchorage has a long history, beginning as an Indigenous village of the Dena'ina Athabascan. Russia sold Alaska to the US in 1867, causing the government to assign employees of the Smithsonian to include that territory among its sweep of Indigenous materials to demonstrate regions within federal authority for the 1876 Centennial. The Government Building at the 1876 Philadelphia Centennial featured numerous objects collected from Indigenous groups in Alaska, uprooted from their cultural significance, causing them to be viewed only as curiosities.

White settlers from the US arrived in Anchorage in 1915, erecting a tent city while the Alaska Railroad was being constructed by the federal government, with Anchorage incorporated as a city in 1920. To commemorate the city's centennial at the Great Alaska Quilt Show, the ALCQ grouped their pictorial quilts into groups of ten decades, a unique approach to centenary quilt displays. Balancing historic photographs with appliquéd fabric collage, the quilters documented landmarks, architecture, landscapes, people, and notable events.

2016: THE INDIANA BICENTENNIAL BARN QUILT

Quilting groups in numerous states have honored historic buildings in their quilts, notably barns, regarded as Americana icons representing our agricultural heritage. These projects can also refer to individual quilt squares painted on barns in "quilt trails" across a specific geographic area, promoting tourism and appreciation of public art in the rural environment. A collaborative effort by the Indiana Barn Foundation, Indiana Landmarks, and Indiana State Quilt Guild created the *Indiana Bicentennial Barn Quilt* in 2016, the two hundredth anniversary of Indiana entering the Union. Joy William, who edited the book accompanying this bicentennial commemoration, explained:

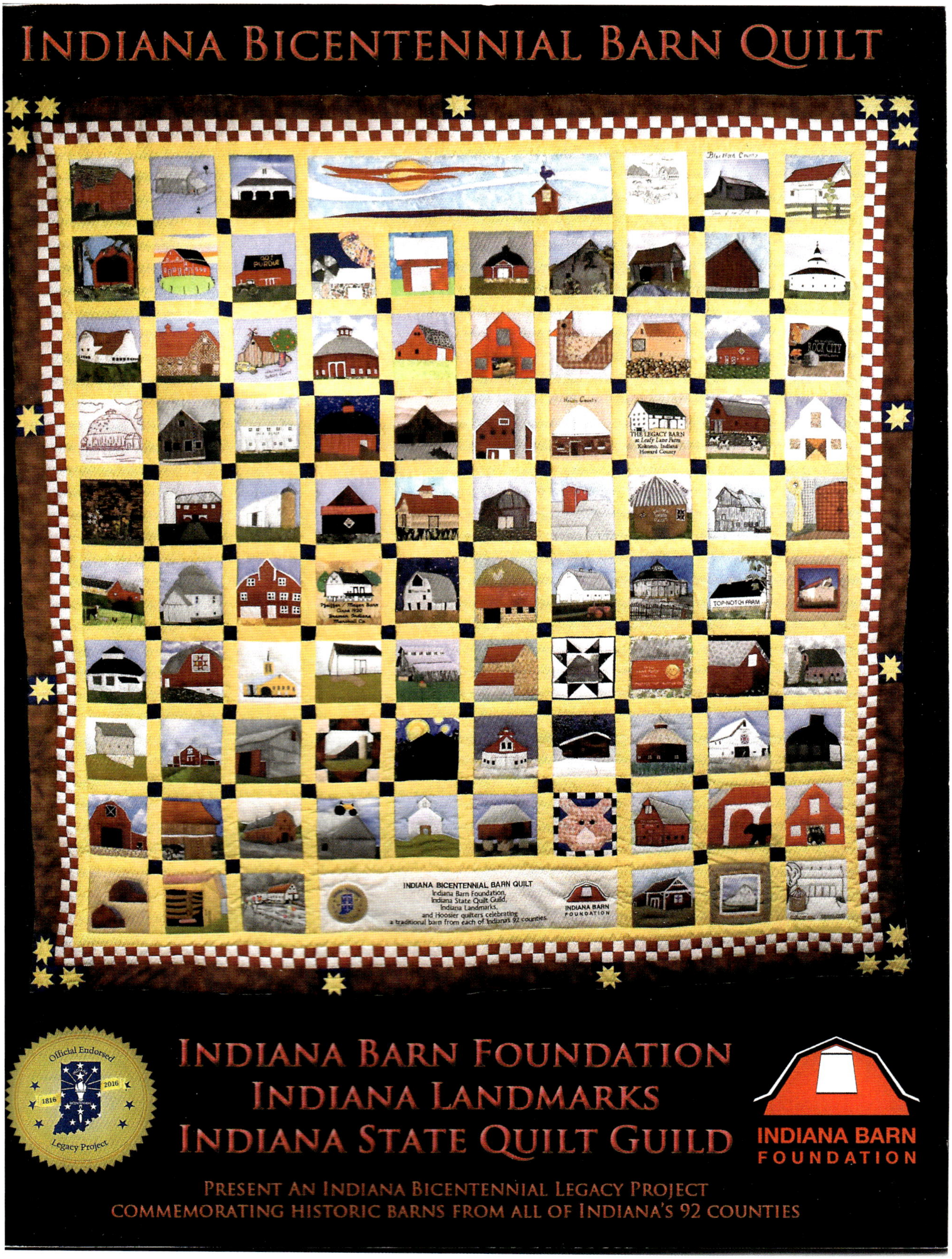

Indiana Bicentennial Barn Quilt

INDIANA BICENTENNIAL BARN QUILT
Indiana Barn Foundation,
Indiana State Quilt Guild,
Indiana Landmarks,
and Hoosier quilters celebrating
a traditional barn from each of Indiana's 92 counties.

Indiana Barn Foundation
Indiana Landmarks
Indiana State Quilt Guild

Present an Indiana Bicentennial Legacy Project
commemorating historic barns from all of Indiana's 92 counties

◀ Joy William, ed., *Indiana Bicentennial Barn Quilt* (Indianapolis, IN: Indiana Barn Foundation, 2016), front cover, quilt measuring 82 × 82 in., quilting by Ruby Borkholder and quilt photography by Albert William

"Our ultimate goals for this project are to commemorate Indiana's heritage represented in its barns and to raise enough funds that we can offer financial help to maintain that heritage through grants to barn owners."[19] The idea for the quilt originated with a woman who suggested it at the Indiana Barn Foundation booth in 2014 at the state fair. Honoring barns from all ninety-two counties, the quilt's imagery includes historic round barns—several now converted into theaters—advertising on barns, barnyards, and barns interpreted as quilt patterns.

A book documenting the project features illustrations of each square, crediting the maker(s). Their quilt-making experience ranged from none at all to decades of expertise, such as with Betty A, Conjalka: "I was introduced to the art of quilting by my mother in 1946. I was immediately intrigued and have continued to design and make quilts over the last 60 years."[20] Stories like this remind us of the very personal aspects of creating quilts, overriding the "anonymous" labels on so many of these objects.

Jennifer Nicolella (San Antonio, Texas), organizer, and Sarah Hood, designer, with *San Antonio Tricentennial Quilt*, 2018, 6 × 10 ft., being presented to the city's mayor and the city council on December 6

2018: TRICENTENNIAL OF SAN ANTONIO, TEXAS

In honor of San Antonio's tricentennial in 2018, two groups in the city were inspired to create quilts commemorating the anniversary of the city and its vibrantly diverse culture. From the time that the presidio and Alamo mission (which became the famous fort) established the town in 1718, San Antonio has been a largely Hispanic community. The African American Quilt Circle of San Antonio, organized in 2017 as part of the Tricentennial projects, created an exhibition of storytelling quilts that related aspects of their history in the city. In addition, many residents of San Antonio volunteered to work on a community Tricentennial quilt, documented by their names embroidered into the pieced rectangles of fabric. Abby's Attic Sewing & Crafting Studio, opened in 2016 by Jennifer Nicolella, organized this project, truly a collaborative effort. Sarah Hood designed the quilt, coordinating the color palette and

Photo by Jennifer Nicolella, Abby's Attic Sewing Studio, San Antonio, Texas

Community group working on the *San Antonio Tricentennial Quilt*, 2018

Photo by Jean Vong

Robin Schwalb (Brooklyn, New York), *Amelia Bloomer: Advocating a Change*, 2019, 48 × 48 in.

sketching a blueprint for the silhouetted skyline; Emily Bruno facilitated the assembly and finishing of the quilt; and Miranda Harris helped children who wanted to add their own stitches to the composition. Landmarks of the city can be recognized in the silhouettes, notably the Tower of the Americas in the center erected for the sesquicentennial Hemisfair in 1968 (see chapter 4).

2019: BICENTENNIAL OF TUSCALOOSA, ALABAMA

Tuscaloosa, meaning "Black Warrior" in Choctaw, served as an Indigenous riverine crossroads for centuries before white settlers claimed the region. The day before Alabama joined the Union in 1819, Tuscaloosa became incorporated. From 1826 to 1846, Tuscaloosa was the capital of Alabama. After recovering from the Civil War, the city developed into a manufacturing center. Storytelling quilter Yvonne Wells, born in Tuscaloosa just before the US entered World War II, organized a team of local quilters to create the Tuscaloosa Bicentennial Quilt. The appliquéd imagery includes Lake Tuscaloosa, the First African Baptist Church (where Martin Luther King Jr. spoke), other architectural landmarks, parks, the profile of an Indigenous man representing Chief Tuscaloosa (repurposed from a vintage purse), and Wells's alma mater, Stillman College.

★

Residents of San Antonio, including children, celebrated by making a community Tricentennial quilt with their names embroidered in.

2020: NINETEENTH AMENDMENT CENTENNIAL, VOTES FOR WOMEN

Several curators and quilting groups made ambitious plans in 2018 and 2019 to celebrate the centennial of the Nineteenth Amendment, by which most women in the US finally were able to cast their votes in federal elections as of 1920. While African Americans, Asian Americans, and Native American women continued to struggle with discrimination and bigoted attitudes from election officials, the Nineteenth Amendment helped make future voting laws to enfranchise additional categories of women possible. Excitement was running high, especially after our 2016 national election, in which a woman almost became president. But then came COVID-19, which shuttered museums and galleries everywhere, much like the shutdowns a century earlier during the 1918 influenza pandemic, which contributed to the delay of the Nineteenth Amendment being passed by Congress. Pam Weeks and I experienced the disappointment of having the art quilt exhibition tour we had spent nearly two years organizing canceled by several closed venues.[21] Other quilt shows commemorating aspects of women's votes and women's rights were canceled as well. Finally, the world began to revive, venues cautiously opened, and our exhibition traveled for two years, including to the Houston International Quilt Festival.

One of the most graphic quilts in the show is by New York artist Robin Schwab, who selected Amanda Bloomer as her suffragist, the first woman in America to own, operate, and publish a newspaper for women. Between 1849 and 1856, her focus on temperance in *The Lily* gradually shifted to support of the suffrage movement. When she sold the newspaper, it had more than six thousand paid subscribers nationwide. Schwab printed her triple image of Amanda Bloomer wearing "bloomers" instead of the traditional long skirt from an 1851 illustration, depicting her in the three symbolic suffragist colors: white, gold, and purple.

2021: TULSA RACE MASSACRE CENTENNIAL

In 2021, Kym Cooper had an artist's residency of four weeks with Queen Rose Art House in conjunction with a Tulsa, Oklahoma, fellowship program. Being in that city during that historic year inspired her to make two art quilts commemorating the 1921 Tulsa Race Massacre. Her quilt depicted here honors the memory of the young African American man who was murdered during the brutal massacre of a prosperous African American community due to unfounded allegations by a white woman. She wrongfully accused a Black man of accosting her in an elevator in downtown Tulsa. The rampant spread of misinformation and endemic white supremacy caused a horrific racial backlash. Within the span of two days, everything the flourishing community of Greenwood had meticulously created was burned to the ground and essentially destroyed. The Tulsa Massacre was one of the worst race riots in American history. Cooper was honoring her ancestors by creating this quilt to express her conviction: "Your ingenious efforts were never forgotten."

Kym Cooper (Greensboro, North Carolina), *Two Days in Tulsa*, 2021, 41 × 32 in., with the artist

Detail of Kym Cooper, *Two Days in Tulsa*

Nancy McFarland, *Lutheran Community Services Northwest Centennial Quilt*, 2021, 62 × 62 in.

2021: LUTHERAN COMMUNITY SERVICES NORTHWEST CENTENNIAL

Based in Tacoma, Washington, the Northwest Branch of Lutheran Community Services opened its doors in 1921. The economic slump for the port city following World War I and societal disruptions of the 1918–1919 influenza pandemic left many residents in need of aid. Desperate conditions worsened during the Great Depression of the 1930s, compounded in the 1940s as Tacoma welcomed refugees fleeing from the chaos of Eastern Europe. As illustrated by their Centennial quilt, the organization in 1921 celebrated "100 years of health, justice, and hope."[22]

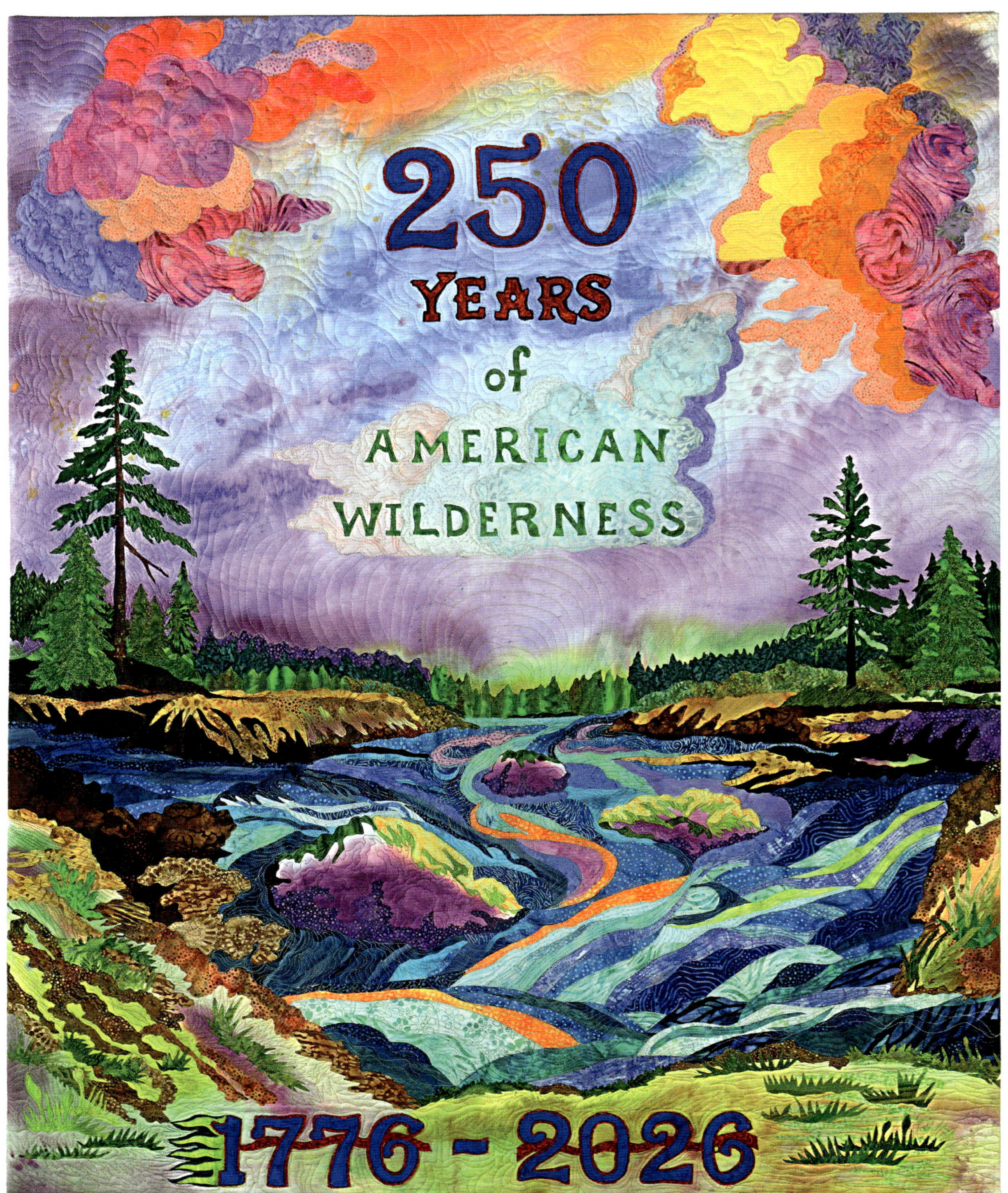

Photo by Paul Rubin

Detail of Luana Rubin, *250 Years of American Wilderness*

Most of the images on the quilt represent services maintained by the office today, including programs for senior companions, military family respite care, dementia services, and refugee resettlement services.

2026: SEMIQUINCENTENNIAL OF THE USA

To commemorate our country's 250th anniversary, Luana Rubin created this art quilt marking the fiftieth anniversary of the Endangered Species Act, intended to protect America's wilderness areas of forests, mountains, prairies, and rivers. In addition to their natural beauty, these pristine landscapes provide habitats for a diversity of wildlife. For more than a century, we have preserved our wild lands with national parks, national wildlife refuges, national conservation lands, national seashores and lakeshores, national trails, and more. What better image to conclude this chapter—the legacy of wild lands that have existed since the very beginnings of our American story.

◀ Luana Rubin, *250 Years of American Wilderness*, 2025, 50 × 40 in.

Conclusion

Quilt culture has played a major role in commemorating public anniversaries in this country. Even so, the number of these quilts would seem insignificant if compared with the thousands of quilts commemorating private anniversaries of births, deaths, graduations, weddings, homes, places of worship, etc. Putting hand to needle and needle to fabric obviously satisfies a basic human urge to express a tangible act of memory through commemoration. What will we be wanting to remember during the fifty years between 2026 and 2076, when America marks its tricentennial?

Perhaps the disasters claiming lives and livelihoods might prompt our memories. Several of these events soon will have their 150th anniversaries, including the Galveston hurricane in 2050, the San Francisco earthquake in 2056, and the Triangle shirtwaist factory fire in 2061. The bicentennial of the Great Chicago Fire will be observed in 2071. If the history of America's cities sparks your interest, we should note that bicentennials will be approaching for Atlanta in 2045, Minneapolis in 2056, Denver in 2067, and more. Miami will celebrate its sesquicentennial in 2046, and St. Louis will celebrate its 250 years in 2073. Then there are birthdays of America's most famous heroes, such as Thomas Paine's tricentennial in 2037 and Harriet Tubman's 250th in 2072.

Will Americans be making quilts by 2076 or will handcrafted art become overwhelmed and replaced by technology? Scholars of aesthetics and material culture have been grappling with this issue for decades, and some of their conclusions, such as research by Gail Kenning, bring good news to quilt makers in the digital age, seeing that "domestic craft-based textile activities have greater innovative potential than has been perceived and that digital media technologies . . . present new opportunities and suggest new sites for creative endeavor."[1]

Statistics from Craft Industry Alliance surveys indicate that the quilting industry grows more robust each year.[2] The market's strength is predicted to exceed $5 billion within the next two years. Many of the ten million quilters in the US prefer online retail sources for their supplies and rely on digital media, especially free videos, for instructions and technical advice. In addition, regional quilting groups and national quilt organizations turn to digital resources for online conferences and other communication. American quilts of all kinds—far from being replaced by digital art—seem to be thriving, as determined by a recent master's thesis from the Fashion Institute of Technology: "With limitless resources available to them thanks to the internet, quilters can learn about methods, block styles, and techniques with a quick Google search, and share ideas with thousands of their peers through social media platforms. Affected by the 1971 Whitney exhibition and the American bicentennial only indirectly, quilters of the last quarter-century comprise the latest generation of the quilting revival era."[3] This generation, which does not know life without digital devices, can choose to set their device aside to pick up a quilting project, letting the device entertain and inform while their hands stay busy with whatever creative tools catch their fancy.

Perhaps our Bicentennial rather than the Centennial might suggest a model for America's Tricentennial commemorative quilts, as Tammy Gordon explained: "The bicentennial was a moment in which 'do-your-own-thing' commemoration applied to everyone. . . . People actively sought out meaning for themselves in the history of the American Revolution. It was a deeply personal event that emphasized the self and one's communities, that realigned how Americans viewed themselves as part of a public."[4] The partisan polarization in our country that today has morphed into hyperpolarization had already commenced by the mid-1970s.[5] Nevertheless, many Americans in 1976 eagerly expressed pride in our past, and in our country's possibilities, a good number of them by making commemorative quilts. Democracy can be challenging. As Winston Churchill famously said in 1947, "Democracy is the worst form of government except for all those other forms that have been tried from time to time." American quilts can shine a spotlight on our complicated democracy, creating exuberant touchstones of American history to remind us that the past truly is prologue, waiting for us to stitch the future.

Notes

Introduction

1. I was twenty-seven at the time and can testify to the Bicentennial fervor, from television programs to parades to special issues of news and photo magazines. New York City hosted Operation Sail, and I was there—but watching the tall ships on television since I was in a friend's apartment, finishing the binding of their Bicentennial quilt. In retrospect, I wonder whether African Americans viewing the replicas of historic ships sailing into New York Harbor perhaps were thinking about ancestors huddled inside those original ships during the Middle Passage.
2. Terry McDonald and Melanie Methot, "That Impulse That Bids a People to Honour Its Past: The Nature and Purpose of Centennial Celebrations," *International Journal of Heritage Studies* 12, no. 4 (July 2006): 307.
3. Ibid., 309.
4. Marie Proeller, "Patriotic Quilts." *Country Living* 19, no. 7 (July 1996): 60. Gale Academic OneFile.
5. Juliana Koenig, "The Public Quilt," *The Clarion,* Spring/Summer 1986, 66. This is a special issue celebrating the Great American Quilt Festival of 1986.
6. J. S. Ingram, *The Centennial Exposition, Described and Illustrated* (Philadelphia: Hubbard Bros., 1876), 29.

Chapter 1

1. Paul Cimbala and Randall M. Miller, eds., *The Great Task Remaining Before Us: Reconstruction as America's Continuing Civil War* (New York: Fordham University Press, 2010), ix.
2. Walter Smith, *The Masterpieces of the Centennial Exhibition Illustrated,* vol. 2 (Philadelphia: Gebbie & Barrie, ca. 1876), 62.
3. Frank Norton, ed., *Frank Leslie's Illustrated Historical Register of the Centennial Exhibition* (New York: Frank Leslie's Publishing House, 1877), 125.
4. William B. Beebe, *Intimate Parallels: The Art, History, and Activism of Civil War–era Women's Quilt Art* (Harvard University ProQuest Dissertations and Theses, 2016), 50. In 2013, the Museum of the Confederacy merged with the American Civil War Museum in Richmond, dropping its name.
5. Beebe, *Intimate Parallels*, 50–51.
6. Stephen Kantrowitz, "White Supremacy, Settler Colonialism, and the Two Citizenships of the Fourteenth Amendment," *Journal of the Civil War Era* 10, no. 1, accessed online.
7. *New York Times*, May 3, 1869, 2.
8. Robert Utley, "Centennial Speech," June 24, 1976, *1876–1976 Centennial Commemoration, Battle of the Little Bighorn*, Custer Battlefield National Monument.
9. William H. Rehnquist, *Centennial Crisis: The Disputed Election of 1876* (New York: Vintage Books, 2004), 17.
10. Mrs. E. D. Gillespie, *A Book of Remembrance* (Philadelphia and London: J. B. Lippincott, 1901), 298.
11. J. S. Ingram, *The Centennial Exposition, Described and Illustrated* (Philadelphia: Hubbard Bros., 1876), 604. I am very grateful to Patty Kennedy-Zafred, who loaned me her copy of this book, which proved invaluable for my research.
12. Ibid., 608.
13. Mrs. Hopkinson, "Some Thoughts on the Completed Century," *Godey's Lady's Book and Magazine* 92 (January–June 1876): 32.
14. Ingram, *The Centennial Exposition*, 605. The possible relevance of Japanese screens will be discussed in chapter 4.
15. Ingram, *The Centennial Exposition*, 645.
16. Available online at https://ohiomemory.org/digital/collec

tion/p16007coll86/id/196.

17. Elizabeth Cady Stanton, Susan B. Anthony, and Matilda Joslyn Gage, eds., *History of Woman Suffrage*, vol. 3, *1876–1885* (Salem, NH: Ayers, 1985), 31.
18. Mary Frances Cordato, "Toward a New Century: Women and the Philadelphia Centennial Exhibition, 1876," *Pennsylvania Magazine of History and Biography* 107, no. 1 (January 1983): 131.
19. Gloria Seaman Allen, "Slaves as Textile Artisans," *Uncoverings* 22 (2001): 10–11.
20. Beebe, *Intimate Parallels*, 52.
21. Philip S. Foner, "Black Participation in the Centennial of 1876," *Negro History Bulletin* 39, no. 2 (February 1976): 535. (From the *People's Advocate*, July 17, 1876.)
22. This statue eventually was accessioned by the Smithsonian.
23. Ingram, *The Centennial Exposition*, 372.
24. It's worth mentioning that during 1794, Philadelphia served as the nation's capital. Although Pennsylvania passed an act in 1780 to abolish slavery, racial discrimination extended into the (white) churches and into the household of President Washington.
25. Mitch Kachun, "Before the Eyes of All Nations: African-American Identity and Historical Memory at the Centennial Exposition of 1876," *Pennsylvania History: A Journal of Mid-Atlantic Studies* 65, no. 3 (Summer 1998): 319–320.
26. Frank Norton, ed., *Frank Leslie's Illustrated Historical* Register, 133. The statue, not purchased during the Centennial, was acquired after the artist's death by the Revoltella Museum in Trieste, Italy.
27. Pat Ferrero, Elaine Hedges, and Julie Silber, *Hearts and Hands: The Influence of Women & Quilts on American Society* (San Francisco: Quilt Digest, 1987), 16.
28. Ibid., 21–23.
29. Jenny Yearous, "Stitches in Time: The Development of Sewing Thread in the Nineteenth Century and Beyond," *Uncoverings* 19 (1998): 155–178, comprehensively discusses this subject.
30. Ingram, *The Centennial Exposition*, 158.
31. Ibid., 368–369. When we discuss inventions by women displayed at the Women's Pavilion in chapter 2, we can judge the validity of his comment about women inventors.
32. Martha C. Halpern, "Germantown Goods: A Survey of the Textile Industry in Germantown, Pennsylvania," *Textile History* 29, no. 2 (1998): 168.
33. "Philadelphia's Textile Industries," *Scientific American* 43, no. 3 (1880): 38.
34. Deborah E. Kraak, "Patchwork Prints in America: 1878–1900," *Uncoverings* 32 (2011): 155.
35. Ingram, *The Centennial Exposition*, 707.
36. Beverly Gordon, "Spinning Wheels, Samplers, and the Modern Priscilla: The Images and Paradoxes of Colonial Revival Needlework," *Winterthur Portfolio* 33 (Summer-Autumn 1998): 163.
37. Doris M. Bowman, *The Smithsonian Treasury: American Quilts* (Washington, DC: Smithsonian Institution Press, 1991), 74–75, including a full-page color image. Analysis of the quilts is by Joan Stephens.
38. Ingram, *The Centennial Exposition*, 363.
39. These textile objects are also called "banners," but the sizes and formats more appropriately fit the category of "bandanas."
40. Hillary Weiss, *The American Bandanna: Culture on Cloth from George Washington to Elvis* (San Francisco: Chronicle Books, 1990), 9. Thanks to Teresa Barkley for the loan of this fascinating book.
41. "Columbia" here means America, the so-called land of Columbus.
42. Karlyn Kohrs Campbell and Kathleen Hall Jamieson, "Inaugurating the Presidency," *Presidential Studies Quarterly* 15 (Spring 1985): 357.
43. "Inaugurations of a Century," *Evening Star* (Washington, DC), March 2, 1889, 14. His entourage entered New York Harbor via a barge.
44. "The Presidents," *Weekly Kansan Republican*, March 7, 1889, 1.
45. "They Want to Take Part: Women Suffragists Annoyed by the Centennial Snub," *The Sun* (New YorkY), April 27, 1889, 5.
46. Quilt Index 11-37-3054, from Massachusetts.
47. "Washington Bicentennial Celebration Unique in History: Coolidge Began Preparation for Great Celebration," *Asbury Park (NJ) Press*, August 31, 1932, 19.
48. "Radio Will Carry Program from Capitol to Every Corner of the Nation," *Carpinteria (CA) Herald*, February 19, 1932, 3.

Chapter 2

1. "Women and the Centennials," *Harper's Bazar* 8, no. 35 (August 28, 1875): 554. This statement certainly applied to upper-class and middle-class women—not so much for women living in poverty. The magazine's name was changed to *Harper's Bazaar* ca. 1929.
2. Mrs. E. D. Gillespie, *A Book of Remembrance* (Philadelphia and London: J. B. Lippincott, 1901), 269. I feel confident about using her autobiography and that of Frances E. Willard as reliable sources because their comments quoted in my book have been confirmed by contemporaneous sources.
3. Ibid., 270.
4. Ibid., 273.
5. Ibid., 275–276.
6. Ibid., 282.

7. "Centennial Tea Party," *Godey's Lady's Book* 88 (February 1874): 190. Mount Vernon houses a few quilts made by Martha Washington, possibly with the assistance of an enslaved person, such as her seamstress Charlotte. One of those quilts may have been the work displayed in 1876.
8. Gillespie, *Book of Remembrance*, 292.
9. *National Cookery Book, Compiled from Original Receipts, for the Women's Centennial Committee of the International Exhibition of 1876* (Philadelphia: Women's Centennial Executive Committee, 1876).
10. Gillespie, *Book of Remembrance*, 295.
11. *National Cookery Book*, 85.
12. Gillespie, *Book of Remembrance*, 292.
13. Frank Norton, ed., *Frank Leslie's Illustrated Historical Register of the Centennial Exhibition* (New York: Frank Leslie's Publishing House, 1877), 63–64.
14. Gillespie, *Book of Remembrance*, 319.
15. Norton, *Leslie's Illustrated Historical Register*, 92.
16. Ibid., 156. It seems that the number of skeins might be exaggerated.
17. Ibid. See chapter 3 for more information about the Royal School of Art Needlework at the Centennial.
18. *International Exhibition 1876 Official Catalogue, Part 1: Main Building and Annexes* (John R. Nagle, 1876), 119. This catalog lists all commercial participants and the products displayed in their sections.
19. Ibid., 121.
20. Exhibition label for the 1876 *Centennial Charm Quilt* by Emma Willey in *Happy Birthday, America* at the New England Quilt Museum in 2006, curated by Sue Reich.
21. Pat L. Nickols, "Charm Quilts: Characteristics and Variations, 1870s–1890s," *Uncoverings* 17 (1996): 196.
22. Ibid., 196.
23. Sue Reich, *"Quilting News of Yesteryear": 1000 Pieces and Counting* (Atglen, PA: Schiffer, 2007), 6.
24. Linda J. Borish, "'A Fair, Without the Fair, Is No Fair at All': Women at the New England Agricultural Fair in the Mid-Nineteenth Century," *Journal of Sport History* 24 (Summer 1997): 160, 162.
25. Rev. Theodore L. Cuyler, "Introduction," in *Centennial Temperance Volume: A Memorial . . .* (New York: National Temperance Society, 1877), 11.
26. Frances E. Willard, *Glimpses of Fifty Years: The Autobiography of an American Woman* (Chicago: Woman's Temperance Publication Association and H. J. Smith, 1889), 352–353.
27. Ricky Clark, George W. Knepper, and Ellice Ronsheim, *Quilts in Community: Ohio's Traditions* (Nashville: Rutledge Hill, 1991), 150.
28. I am very grateful to Nancy Schultz, archivist for the Frances Willard House Museum in Evanston, Illinois, for information about this quilt and the WCTU in general. We spoke during a phone interview on August 16, 2024. Another WCTU "mystery" quilt was created for 1976, with the message to be opened and read in 2076.
29. Mary Rose Williams, "A Re-Conceptualization of Protest Rhetoric: Characteristics of Quilts as Protest" (PhD diss., University of Oregon, 1990), 2.
30. Ibid., 84n10. Her dissertation includes a thorough description of the physical quilt.
31. Willard, *Glimpses of Fifty Years*, 77.
32. Pat Ferrero, Elaine Hedges, and Julie Silber, *Hearts and Hands: The Influence of Women & Quilts on American Society* (San Francisco: Quilt Digest, 1987), 87. It's probably safe to assume that blue-and-white quilts in the *Drunkard's Path* pattern or incorporating all-over "T" blocks for "Temperance" around this time expressed support of the WCTU's initiatives.
33. Beverly Gordon, "Spinning Wheels, Samplers, and the Modern Priscilla: The Images and Paradoxes of Colonial Revival Needlework," *Winterthur Portfolio* 33 (Summer/Autumn 1998): 166.
34. "Some of the Exhibits" in "The State Fair," *Sacramento Daily Record-Union*, September 12, 1883, 2.
35. "The Third Day," *Daily Press*, October 8, 1886, 3.
36. "A Novel New England Industry: Over 700,000 Bed Quilts Manufactured Last Year in One Connecticut Village," *The Sun*, June 21, 1885, 6.
37. "Crazy Quilt Politicians," *Semi-Weekly Miner* (Butte, MT), April 12, 1884, 3.
38. "Full List of Premiums, *Helena (MT) Daily Herald*, August 31, 1885, 2.
39. "A Wonderful . . . [page torn]," *Missoula County (MT) Times*, February 6, 1884, 3.
40. "Old Fashioned Industries Revived," *Quachita Telegraph* (Monroe, LA), September 2, 1882, 1.
41. "A Poem in Patches," *Times-Picayune* (New Orleans, LA), May 25, 1883, 8.
42. "Woman and Home . . ." *The Times*, December 9, 1883, 2. The maker was Ellen Harding Baker, who taught science in rural Iowa. Her embroidered and appliquéd quilt now resides in the Smithsonian.
43. "Osage County Fair: Immense Gathering of the People," *Burlingame (KS) Herald*, September 22, 1883, 2.
44. "Fifth Annual Fair!," *Weekly Eagle* (Wichita, KS), October 4, 1877, 2.
45. "The Fair," *Fort Scott (KS) Tribune*, October 15, 1885, 6.
46. "The Beauties of Patchwork," *Leavenworth (KS) Times*, August 22, 1880, 3.
47. "A Remarkable Quilt," *St. Louis Globe-Dispatch*, September 25, 1880, 9.

48. "Noah's Ark Quilt," *Iron County (MO) Register*, July 29, 1886, 3.
49. "The Quilt Drawing," *Austin-American Statesman*, March 22, 1884, 4. The quilter's name is spelled "Harn" in other newspapers.
50. "Something Worth Looking Upon," *Galveston (TX) Daily News*, July 13, 1884, 12.
51. *Austin Weekly Statesman*, May 6, 1880, 4.
52. "Patchwork: The Great Crazy Quilt Exposition . . . ," *Memphis Daily Appeal*, December 17, 1885, 4.
53. "A Useful Invention," *Southern Standard* (McMinnville, TN), February 27, 1886, 1.
54. "Making Crazy Quilts," *Harrisburg (PA) Daily Independent*, October 6, 1884, 4,
55. "Home Topics: Warm Coverlets," *Philadelphia Times*, November 2, 1879, 2.
56. Mary E. Carswell's spectacular quilt is in the collection of the Mattatuck Museum in Waterbury, Connecticut.
57. "Exhibiting Crazy Work: A Dazzling Display Opened in the Masonic Temple, Curious Handwork Executed by Old and Young Men and Women in All Parts of the Country," *New York Times*, November 18, 1885, 8.

Chapter 3

1. This date is supplied by Sue Reich in an email to the author dated July 28, 2024. Her generous advice has very much improved this chapter. All errors rest with me.
2. Cindy Brick, *Crazy Quilts: History, Techniques, Embroidery Motifs* (St. Paul, MN: Voyageur, 2008), 29.
3. Even when a quilt's content might suggest a date of completion, we need to be careful about assigning a date, such as for the Metropolitan Museum of Art's crazy quilt made by Tamar Horton Harris North as a memorial to her daughter Grace, who died in 1877. The museum gives "ca. 1877" as the proposed date. But contemporaneous accounts repeatedly inform us that some women spent quite a long time working on their crazy quilts, and this particular quilt features a spectacular amount of handwork.
4. Brick, *Crazy Quilts*, 45.
5. Robert Shaw, *American Quilts: The Democratic Art, 1780–2007* (New York and London: Sterling, 2009), 150.
6. Van E. Hillard, "Census, Consensus, and the Commodification of Form," in Cheryl B. Torsney and Judy Elsley, eds., *Quilt Culture: Tracing the Pattern* (Columbia: University of Missouri Press, 1994), 122–123. (Most of her article concerns the NAMES Project AIDS Memorial Quilt.)
7. "Crazy Quilts: A Feminine Mania Which Has Many Sides," *San Francisco Chronicle*, September 28, 1883, 3.
8. Ibid.
9. "Bubbles and Quilts: To-Night at the Art Loan," *Atlanta Constitution*, November 9, 1883, 7.
10. One of four stanzas in an anonymous poem from *Good Housekeeping* (October 25, 1980), 310. The entire poem is reprinted in McMorris, *Crazy Quilts*, 7.
11. Connecticut Quilt Search Project, *Quilts and Quiltmakers Covering Connecticut* (Atglen, PA: Schiffer, 2002), 98–99.
12. Penny McMorris, *Crazy Quilts* (New York: E. P. Dutton, 1984), 13–15, describes Victorian home decor, with a photograph of a Victorian drawing room in Chicago.
13. Shaw, *American Quilts*, 150–153.
14. According to a 2024 email exchange with the archivist of the Royal School of Needlework (their name since 1922), some of the works displayed at the 1876 booth never made it back to England, including the door curtain. Their location remains unknown.
15. Candace Wheeler, *The Development of Embroidery in America* (New York and London: Harper & Brothers, 1921), 107–108.
16. Walter Smith, *The Masterpieces of the Centennial Exhibition Illustrated*, vol. 2 (Philadelphia: Gebbie & Barrie, ca. 1876), 278. The training proposed by Smith was not for sweatshop-type labor, but for the sort of atelier work created by the Arts and Crafts movement in Britain.
17. Candace Wheeler, *Yesterdays in a Busy Life* (New York and London: Harper & Brothers, 1918), 211.
18. Candace Wheeler, "A Chapter on Artistic Poetry," *Harper's Bazaar* 22, no. 11 (March 16, 1889): 196.
19. Shaw, *American Quilts*, 156. A comprehensive analysis of the aesthetic influence can be found in Virginia Gunn, "Crazy Quilts and Outline Quilts: Popular Response to the Decorative Art / Art Needlework Movement, 1876–1893," *Uncoverings* 5 (1984): 131–152.
20. Brick, *Crazy Quilts*, 54.
21. McMorris, *Crazy Quilts*, 31–25.
22. Brick, *Crazy Quilts*, 47, depicting both sides of the card.
23. McMorris, *Crazy Quilts*, 57.
24. T. Edward Parker, *Ornamental Stitches for Embroidery* (Lynn, MA: Nonotuck Silk, 1885), 3.
25. Ibid., 15.
26. Jane Przybysz, "The Victorian Crazy Quilt as Comfort and Discomfort," *Quilt Journal* 3, no. 2 (1994): 9.
27. Marin F. Hanson, "Modern, Yet Anti-Modern: Two Sides of Late-Nineteenth- and Early-Twentieth-Century Quiltmaking," *Uncoverings* 29 (2008): 105.
28. Ibid., 120.
29. Parker, *Ornamental Stitches*, 3. As far as I have been able to tell, this author was not associated with Parker Pens, founded in 1888 in Wisconsin. His assertion that crazy

work derived its name from crackled porcelain is not supported by any evidence.

30. "The Display of Needlework and Embroidery," *Godey's Lady's Book* 93 (July–December 1876): 95, describes several of these items on view in the Women's Pavilion, crediting the makers: "As this is an interesting subject to ladies, we give a brief account of some of the most prominent articles on exhibition."
31. Frank Norton, ed., *Frank Leslie's Illustrated Historical Register of the Centennial Exhibition* (New York: Frank Leslie's Publishing House, 1877), 251.
32. Jill Liddell and Yuko Watanabe, *Japanese Quilts* (New York: E. P. Dutton, 1988), 16.
33. Ibid., 19 (caption).
34. McMorris, *Crazy Quilts*, 12. Italics by McMorris.
35. Smith, *Masterpieces*, 170–171.
36. Ibid., 51.
37. Clarence Cook, *The House Beautiful* (New York: Scribner, Armstrong, 1878), 141–142. My italics.
38. "Art Needlework," *Art Amateur* 7, no. 5 (October 1882): 108.
39. Brick, *Crazy Quilts*, 42–43.
40. Smith, *Masterpieces*, 176–178.
41. Ibid., 239. My italics.
42. Ibid., 367. My italics.
43. Ibid., 25.
44. Ibid., 86.
45. Ibid., 390.
46. Nelson Klose, "Sericulture in the United States," *Agricultural History* 37, no. 4 (October 1963): 225.
47. Carrie Williams, *Complete Instruction in Rearing Silkworms* (San Francisco: Whitaker and Ray, 1902), 119.
48. L. O. Howard, "The United State Department of Agriculture and Silk Culture," USDA, *Yearbook*, 1903, 142–143.
49. Norton, *Frank Leslie's Illustrated*, 282: $21,120,428 worth of US silk and $23,996,782 of foreign silk.
50. Norton, *Frank Leslie's Illustrated*, 282.
51. Silk Association of America, *Annual Report: Wednesday, April 26th, 1876* (New York, 1876), 154.
52. Didi Barrett, "Quilt Dealer to the Stars," *The Clarion*, Spring/Summer 1986, 49. This was a special issue celebrating the Great American Quilt Festival.
53. Beverly Gordon, "Playing at Being Powerless: New England Ladies Fairs, 1830–1930, *Massachusetts Review* 27, no. 1 (Spring 1986): 154.
54. Beverly Gordon, "Crazy Quilts as an Expression of 'Fairyland,'" *Uncoverings* 27 (2006): 27, 31.
55. Gordon, "Crazy Quilts," 38.
56. In 2009 the Design Gallery at the University of Wisconsin in Madison mounted an exhibition titled *A Fairyland of Fabrics: The Victorian Crazy Quilt*, curated by quilt historian Beverly Gordon.
57. Daniel Walker Howe, "American Victorianism as a Culture," *American* Quarterly 27, no. 5 (December 1975): 527.
58. Elaine Hedges, "Quilts and Women's Culture," *Radical Teacher* 4 (March 1977): 10.
59. Smith, *Masterpieces*, 96. My italics. This is not the only patronizing comment in Smith's volume.
60. Beverly Gordon, "Woman's Domestic Body: The Conceptual Conflation of Women and Interiors in the Industrial Age, *Winterthur Portfolio* 31, no. 4 (Winter 1996): 282.
61. Ibid., 286.
62. Ellen DuBois, Marijo Buhle, Temma Kaplan, Gerda Lerner, and Carroll Smith-Rosenberg, "Politics and Culture in Women's History: A Symposium," *Feminist Studies* 6 (Spring 1980): 26–64.
63. Sue Reich, *Quilting Notes of Yesteryear: Crazy as a Bed Quilt* (Atglen, PA: Schiffer, 2007). It's interesting to note that crazy quilts fell out of fashion around the time of ratification of the Nineteenth Amendment, granting suffrage to women in 1920.
64. Margaret E. Sangster, "The Crazy Quilt," *Harper's Bazar*, January 12, 1884, 27. This is the first stanza of her poem. Sangster was editor of the magazine during the 1890s.

Chapter 4

1. For thorough information about US world's fairs in general, see Robert W. Rydell, John E. Findling, and Kimberly D. Page, *Fair America: World's Fairs in the United States* (Washington, DC, and New York: Smithsonian Books, 2000).
2. Sara S. Cromwell, "Fair Treatment? African-American Presence at International Expositions in the South" (master's thesis, Wake Forest University, 2010), 17–39, which includes a thorough discussion of the 1884 Cotton Centennial. Accessed online: https://wakespace.lib.wfu.edu/bitstream/handle/10339/30396/Cromwell_wfu_0248M_10035.pdf.
3. Ibid., 31.
4. "The Colored People of Louisiana," *Times Picayune* (New Orleans, LA), February 24, 1885, 3.
5. Miki Pfeffer, *Southern Ladies and Suffragists: Julia Ward Howe and Women's Rights at the 1884 New Orleans World's Fair* (Jackson: University Press of Mississippi, 2014), 7.
6. Ibid., 10.
7. Terry McDonald and Melanie Methot, "That Impulse That Bids a People to Honour Its Past: The Nature and Purpose of Centennial Celebrations," *International Journal of Heritage Studies* 12, no. 4 (July 2006): 311.
8. Candace Wheeler, *The Development of Embroidery in America* (New York and London: Harper & Brothers, 1921), 108–109.
9. Candace Wheeler, "Applied Arts in the Woman's Building,"

in Maud Howe Elliott, ed., *Art and Handicraft in the Woman's Building of the World's Columbian Exposition* (Chicago and New York: Rand, McNally, 1894), 84.

10. "Wrought by Needles," *Chicago Tribune*, February 11, 1893, 16.
11. "White City Chips," *Daily Inter Ocean* (Chicago), July 7, 1893, 6.
12. Maud Howe Elliott, *Art and Handicraft in the Woman's Building of the World's Columbian Exposition, Chicago, 1893* (Paris and New York: Goupil, 1893).
13. Barbara Brackman, "Quilts at Chicago's World's Fairs," *Uncoverings* 2 (1981): 65.
14. "In the Children's Building," *Nashville Banner*, June 7, 1897, 1.
15. "Government Building," *Nashville Banner*, May 17, 1897, 7.
16. *Tennessee Centennial Exposition* (Nashville, 1897), 12.
17. "The Negro Department," *The Tennessean*, February 10, 1897, 5.
18. *Tennessee Centennial Exposition*, 19.
19. "Rose Marion Sees Trouble Ahead for Comr. Bonfoey, Who Will Have to Judge Handiwork of Missouri Women," *St. Louis Post-Dispatch*, June 12, 1904, 27.
20. "Creations of Needle and Brush Shown at the Fair Attract Much Attention," *St. Louis Republic*, July 31, 1904, 11.
21. "Valuable Quilt Mutilated by Vandals," *St. Louis Republic*, October 27, 1904, 14.
22. *Jamestown Ter-Centennial Exposition* (Norfolk, 1907), iv.
23. *Jamestown Exposition on Hampton Roads, 1907: Official Classification of Exhibit Departments* (n.p.), 22–23.
24. Frederic W. Gleach, "Pocahontas at the Fair: Crafting Identities at the 1907 Jamestown Exposition," *Ethnohistory* 50 (Summer 2003): 427.
25. "Jamestown Exposition Grounds," *Richmond Times-Dispatch*, August 4, 1907, 10. In passing, it is worth noting that Booker T. Washington studied oratory at Hampton Institute and had achieved fame as an orator years before he became an advisor to Theodore Roosevelt. We might question who influenced whom.
26. "Hessian Barracks Replica at Sesqui," *Philadelphia Inquirer*, August 15, 1926, 7.
27. "Relics Put on View for Sesqui Visitors," *Philadelphia Inquirer*, June 27, 1926, 11.
28. Merikay Waldvogel and Barbara Brackman, *Patchwork Souvenirs of the 1933 World's Fair* (Nashville: Rutledge Hill, 1993), 7.
29. Robert Shaw, *American Quilts: The Democratic Art, 1780–2007* (New York and London: Sterling, 2009), 232.
30. Brackman, "Quilts at Chicago's World's Fairs," 68.
31. Rhea Seeger, "Modern Quilt Patterns Vie with Favorites," *Chicago Daily Tribune*, May 20, 1933, 17.
32. Waldvogel and Brackman, *Patchwork Souvenirs*, 43.
33. Display ad: "'Century of Progress' Quilt Show," *Chicago Tribune*, June 1, 1933, 11.
34. "Piece of Art to Be Exhibited at Century of Progress," *Daily Clarion-Ledger* (Jackson, MS), May 5, 1933, 14.
35. W. G. MacFarlane, ed., *The Texas Centennial and Dallas Exposition, 1836–1936* (Chicago: American Autochrome, 1936), 4–5.
36. Suzanne Yabsley, "Quilting," Texas State Historical Association, accessed online: https://www.tshaonline.org/handbook/entries/quilting.
37. Jesse O. Thomas, *Negro Participation in the Texas Centennial Exposition* (Boston: Christopher, 1938), 40.
38. Email on September 24, 2024.
39. "Allegheny Woman Wins Quilt Contest . . . ," *New York Times*, May 11, 1939, 11.
40. Joyce R. Gross, "Bertha Stenge," *Quilters' Journal* 2 (Summer 1979): 1–5, 7.
41. "Over 40 Nations in Boulevards of the World," *Filipino Forum*, April 18, 1962, 1. Seattle had a large Filipino population, and the Philippines were well represented and publicized, as were Filipino merchants with businesses in Seattle.
42. "The Philippines Among over Forty Nations in World's Fair," *Filipino Forum*, May 11, 1962, 2.
43. *Century 21 Exposition: Seattle World's Fair 1962* (Seattle, WA: First National Bank, 1962), 26. This was the official souvenir program for the event, which concentrated mostly on science.
44. The pavilions are described via photographs and summaries of their contents online: www.worldsfairphotos.com.
45. *The Hemisfair 1968 Official Souvenir Guidebook* (San Antonio, 1968), 51.
46. Ibid., 74.
47. Nancy Baker Jones, "The Way We Were: Gender and the Woman's Pavilion Hemisfair '68," *Southwestern Historical Quarterly* 199 (April 2016): 341.
48. Shaw, *American Quilts: The Democratic Art*, 253.

Chapter 5

1. "Sent Taft a Quilt," *Pittsburg Daily Highlight*, February 4, 1913, 2. There is some confusion about the source of this quilt because the Associated Press picked up the story, reported in various newspapers as made by Mr. Reed, Mr. Reid, or Mrs. H. C. Reed and containing 5,082 pieces.
2. "1600 Pieces of Silk in Quilt," *Richmond Times Dispatch*, March 1, 1913, 10. The term "Old Glory" means the US flag.
3. Heartfelt thanks to Andrew Phillips, curator of the Woodrow Wilson Presidential Library in Staunton, Virginia, who

kindly photographed these two quilts for my book. He photographed them on the very bed where Woodrow Wilson was born. Email of October 9, 2024.

4. "Harding Quilt Brings $150," *Pittsburgh Gazette*, November 2, 1922, 1.
5. Sue Reich, *Quilts Presidential and Patriotic* (Atglen, PA: Schiffer, 2016), 140.
6. Ibid., 144. An eagle has also represented the Republican Party in quilts, and a rooster the Democratic Party.
7. Robert Shaw, *American Quilts: The Democratic Art, 1780–2007* (New York and London: Sterling, 2009), 145.
8. "Quilt for Kennedy," *Kansas City Times*, September 6, 1961, 4. Her quilt is illustrated above the fold.
9. *Corbin Daily Tribune*, October 21, 1969, 3.
10. "Quilt Bears Signatures," *Oregonian*, February 24, 1970, 1.
11. "Mississippians' Quilt to Get Special Place," *Advocate* (Baton Rouge, LA), December 3, 1971, 6.
12. Shaw, *American Quilts*, 188. The International Quilt Museum, University of Nebraska–Lincoln, owns a replica of this quilt made to scale by Hortense Beck, 1990–1991. Carolyn Ducey, Ardis B. James Curator of Collections, explained in an email dated September 30, 2024, that Beck made reproductions of historic quilts, such as this one. I was unable to locate the original Blackhorse quilt. For those wishing to study Native American work, the National Museum of the American Indian has an outstanding collection of more than 125 quilts.
13. Email from Larry Belitz, October 4, 2024, mentioning that he was adopted by two families whose names are on the quilt—Blue Legs and Pipe on Head families of porcupine quillwork fame. At the end of the 1973 siege, the Sioux Indian Museum and trading post, used as bunkers and headquarters of AIM protestors, were looted, then burned to the ground. Only several historic museum items miraculously survived. Artifacts surviving the AIM takeover are displayed at the Belitz Ranch in the Lakota Cultural Museum. Belitz founded Sioux Replications, where he instructs and demonstrates skills of the prereservation era such as bow making, hide tanning, parfleche work, porcupine quillwork, lazy-stitch beadwork, and constructing hide tipis (teepees). He has constructed sixty-five hide tipis and guided the Northern Cheyenne and also Arapaho on tanning and constructing their first buffalo hide tipis in over a century.
14. Teresa Duryea Wong, "Giving Them All Away: Rosebud Reservation Quilters," *Quiltfolk* 24 (2016): 93, illustrating a red, white, and blue star quilt by Velda Bear Shield and gifted in 1977 to the Veterans of Foreign Wars Hall in Gregory, South Dakota, where it currently is on display.
15. Wasaja N.E.W.S. Bureau, "Divided Opinion on Bicentennial," *San Francisco Chronicle*, October 1, 1975, 8.
16. "State Suffrage Work," *Emporia (KS) Gazette*, August 5, 1912, 1. As in several other places in this book, I am grateful to Sue Reich for her tireless research in newspapers that has revealed gems such as this.
17. "Auction Brings $2,000," *Burlingame (KS) Enterprise*, April 4, 1918, 4.
18. "Big Time at Quilt Sale," *Times-Journal* (Mound Valley, KS), November 15, 1918, 3. At this time, the Red Cross was focusing on the flu pandemic as well as on war relief projects.
19. For quilt images, see Sue Reich, *World War I Quilts* (Atglen, PA: Schiffer, 2014), 158–159.
20. "Beautiful Patriotic Quilt," *Leavenworth (KS) Times*, October 16, 1918, 5. The quilt's fabric was delaine, French for "of wool," a high-grade woolen fabric.
21. Reich, *World War I Quilts*, 165–166.
22. "Beautiful Poppy Quilt," *Tampa Tribune*, December 15, 1917, 5.
23. "Awards Announced for Poppy Poster Contest," *The Tennessean*, May 18, 1930, 20.
24. Alice Brooks, "Household Arts: Scrap Quilt," *Fresno (CA) Bee*, January 9, 1943, 4. The pattern number was 7419.
25. "Makes Patriotic Quilt," *Schuyler (NE) Sun*, May 28, 1942, 5.
26. "Has Patriotic Quilt," *Kansas City Star*, January 29, 1942, 18.
27. "Patriotic Quilt Is Shown to Kiwanians," *North Platte (NE) Telegraph*, July 1, 1943, 3.
28. "Want Owner to Get Patriotic Quilt," *Cherokee (OK) Messenger*, July 6, 1943, 1.
29. "$2,650 for Patriotic Quilt," *Newkirk (OK) Herald Journal*, November 4, 1943, 6.
30. Sue Reich, *World War II Quilts* (Atglen, PA: Schiffer, 2010), 153.
31. "Sunflower Club's Victory Quilt Brings Large Sum," *Benkelman-Post (NE) and News Chronicle*, April 2, 1943, 1. A stylized star pattern can be formed by setting the Vs in different directions.
32. Joan Gilmore, "'Soc' Takes In Fair Exhibits, Finds Interesting Items in Every Hall," *Muskogee (OK) Daily Phoenix and Times-Democrat*, October 4, 1951, 6.
33. "Stars and Stripes in Stitches," *Star Tribune* [Minneapolis], July 4, 1953, 31, with a three-quarter-page photo of the quilt above the fold for this Sunday issue on the Fourth of July, two weeks before the Korean War ended.
34. "VFW Auxiliary Meets," *Beckley (WV) Post-Herald*, November 23, 1958. 4,
35. Barbara Golz, "Quilts Offer Homespun Beauty from Nimble Fingers," *Amarillo (TX) Globe-Times*, September 20, 1961, 16. Another exhibitor made a patriotic eagle quilt from

a kit.

36. "State Fair's Patriotic Quilt Took Three Years," *Bucyrus (OH) Telegraph-Forum*, August 15, 1962, 29. This was the year when John Glenn became the first US astronaut to orbit the earth. This quilt is illustrated in Ricky Clark, George W. Knepper, and Ellice Ronsheim, *Quilts in Community: Ohio's Traditions* (Nashville: Rutledge Hill, 1991), 160.
37. Martha Mahaffey, "Small Talk," *Parsons (KS) Sun*, September 18, 1963, 3.
38. "Public Law 89-491, 89th Congress, July 4, 1966, as amended through October 23, 1972," in *United States of America, 1776–1976: Official Documents of the American Revolution Bicentennial Commission* (New Haven, CT: University of Michigan Reprints, 2024), 4.
39. Ibid., 20.
40. "The City," *San Francisco Examiner*, June 8, 1975, 154. The proposed Freedom Train that was to be parked near the Presidio is not the American Freedom Train of twenty-six cars that toured through several states.
41. "Public Law 89-491," 21.
42. Tammy S. Gordon, *The Spirit of 1976: Commerce, Community, and the Politics of Commemoration* (Amherst and Boston: University of Massachusetts Press, 2013), 4.
43. Gordon, *The Spirit of 1976*, 82.

Chapter 6

1. *Index of Bicentennial Activities: Titles of Projects and Events, Listed by City and State* (Washington, DC: American Revolution Bicentennial Administration, February 1976).
2. "Area Shares Honors in Quilting for Bi-C," *Flint (MI) Journal*, August 24, 1976, 4.
3. Robert Shaw, *American Quilts: The Democratic Art, 1780–2007* (New York and London: Sterling, 2009), 277.
4. Tanana Valley State Fair Association, *Premium List: 1976 Alaska State Fair* (1976), 16.
5. Anne Kuchejda and Eleanore Taylor, eds., *Signode's Bicentennial Sampler . . . A Crazy Quilt of Good Eating* (n.p. [Signode Steel Strapping Co.], 1976) (inside front cover, letter from Thomas Schanck, president). This title was the finalist from more than seventy-five submitted by Signode employees.
6. A search in newspapers.com reveals Bicentennial album quilts in almost every state of the US.
7. Jeannette Lewis, director, women's activities, Ohio State Grange, in *Ohio State Grange Cookbook* (Columbus: Ohio State Grange, 1976), iv.
8. *Ohio State Grange Cookbook*, ii, extrapolating from the Ohio State Grange text.
9. Mardi Marsh, ed., *Quilter's Cookbook: Calaveras County Bicentennial Quilt* (Kansas City, MO, 1976), i. The quilt's story is discussed below.
10. Interview by phone with Glady Boalt, February 20, 2024.
11. Made by the Walsh Quilters of Park River, illustrated on a postcard.
12. Emails to the author, May 23, 2024. Dr. Gates Carlisle's tribute to her mother enriches the creation story of this quilt: "Mamma felt the policies and curriculum were racist, so every year I had independent study in February and made a presentation to the School Board. The ladies didn't want the legacy of Black excellence erased. From Pedro Alonso Niño and James Beckworth, from Crispus Attucks and Salem Poor, Blacks were active participants in the American story. . . . Mamma was an *incredible* woman. Her interest in history was a legacy of her father, a Spanish American war hero and evangelist, one of the only Blacks buried in Chalmette National Cemetery before the Civil Rights era. She got an MBA from NYU, Class of '50, and taught and practiced accounting. She was a successful plaintiff in a class-action lawsuit against Georgia-Pacific. . . . She donated her settlement to support multi-cultural education by bringing John Hope Franklin and Helen Edmonds to teach for two weeks every summer. She also established the Gates Collection at Portland State." Our image here of the quilt was taken before it was damaged by vandalism.
13. "The flag most generally attributed to Betsy Ross contains the traditional 13 red and white stripes with 13 five-pointed stars arranged in a circle in the canton. Although most scholars now doubt the story advanced by Ross's grandson William Canby that Ross designed the first American flag, she and her descendants certainly made flags, and it is common to refer to a flag with 13 alternating red and white stripes and a canton with 13 stars arranged in a circle as a Betsy Ross flag. The earliest flag legislation did not specify how stars were to be arranged, and this Betsy Ross pattern remains one of the most popular flag designs. It was widely reproduced during the nation's centennial and bicentennial celebrations." John R. Vile, *The American Flag: An Encyclopedia of the Stars and Stripes in U.S. History, Culture, and Law* (Santa Barbara, CA, and Denver, CO: ABC-CLIO, 2018), 107.
14. "Artex Firm Expansion Continues," *Lima (OH) News*, February 29, 1976, 24.
15. *McCall's Bicentennial Quilt Book*, 1976, 33 (completed quilt) and 42–44 (pattern).
16. Jo Ann Knout, "Mary's Quilts Stitch History," *Dayton (OH) Daily News*, July 30, 1975, 29.
17. Tammy Ayers, "Naches Woman Put Life on Hold in 1976 for

the Bicentennial Wagon Train Pilgrimage," *TCA Regional News* (Chicago), June 27, 2016 (wire feed). Marilyn "Micki" Robison was the Naches woman who helped organize the event, also participating in its fortieth-year reunion in 2016, which celebrated the centennial of the National Park Service. She commented about her Bicentennial experience: "'Nobody dreamed that it would get as big as it did,' Robison said. In every sense of the cliche, it was the journey of a lifetime. She met a descendant of Sacagawea, country singer Loretta Lynn and her daughters; the president and his daughter. She met most of the governors."

18. Email to the author, February 21, 2024.
19. Email to the author, March 4, 2024.
20. Email to the author, December 2, 2024.
21. Website of browngrotta arts, https://browngrotta.com/artists/katherine-westphal.
22. Margaret Carroll, "A Sew-Journ into Patriotism," *Chicago Tribune*, June 14, 1975, 56.
23. Whitney Chadwick, *Women, Art, and Society* (London: Thames and Hudson, 1990), 316.
24. Lisa E. Farrington, *Faith Ringgold* (San Francisco: Pomegranate, 2004), 63.
25. Gary Blonston, "Now You Can Buy Yourself Patriotism," *San Francisco Examiner*, April 27, 1975, 27.
26. The PBC became today's Foundation for Economic Trends (office of Jeremy Rifkin).
27. Connie Young Yu, *The People's BiCentennial Quilt: A Patchwork History* (East Palo Alto, CA: Up Press, 1976).
28. "The Bicentennial Quilt Boom," *Lady's Circle Patchwork Quilts* 4 (1976): 4.
29. George Gallup, "Bicentennial Travel Carries Little Appeal," *Cincinnati Inquirer*, July 1, 1976, 46.
30. Email to the author, February 21, 2024. Jinny Beyer's *Ray of Light* quilt won First Prize in the Great American Quilt Contest mentioned here.
31. Email to the author, February 21, 2024.

Chapter 7

1. Charles Counts and his wife, Rubynelle Counts, made sure to credit the Rising Fawn Quilters for their work, and Ed Larson credited his quilters by having them embroider their names along with his on each quilt. In my phone interview with Larson in March 2008, he asked me to mention that two of his regular quilters were Wanie Thomas and Carolyn Whelan.
2. An interesting sidelight in these publications is the gendering of new quilt patterns, such as "Out of This World Quilt for the Little [male] Astronaut's Room," a simple spool pattern, and "Quilt for the Little Princess," a "perky appliquéd flower quilt." These patterns appeared in *15 Quilts for Today's Living* (Graphic Enterprises, 1968), 26–27 and 28–29, respectively.
3. Ruby Short McKim, *One Hundred and One Patchwork Patterns* (New York: Dover, 1962).
4. Marguerite Ickis, *The Standard Book of Quilt Making and Collecting* (New York: Dover, 1972).
5. Donna Renshaw, *Quilting, a Revived Art: Cultivate the Art of Making Something with Your Own Hands* (Los Altos, CA: Donna Renshaw, ca. 1975). This was a modest production, using a typewriter and with black-and-white illustrations, covered in a paper wrapper. Its price was $3.00. Until 1974, Renshaw owned the Quilting Bee, a store in Los Altos.
6. Renshaw, *Quilting, a Revived Art*, i.
7. Alyson Smith Gonsalves, ed., *Quilting and Patchwork* (Menlo Park, CA: Lane Magazine and Book, 1973). Donna Renshaw was an advisor for this publication.
8. Mazloomi treasures her copy of *Quilting and Patchwork*: "The book is like a dear old friend! Its pages well worn, it's enshrined in a special place in my studio" (email to the author, March 17, 2008).
9. Quilt seams should measure no wider than ¼ inch, unless the artist is purposefully manipulating the seams for a special effect. Clothing seams are usually 5/8 inch.
10. Judy Brittain, ed., *Vogue Guide to Patchwork and Quilting* (New York: Galahad Books, 1973).
11. The 1960s and 1970s perpetuated the assumption, which we now know to be false, that all antique quilts were made from scraps of fabric.
12. The *Progressive Farmer* was the only magazine seen by most of the quilt makers living near Gee's Bend, Alabama, during the 19670s and 1970s. This fact is based on an interview with Tinnie Pettway and her sister Minnie Pettway that took place in person in Boykin, Alabama, on January 15, 2008. I am very grateful to them, and to Rennie Miller, for their generosity in sharing information about quilting in their Black community, and about the original Freedom Quilting Bee.
13. Gross was one of the organizers of the American Quilt Study Group in 1980. Her collection of quilts and other items pertaining to twentieth-century quilts was acquired by the Center for American History at the University of Texas, Austin.
14. The name was changed as of the July 1974 issue.
15. In the mid-1970s, the author taught a traditional quilt-making workshop in Champaign-Urbana, Illinois.
16. By the early 1980s, quilt artists who lectured and taught in workshops were traveling throughout much of the US.
17. Renamed the Oregon College of Arts and Crafts, which closed in 2019.
18. Marie Lyman was assistant head of the Fibers/Textiles Department from 1978 to 1980. She also taught at the

University of Oregon, Eugene, in the spring of 1978 and gave workshops in Seattle in 1979. This information was provided in Lyman's c.v., mailed to me by her husband, William McLaughlin, in March 2008. I am grateful to Mr. McLaughlin for generously sharing his deceased wife's images, documents, and publications. Readers should note that as of 1992, Lyman began calling herself Nyx Philomela Lymann. She died on October 28, 2000.

19. Email to the author, May 9, 2008.
20. Artist's typed survey, 2007.
21. See *Quilter's Newsletter Magazine* 5, no. 4 (April 1974): 4, announcing that the University of Pittsburgh "will offer a course in Needlework as a Social History of Women this fall. The course is being sponsored jointly by the Women Studies Program and the Fine Arts Department," taught by Rachel Maines.
22. Jinny Beyer, *Patchwork Patterns* (McLean, VA: EPM Publications, 1979).
23. Robert Shaw, *The Art Quilt* (Hugh Lauter Levin, 1997), 54.
24. Rita Reif, "Quilting Is No Longer Just Another Pastime," *New York Times*, April 25, 1972; accessed online in the newspaper's archives, http://www.newyorktimes.com. The article discusses several women involved with traditional quilt making, including two who were successfully marketing kits for crib quilts to New York department stores such as Altman's and Saks Fifth Avenue. Beth Gutcheon is pictured behind a fabric-covered worktable, with her pieced quilt *Crazy Ann* partially visible on the wall behind her (quilt identified by this author from the reproduction on p. 65 of Beth Gutcheon, *The Perfect Patchwork Primer*, 1973). This article was an appealing presentation of Gutcheon and her work, most likely prompting students to enroll in the quilting classes.
25. Elsa Brown, *Creative Quilting* (New York: Watson-Guptill, 1975), 33.
26. Ann-Sargent Wooster, *Quilt Making: The Modern Approach to a Traditional Craft* (New York: Drake, 1972), x.
27. While she was teaching studio art at the Catholic University of America in Washington, DC, Sonnemann was a formative influence on Martin Puryear, who was one of her students.
28. Thelma R. Newman, *Quilting, Patchwork, Appliqué, and Trapunto: Traditional Methods and Original Designs* (New York: Crown, 1974), vii.
29. Email to the author, February 12, 2008.
30. Audrey Heard and Beverly Prior, *The Complete Guide to Quilting* (Des Moines, IA: Creative Home Library (in association with Better Homes and Gardens, 1974), 8.
31. Michael James was and continues to be an important influence. Michael Cummings, for example, stated in an email of January 22, 2002, that "Michael James and Faith Ringgold have been my role models for reaching my goal as a quilter. Michael because he was the only male with a high profile making art quilts. Faith because . . . I have always enjoyed her creative spirit."
32. Beth Gutcheon, *The Perfect Patchwork Primer* (Baltimore: Penguin Books, 1973), 22. On pp. 250–252, Gutcheon mentioned three large quilt cooperatives whose quilts were being marketed in urban retail stores: Mountain Artisans (West Virginia mountain women), Dakotah Handicrafts (Sioux Native Americans and Caucasians), and the Martin Luther King Freedom Quilting Bee (Black women near Gee's Bend, Alabama). Interestingly, she explained that while the first two groups were producing quilts designed by others, the members of the Freedom Quilting Bee "designed their own quilts instead of working with a professional, and the quality of the design was outstanding." But because much of the work evidently was offered on speculation, the group was not very successful. The Freedom Quilting Bee was revived, along with a new company, That's Sew Gee's Bend, with purchasers eagerly acquiring recent Gee's Bend original quilts.
33. Michael James, *The Quilt Maker's Handbook* (Mountain View, CA: Leone, 1993, reprint), 1.
34. Jane Przybysz, "Competing Cultural Values at the Great American Quilt Festival," *Uncoverings* 8 (1987): 119, an interview with Georgia quilter Barbara Thurman Butler, who commented that seeing quilts at the time of the 1976 Bicentennial first inspired her to quilt.
35. Chatterton's comment about Colby's quilt surely must be one of the most extreme understatements in quilt criticism: "Sas Colby makes interesting use of printed and plain fabrics to create her designs" (p. 47).
36. Mariska Karasz, *Adventures in Stitches: A New Art of Embroidery* (New York: Funk & Wagnalls, 1949), 9.
37. David B. van Dommelen, *Decorative Wall Hangings: Art with Fabric* (New York: Funk & Wagnalls, 1962). The book includes an installation shot of the fabled *Invention with Thread II* 1961 exhibition at the Montclair (New Jersey) Art Museum on p. 107.
38. Jean Ray Laury, *Applique Stitchery* (New York: Van Nostrand Reinhold, 1966), 11.
39. Laury, *Applique Stitchery*, 28.
40. Carolyn Vosburg Hall, *Stitched and Stuffed Art: Contemporary Designs for Quilts, Toys, Pillows, Soft Sculpture and Wall Hangings* (Garden City, NY: Doubleday, 1974).
41. Lisa Hammel, "Handcrafts: Show and Tell," *New York Times*, October 17, 1974; accessed online via the newspaper's website, http://www.newyorktimes.com.
42. She had no idea how the editors planned to use the image of her quilt, but agreed to make it because this was the first time she knew of that the magazine had shown any

interest in handicrafts. Typed note (n.d.) on Mylar envelope containing an offprint of the page, loaned to the author by Laury.

43. Autograph note (n.d.) on Post-it, on Mylar envelope containing an offprint of the article, loaned to the author by Laury.

44. Twyla Dell, "A Heart to Heart Talk with Jean Ray Laury," *Quilt World*, September/October 1979, 10–12.

45. Email to the author, March 16, 2008.

46. *Quilter's Newsletter Magazine* 1, nos. 21–22 (1971): 24. Unless noted otherwise, the art-related items were published in the "What's New—and News—in Quilting" column.

47. This is the first instance that I know of quilt making being referred to as a "revived home *art*."

48. *Quilter's Newsletter Magazine* 7, no. 5 (1976): 16–17.

49. *Quilter's Newsletter Magazine* 7, no. 6 (1976), with pp. 23–25 giving instructions on how to make a batik quilt.

50. Michael James, "Color in Quilts," *Quilter's Newsletter Magazine* 8, no. 3 (1977): 16–17. First article in a three-part series.

51. I am extremely grateful to the staff of the ACC Library (then located in New York City), who facilitated my research there.

52. *Craft Horizons* was a prime resource for Patricia Malarcher as she prepared her presentation on surface design in contemporary quilts of the 1960s and 1970s for a panel organized by me for the 2008 annual conference of the College Art Association. In that same session, Michael James spoke about the history of the movement, and I presented a paper on politics and contemporary quilt art from 1960 to 1980. The title of the session was *The Evolution of Contemporary Quilt Art*, a voice recording of which was available at the time in a CD set of two disks (CA08-043) from the College Art Association, http://www.collegeart.org.

53. *Craft Horizons*, June 1966, 81.

54. *Craft Horizons*, June 1974, 33.

55. *Craft Horizons*, February 1977, 29.

56. Joan Schulze was among the many students who benefited from her workshops.

57. Ed Rossbach, "Trude Guermonprez, 1910–1976" [obituary], *Craft Horizons*, August 1976, 10. Black Mountain College runs like a refrain through the fiber art of the 1960s and 1970s, with several artists having studied there or having studied under teachers who were alumni.

58. See Nancy Bavor, "Common Threads: Nine California Art Quilt Pioneers," *Uncoverings* 33 (2021): 7–38.

59. February/March, 70.

60. April/May, 69.

61. June/July, 74.

62. October/November, 4 and 71, respectively.

63. August/September, 39.

64. *Craft Horizons*, August 1977, 65.

65. The quilts were from the collection of Mary Woodard, organizer of the Santa Fe Textile Workshops (pp. 8–9). The title of the magazine was changed in 2004 to *FiberARTS: Contemporary Textile Art and Craft*. The magazine went out of business in 2011, and its archives were donated to the Morgan Library and Museum in New York.

66. The 1979 *Fiberarts Equipment Directory* had thirty pages of looms and eleven pages of spinning wheels.

67. Amy Zaffarano Rowland, "Building on Experience: Virginia Jacobs' Fabric Constructions," *Fiberarts*, July/August 1980, 39–43. Interestingly, Jacobs mentioned that she listens to music while she works because it helps free her creativity. The same comment was made by most of the artists who responded to the survey concerning my research between 2008 and 2010.

68. This lecture was part of a quilt seminar at the Old Amherst Colony Museum Park (Amherst, New York), an annual event since the mid-1970s under the auspices of the Amherst Quilters Guild.

69. In 1987, Nancy Crow and Linda Fowler organized Art Quilt Network in Ohio. This group inspired spin-off organizations, such as Art Quilt Network / New York.

70. The National Quilter's Association was established in 1969, but the American Quilter's Society was not founded until 1985. Both these organizations focused on traditional quilters. The International Quilt Association, promoting all types of quilts, was founded in 1979 and closed in 2020.

71. Located in the San Francisco Bay Area.

72. Email to the author, March 14, 2008. Tafi Brown also mentioned the importance for her early quilts of "one fabric store in Peterborough, NH (Joseph's Coat), that had wonderful and unusual fabrics. The employees were well educated, extremely creative, gifted and supportive with diverse backgrounds. (One of them had taken one of Nancy Crow's workshops in the early '70s.) I make this notation because of the visual stimulation, collegiality and support of this place and its employees." This book does not attempt to analyze the effects of local fabric and quilt dealers on the development of contemporary quilt art between 1960 and the early 1980s. This is, however, a subject well worth investigating.

73. Phone interview in March 2008.

74. Email to the author, March 9, 2008.

75. For succinct information on textile art in and near San Francisco before 1960, see Jan Janeiro, "Before the '60s: The Early History of Bay Area Textiles," *Fiberarts*, January/February 1993, 32–35.

76. Louise O. Townsend, "What Was New and News in Quilting 1969 Through 1984," *Quilter's Newsletter Magazine*, Special 15th Anniversary Issue, 1984, 17.

77. See the timelines for "1960s–1970s: Emergence of the Movement," and "1980s: Art Quilts Go National in Publications and Exhibitions," in Sandra Sider, ed., with Nancy Bavor, Lisa Ellis, and Martha Sielman, *Art Quilts Unfolding: 50 Years of Innovation* (Atglen, PA: Schiffer, 2018), 14–17 and 74–74.

78. Alan Meisel, "Letter from San Francisco," *Craft Horizons* 26 (June 1966): 87–88.

79. Jonathan Holstein, *Abstract Design in American Quilts: A Biography of an Exhibition* [re-creation at the Louisville Museum of History and Science of the 1971 Whitney exhibition] (Louisville, KY: Kentucky Quilt Projector, 1991), 216–217. The original 1971 catalog has only sixteen pages, with seven illustrations. It is interesting to note that the 1971 exhibition and catalog were dedicated to Holstein and van der Hoof's friend, the abstract painter Barnett Newman (died 1970), who had encouraged them to exhibit the quilts in a museum in New York City. Quilts from the Holstein–van der Hoof collection were also exhibited in museums in Paris and Lausanne (1972), Bristol (1975), and Kyoto (1976).

80. Holstein, *Abstract Design in American Quilts*, 214.

81. Ibid., 21.

82. The International Quilt Museum, University of Nebraska–Lincoln, reprised the exhibition in 2021 to commemorate the event's fiftieth anniversary. The IQM now owns the quilt collection.

83. The combination of quilts and wood, ceramics, or glass was utilized in several exhibitions during the 1970s, such as the large-scale quilts of Susan Zucker and the "architectural" wooden structures of David Durst, shown together at the Hudson River Museum in 1979.

84. Nancy Halpern, *Northern Comfort: Three Hundred and Fifty Years of New England Quilts* (unpublished manuscript, completed in 1983), chapter IX, 11.

85. On July 4, 1976, the author was in New York City, sewing the binding on a traditional *Moon over the Mountain* Bicentennial quilt created for a friend who lived in the city. That commission resulted in the opportunity to view *The New American Quilt*.

86. Phone interview of May 27, 2008.

87. Halpern, *Northern Comfort*, chapter IX, 12.

88. Erica Wilson, *Erica Wilson's Quilts of America* (Birmingham, AL: Oxmoor House, 1979), 1.

89. Amanda Sikarsie, "Erica Wilson and the Quilt Revival," *Uncoverings* 36 (2015): 95–96.

90. Lisa Hammel, "Quilts: A Folk Idiom That Has Come of Age," *New York Times*, April 9, 1976, http://www.newyorktimes.com.

91. Jean Libman Block, "A Quilt Is Built," *Craft Horizons* 36 (April 1976): 31.

92. N. F. Karlins, "New & Newer Quilts," *Quilter's Newsletter Magazine* 7 (August 1976): 19–21.

93. Gayle Pritchard, *Uncommon Threads: Ohio's Art Quilt Revolution* (Athens: Ohio University Press, 2006), 11. This excellent book is a fount of information about the contemporary quilt art movement in Ohio.

94. Email from Karey Bresenhan to the author, July 8, 2008: "The first special exhibit at Festival to feature art quilts was the 1984 exhibit "New Directions for an American Tradition," which was the Quilt National 1983 touring exhibit. All of the brochures prior to 1984 mention antique/traditional quilt exhibits only." As for the International Quilting Association exhibitions, she recalls that in 1982, a quilt by Katie Pasquini Masopust won Best of Show, which may have been the first time that a studio quilt was awarded that honor..

95. David L. Shirey, "A Bright New Wrinkle for Quilts," *New York Times*, (February 27, 1977; accessed online in the newspaper's archives, http://www.newyorktimes.com.

96. Glen Kaufman, "Fiber," in "Young Americans: Fiber/Wood/Plastic/Leather," *Craft Horizons* 37 (June 1977): 15, 69–70.

97. There unfortunately was no published catalog. The jurors were Michael James (a quilt artist), Gary Schwindler (an art history professor), and Renee Steidle (a gallery owner).

98. Beth Gutcheon, "Quilt National '79," *Fiberarts*, September/October 1979, 80.

99. Gutcheon, "Quilt National '79," 80.

100. Pritchard, *Uncommon Threads*, 48.

101. Pattie Chase, "Radka Donnell: Patchwork Quilts," *Fiberarts*, September/October 1980, 76–77.

Chapter 3

1. Terry McDonald and Melanie Methot, "That Impulse That Bids a People to Honour Its Past: The Nature and Purpose of Centennial Celebrations," *International Journal of Heritage Studies* 12, no. 4 (July 2006): 308–309.

2. Anne Dawson, "The 1876 Centennial Quilt Project," *Quiltfolk* 32, *State of Washington* (2024), 142. Entire article: 142–147.

3. The Houston exhibition can be viewed online on YouTube: https://www.youtube.com/watch?v=ssny-unntOY.

4. Her quilt is in the Smithsonian American Art Museum.

5. His painting *Unveiling the Statue of Liberty Enlightening the World* is in the Museum of the City of New York.

6. Robert Bishop and Carter Houck, *All Flags Flying: American*

Patriotic Quilts as Expressions of Liberty (New York: E. P. Dutton in association with the Museum of American Folk Art, 1986), 2–3.

7. For a more complete analysis of problematic aspects of this contest within American quilt culture, see Jane Przybysz, "Competing Cultural Values at the Great American Quilt Festival," *Uncoverings* 8 (1987): 107–127.
8. Tammy S. Gordon, *The Spirit of 1976: Commerce, Community, and the Politics of Commemoration* (Amherst and Boston: University of Massachusetts Press, 2013), 134.
9. Phone conversation with her daughter Diane H. Waanders on November 27, 2024, plus subsequent texts and emails about the project. Waanders supplied the quilt photo taken at the Topeka–Shawnee County Library.
10. Email to the author dated October 28, 2024.
11. Catalog ID: 2020.12.1.
12. Nancyann Johanson Twelker, *Women and Their Quilts: A Washington State Centennial Tribute* (Bothell, WA: That Patchwork Place, 1988), with a foreword by Carter Houck.
13. Ibid., 20.
14. Carolyn O'Bagy Davis and Helen Young Frost, eds., *100 Years—100 Quilts: Arizona Centennial Quilt Project* (Tucson: Arizona Historical Society, 2012).
15. Ibid., 101.
16. *Grand Central Terminal Centennial Quilt Challenge* (New York: City Quilters, 2014), exhibition catalog, 1. I am grateful to Teresa Barkley for gifting me her extra copy of the booklet. She had a quilt in the exhibition.
17. Walker Rumble, "Gutzon Borglum: Mount Rushmore and the American Tradition," *Pacific Northwest Quarterly* 59, no. 3 (July 1968): 121.
18. Artist's statement accompanying the quilt.
19. Joy William, ed., *Indiana Bicentennial Barn Quilt* (Indianapolis, IN: Indiana Barn Foundation, 2016), 1.
20. Ibid., 33.
21. Sandra Sider and Pamela Weeks, *"Deeds Not Words": Celebrating 100 Years of Women's Suffrage* (Atglen, PA: Schiffer, 2020).
22. The quilt is on permanent display in the organization's office at 3848 S. Junett Street, Tacoma, Washington, 98509.

Conclusion

1. Gail Kenning, "Creative Craft-Based Textile Activity in the Age of Digital Systems and Practices," *Leonardo* 48, no. 5 (2015): 455.
2. Abby Glassenberg, "The Size of the Quilting Market: Quilting Trends Survey Results, 2024," accessed online: https://craftindustryalliance.org/the-size-of-the-quilting-market-quilting-trends-survey-results-2024/.
3. Hayden Lees Cubas, *From Revival to Reinvention: Quilting in America, 1971–2023* (master of arts qualifying paper for the Fashion Institute of Technology, SUNY, 2023), 52.
4. Tammy S. Gordon, *The Spirit of 1976: Commerce, Community, and the Politics of Commemoration* (Amherst and Boston: University of Massachusetts Press, 2013), 148.
5. Richard H. Pildes, "Why the Center Does Not Hold: The Causes of Hyperpolarized Democracy in America," *Columbia Law Review* 99, no. 2 (April 2011): 273–333.

Bibliography

Beebe, William B. *Intimate Parallels: The Art, History, and Activism of Civil War–Era Women's Quilt Art.* Harvard University ProQuest Dissertations and Theses, 2016.

Beyer, Jinny. *Patchwork Patterns.* McLean, VA: EPM Publications, 1979.

Bishop, Robert, and Carter Houck. *All Flags Flying: American Patriotic Quilts as Expressions of Liberty.* New York: E. P. Dutton in association with the Museum of American Folk Art, 1986.

Brackman, Barbara. "Quilts at Chicago's World's Fairs." *Uncoverings* 2 (1981): 63–75.

Brick, Cindy. *Crazy Quilts: History, Techniques, Embroidery Motifs.* St. Paul, MN: Voyageur, 2008.

Brittain, Judy, ed. *Vogue Guide to Patchwork and Quilting.* New York: Galahad Books, 1973.

Brown, Elsa. *Creative Quilting.* New York: Watson-Guptill, 1975.

Collins, Herbert Ridgeway. *Threads of History: Americana Recorded on Cloth 1775 to the Present.* Washington, DC: Smithsonian Institution Press, 1979.

Davis, Carolyn O'Bagy, and Helen Young Frost, eds. *100 Years ~ 100 Quilts: Arizona Centennial Quilt Project.* Tucson: Arizona Historical Society, 2012.

Dawson, Anne. "The 1876 Centennial Quilt Project." *Quiltfolk* 32, *State of Washington* (2024): 142–147.

Elliott, Maud Howe. *Art and Handicraft in the Woman's Building of the World's Columbian Exposition, Chicago, 1893.* Paris and New York: Goupil, 1893.

Ferrero, Pat, Elaine Hedges, and Julie Silber. *Hearts and Hands: The Influence of Women & Quilts on American Society.* San Francisco: Quilt Digest, 1987.

Gillespie, Mrs. E. D. *A Book of Remembrance.* Philadelphia and London: J. B. Lippincott, 1901.

Gordon, Beverly. "Crazy Quilts as an Expression of 'Fairyland.'" *Uncoverings 27 (2006)*: 29–58.

Gordon, Tammy S. *The Spirit of 1976: Commerce, Community, and the Politics of Commemoration.* Amherst and Boston: University of Massachusetts Press, 2013.

Grand Central Terminal Centennial Quilt Challenge. New York: City Quilters, 2014.

Gross, Joyce R. "Bertha Stenge." *Quilters' Journal* 2 (Summer 1979): 1–5, 7.

Gutcheon, Beth. *The Perfect Patchwork Primer.* Baltimore: Penguin Books, 1973.

Hanson, Marin F. "Modern, Yet Anti-Modern: Two Sides of Late-Nineteenth- and Early-Twentieth-Century Quiltmaking," *Uncoverings* 29 (2008): 105–135.

Heard, Audrey, and Beverly Prior. *The Complete Guide to Quilting.* Des Moines, IA: Creative Home Library in association with Better Homes and Gardens, 1974.

Holstein, Jonathan. *Abstract Design in American Quilts: A Biography of an Exhibition* [re-creation at the Louisville Museum of History and Science of the 1971 Whitney exhibition]. Louisville, KY: Kentucky Quilt Projector, 1991.

Home Efficiency Club. *The Bicentennial Quilt of Springfield, Vermont* (ca. 1977). Photos by Bernie Lashua, printed by Joseph A. Dellamano.

Index of Bicentennial Activities: Titles of Projects and Events, Listed by City and State. Washington, DC: American Revolution Bicentennial Administration, February 1976.

Ingram, J. S. *The Centennial Exposition, Described and Illustrated.* Philadelphia: Hubbard Bros., 1876.

International Exhibition 1876 Official Catalogue. Part 1, Main Building and Annexes. Philadelphia: John R. Nagle, 1876.

James, Michael. "Color in Quilts." *Quilter's Newsletter Magazine* 8, no. 3 (1977): 16–17.

James, Michael. *The Quilt Maker's Handbook.* Mountain View, CA: Leone, 1993 (reprint).

Karlins, N. F. "New & Newer Quilts." *Quilter's Newsletter Magazine* 7, no. 8 (August 1976): 19–21.

Laury, Jean Ray. *Applique Stitchery.* New York: Van Nostrand Reinhold, 1966.

McDonald, Terry, and Melanie Methot. "That Impulse That Bids a People to Honour Its Past: The Nature and Purpose of Centennial Celebrations." *International Journal of Heritage Studies* 12, no. 4 (July 2006): 307–320.

McMorris, Penny. *Crazy Quilts.* New York: E. P. Dutton, 1984.

Newman, Thelma R. *Quilting, Patchwork, Appliqué, and Trapunto: Traditional Methods and Original Designs.* New York: Crown, 1974.

Norton, Frank, ed. *Frank Leslie's Illustrated Historical Register of the Centennial Exhibition.* New York: Frank Leslie's Publishing House, 1877.

Pfeffer, Mike. *Southern Ladies and Suffragists: Julia Ward Howe and Women's Rights at the 1884 New Orleans World's Fair.* Jackson: University Press of Mississippi, 2014.

Pritchard, Gayle. *Uncommon Threads: Ohio's Art Quilt Revolution.* Athens: Ohio University Press, 2006.

Przybysz, Jane. "Competing Cultural Values at the Great American Quilt Festival." *Uncoverings* 8 (1987): 107–127.

Rehnquist, William H. *Centennial Crisis: The Disputed Election of 1876.* New York: Vintage Books, 2004.

Reich, Sue. *Quilts Presidential and Patriotic.* Atglen, PA: Schiffer, 2016.

Reich, Sue. *"Quilting News of Yesteryear": 1000 Pieces and Counting.* Atglen, PA: Schiffer, 2007.

Reich, Sue. *World War II Quilts.* Atglen, PA: Schiffer, 2010.

Rowland, Amy Zaffarano. "Building on Experience: Virginia Jacobs' Fabric Constructions." *Fiberarts,* July/August 1980, 39–43.

Rydell, Robert W., John E. Findling, and Kimberly D. Page. *Fair America: World's Fairs in the United States.* Washington, DC, and New York: Smithsonian Books, 2000.

Shaw, Robert. *American Quilts: The Democratic Art, 1780–2007.* New York and London: Sterling, 2009.

Shaw, Robert. *The Art Quilt.* Hugh Lauter Levin Associates, 1997.

Sider, Sandra, ed., with Nancy Bavor, Lisa Ellis, and Martha Sielman. *Art Quilts Unfolding: 50 Years of Innovation.* Atglen, PA: Schiffer, 2018.

Sikarsie, Amanda. "Erica Wilson and the Quilt Revival." *Uncoverings* 36 (2015): 93–114.

Smith, Walter. *The Masterpieces of the Centennial Exhibition Illustrated. Vol. 2.* Philadelphia: Gebbie & Barrie, ca. 1876.

Thomas, Jesse O. *Negro Participation in the Texas Centennial Exposition.* Boston: Christopher, 1938.

Twelker, Nancyann Johanson. *Women and Their Quilts: A Washington State Centennial Tribute.* Bothell, WA: That Patchwork Place, 1988.

Waldvogel, Merikay, and Barbara Brackman. *Patchwork Souvenirs of the 1933 World's Fair.* Nashville: Rutledge Hill, 1993.

Weiss, Hillary. *The American Bandanna: Culture on Cloth from George Washington to Elvis.* San Francisco: Chronicle Books, 1990.

Wheeler, Candace. "Applied Arts in the Woman's Building." In *Art and Handicraft in the Woman's Building of the World's Columbian Exposition.* Edited by Maud Howe Elliott, 79–88. Chicago and New York: Rand, McNally, 1894.

Wheeler, Candace. *The Development of Embroidery in America.* New York and London: Harper & Brothers, 1921.

Willard, Frances E. *Glimpses of Fifty Years: The Autobiography of an American Woman.* Chicago: Woman's Temperance Publication Association and H. J. Smith, 1889.

William, Joy, ed. *Indiana Bicentennial Barn Quilt.* Indianapolis, IN: Indiana Barn Foundation, 2016.

Williams, Mary Rose. "*A Re-Conceptualization of Protest Rhetoric: Characteristics of Quilts as Protest.*" PhD diss., University of Oregon, 1990.

Wilson, Erica. *Erica Wilson's Quilts of America.* Birmingham, AL: Oxmoor House, 1979.

Wooster, Ann-Sargent. *Quilt Making: The Modern Approach to a Traditional Craft.* New York: Drake, 1972.

Yearous, Jenny. "Stitches in Time: The Development of Sewing Thread in the Nineteenth Century and Beyond." *Uncoverings* 19 (1998): 155–178.

Young Yu, Connie. *The People's BiCentennial Quilt: A Patchwork History.* East Palo Alto, CA: Up Press, 1976.

Index

Page numbers in italics refer to images.

ABC. *See* Afro-American Bicentennial Corporation
Abstract Design in American Quilts, 193
ACC. *See* American Craft Council
African Americans, 9–11, 96, 101–11, 118, 142, 169–70, 219, 223
  and 1876 Centennial, 28–31
  Nineteenth Amendment centennial, 225–26
  and *People's BiCentennial Quilt*, 170–72
  and Tulsa Race Massacre centennial, 226
  at World's Columbian Fair (1893), 97–99
African Beauty (Quilt), 96
African Methodist Episcopal Church (AME), 29
Afro-American Bicentennial Corporation (ABC), 141
Afro-American Heritage Bicentennial Commemorative Quilt, The, 148, *149*
Agricultural Society, 9
AIM. *See* American Indian Movement
Airplane Quilt, *132*
Alaska State Fair, *144*
album quilts
  American history as seen on quilts, 153–61
  group projects, 145–51
  individual makers, 151–61
All American Signature Quilt, The, *173*
Allen, Richard, 28
alphabet quilt, 123
Alphabet Quilt, *122*
Amarillo Tri-State Fair, 139
AME. *See* African Methodist Episcopal Church
America, unifying, 22–24
Americana (as seen on quilts), 153–61
American Craft, 99, 188, 197
American Craft Council (ACC), 192, 199
American history (as seen on quilts), 153–61
American Indian Movement (AIM), 118, 141
American Patchwork & Quilting magazine, 217
American Red Cross, 130–31, 135, 138, 139, 151
American Revolution, 142, 207, 231
American Revolution Bicentennial Administration (ARBA), 142, 144
American Revolution Bicentennial Commission, 140
America Through the Needle's Eye, 112
"America Welcomes the World" (poster), *107*
Amnesty Act, 31
Anchorage, Alaska, centennial quilt, 221
Anthony, Susan B., 26, 129–30
Applegate Trail, 157
Applegate Wagon Train, 157
appliqué, 46, 65, 77, 142, 151, 162, 182, 186, 191–94, 196
ARBA. *See* American Revolution Bicentennial Administration
Arizona Centennial Commemorative Quilt, 215–17, *216*
Arizona Centennial Quilt Project, 215–17
Artex Bicentennial quilts, 154
Artex Hobby Products, 153–54, 157
Ashland, Kansas, railroad centennial in, 205
Ashland Railroad Centennial Quilt, *204, 205*
Ashley, Laura, 202, 205, 208
asymmetrical patterning, 71

Baker, M., 64
bandana (as souvenir), *23, 24, 27, 44, 116*
Barkley, Teresa, 117, 153, 197, 206
Barton, Clara, 130
Barton, Mary Pemble, 154, *159*
Battle of the Little Bighorn, 22
Bed and Board, 194
Beebe, William B., 18
Belitz, Larry, 129
Bell, Graham, 29
Benner, Sue, *182*, 185
Bearden, Romare, 182
Better Living in The World of Tomorrow, 112
Beyer, Jinny, 180, 211
Bicentennial Applegate Trail / Applegate Wagon Train Quilt, 157, *160, 161*
Bicentennial Bride's Quilt, 153, *155*
Bicentennial Cook Book, 145
Bicentennial Heritage Quilt, 154, *159*
Bicentennial Quilt, 151, *153, 156*
Bicentennial Quilt of Springfield, Vermont, The, *148*
Bicentennial Star Quilt, *141*, 142
Bicentennial Wagon Train Pilgrimage, 161
Birthplace Centennial Quilt, 219, *220*
Bister, Donna, 170
Bitar, Helen, 182, 188, 193, 197
Black Hawk War, 107
Blackhorse, Rebecca, 124, *126*
Black people. *See* African Americans
Blair, Henry, 29
Bloomer: Advocating a Change, *224*
Blues, *192*
Boalt, Gladys C., 147
Bonaparte, Napoleon, 104
Bonfoey, Beverly H., 102
bookmark (as souvenir), *6, 94*
Book of Remembrance, *54*
books
  creating original quilt designs, 180–86
  quilt making and, 176–78
Booth, Mary Louise, 96
Borish, Linda, 59
Borkowski, Mary, 139, 157, 161, 187
Boston Tea Party, 54, 154
Boyd, Henry, 29
Brackman, Barbara, 66, 99, 107
Bradbury, John, 37
Breyer, Jinny, 196
Brick, Cindy, 77
Brockett, Linus Pierpont, 86
Brother Jonathan (character), *21*
Brown, Eliza Kay, 182, 208
Brown, Isa, *181*
Brown, Solomon, 29
Brown, Tafi, 188, 191, 192, 197, 199
Bruno, Emily, 225

Cabot, Nancy, 109
Calaveras County Bicentennial Quilt, 145, *146*
California, *191*
California, sesquicentennial of, 213–15
California Sesquincentennial Quilt, 213, *214, 215*
California Silk Center Association, 85
Carlisle, Dr. Sylvia Gates, 148
Carney, Beth, 217
Carpenter, Anna E., 102
Carswell, Mary E., 6, 8
Carswell, N. W., 66
Carter, Jimmy, 151
Castine, Maine, bicentennial, 212
Castine Community Bicentennial Quilt, *211, 212–13*
categories (of quilts), 37–41, 46
Centennial bandanas, *45*, 165
centennial calico, 38
Centennial Center Medallion Eagle, *42*
Centennial Commission, 24, 28. *See also* US Centennial
Centennial Exhibition. *See also* US Centennial
Centennial Exposition, Described and Illustrated, The, *25–26, 32*

Centennial Quilt, 18, *19, 20,* 21
"Centennial" quilt, defining, 37–38
centennial stock certificate, *53*
Century 21 Exposition, 112–14
Century of Progress (1933), 107–9
charm quilts, 58–59
Chasms 16: Under the Stars, *217*
Chatterton, Pauline, 185
cheater cloth, 34
Chicago, Illinois. *See* Century of Progress (1933); World's Columbian Fair (1893)
Chicago Historical Society, 99
Chicago World's Fair, 39, 40, 111
Chill, Janet, 179
Christopher Columbus Quincentennial Jubilee Commission, 208–11
Churchill, Winston, 138
Civil Rights Act, 117
Civil War, 22, 94, 130
classes
  creating original quilt designs, 191–93
  quilt making and, 179–80
cloth, patriotic imagery on, 37
Cocheco Manufacturing Company, 35
Cocheco Print Works, 82
Colby, Averil, 177–78, 185
Collord, Myrtle Louise Black, 114
colonialism, national mood of, 21–22
Colorado Centennial Quilt, *152,* 153
Colored Ladies Centennial Association, 96
Colored People's Department. *See* World's Industrial and Cotton Centennial Exposition (1884)
color scheme (of Bicentennial quilts), 162–70
Columbian Quincentennial bandana, *210*
Columbus, Christopher, *98*
  quincentennial jubilee, 208–11
  World's Columbian Fair (1893), 97–99
Columbus Quilt, 211
"combination" quilt, 65
Comer, Bobby, 147
Commemorative of Our Nation's Bicentennial, 145
community, term, 145
Concord/Fairfield Processing Fashion Show, 193
Confederacy, 18, 22, 104, 217, 219
Content, Judith, 199
contests. *See entries by name*
Cook, Clarence, 81
cookbooks, 54–55, 145, *146*
Cooke, Rose Terry, 89, 93
Coolidge, Calvin, 49, 121
Cooper, Kym, *226*
Cornucopia (quilt), *113*
Cotton Centennial (1884). *See* World's Industrial and Cotton Centennial Exposition
Cotton States and International Exposition, Atlanta (1895), 94
Counts, Charles, 177, 182
Counts, Rubynelle, 188
Cox, Sam, 135
Craft Horizons, 99, 188, 197
Crane, Walter, 72, 75
crazy, term, 71. *See also* crazy quilts
Crazy Quilt, *68–70*
Crazy Quilt (Fligelman), *90–91*
Crazy Quilt (New England), *76*
Crazy Quilt of Good Eating, 145
crazy quilts, 37
  appeal of, 65–66
  fairyland imagery, 89–91
  within Gilded Age society, 91–93
  Gilded Age style of, 71–72
  Japanese style, 78–82
  in New York City, 66
  other possible inspirations for, 82–85
  overview of, 68–71
  patterns for, 77–78
  perception of, 66
  Royal School of Art Needlework, 72–77
  silk industry and, 85–88
  as "textile scrapbooks," 75, 77
Crazy Quilt with Animals, *78*
crescent moon and star, crazy quilt block with, *92*
Crosby, W. E., 65–66
Crosby's Dime Museum, 65–66
Crow, Nancy, 188
Crow Quilt, *187*
Crusade Mystery Quilt, 60–61
Cusack, Margaret, 183
Custer, George Armstrong, 22
Cyr, Stephanie, 182

Dallas, Texas. *See* Texas Centennial (1936)
Dallas Exposition. *See* Texas Centennial (1936)
dates, depicting on quilts, 14, *17,* 46
Davis, Garrett, 64
Davis, Jefferson, 18
Davis, Lenore, 182, 197
Davis, Varina Howell, 18
Davis Stars, quilt, 18
Death of Cleopatra, 29
Declaration of Independence, 2, 11, 34, 154
  commemorating, 37–38
  quilts containing text of, 37
  reading during Centennial celebration, 28
  as souvenir bandana, *27*
Declaration of Sentiments, 119
"Declaration of the Rights of Women," 26
Democrat campaign handkerchief, *121*
"dime" museums, 65–66
Dommelen, David van, 186
Donnell, Radka, 188, 194, 197, 199
Dorcas Sunday School Class, 135
Douglass, Frederick, 14, 148
Drunkard's Path, 61
Dudley, Mary Birch, 64
Dwight D. Eisenhower Library & Museum, 123

Edison, Thomas, 29
Edmonds, Chris, 193
1876 Centennial Quilt, The, 200, *201*
1864 Maryland Sesquicentennial Slave Emancipation Proclamation Quilt, 217–19, *218*
Einstein, Sylvia, 194
Eisenhower, Dwight E., 123
Emancipation Proclamation, 28
Emancipation Proclamation sesquicentennial, 217–19
embroidery, 10, 31, 49, 56, 58, 63, 65–66, 68, 71, 74–75, 77–77, 81, 98–99, 101, 105, 120, 151, 185
Erica Wilson's Quilts of America, 196
Erickson, Nancy, 196
Estrada, William, 215
Exeter Bicentennial Quilt, 147
exhibitions. *See also* US Centennial
  Century 21 Exposition, 112–14
  Century of Progress, 107–9
  Jamestown Ter-Centennial Exposition (1907), 104–5
  Louisiana Purchase Exposition, 101–4
  New York World's Fair (1939–40), 111–12
  New York World's Fair (1964–65), 114–15
  San Antonio World's Fair (1968), 115–17
  Sesquicentennial International Exposition, 106–7
  Tennessee Centennial and International Exposition, 100–101
  Texas Centennial (1936), 109–11
  World's Columbian Fair (1893), 97–99
  World's Industrial and Cotton Centennial Exposition (1884), 94–97

Fairmount Park, 52
Fairy at School, A, 89
fairyland, imagery of, 89–91
feed-sack fabric, *122*
Ferrero, Pat, 31
Festival USA, 140–42
Fiberarts magazine, 191, 199
Fiberworks Center for the Textile Arts, 193
Fifteenth Amendment, 21, 31
Filipino Forum, 114
Filipino Pavilion. *See* Century 21 Exposition
First Annual Western Craft Competition, 193
First Nations. *See* Native Americans
Fisk Jubilee Singers, 105
Flag Quilt, *102*
Fligelman, Minnie Weinzweig, 88, *90–91*
Fons, Marianne, 202
Ford, Gerald, 2, 161
Fourteenth Amendment, 21
Fraas, Gayle, 187, 197
Fraley Quilting Attachment, 66
Frances, David R., 102
Franklin, Benjamin, 153
Franklin, Deborah and Benjamin, 52
Freed Slave, The, 29, *30*
Frentz, Margaret E., 17
From 1833 to 1933 (quilt), *110*

funding (for US Centennial), 54–55
fundraising, raffles for, 65
fundraising banner, honoring Theodore Roosevelt with, 47–49

Gaither, Joan M. E., 217–19
Gallup, George, 172
Gates, Jeannette McPherson, 148
General Federation of Women's Clubs, 139
Gentry, Caryl Bryer Fallert, 191
George Washington Bicentennial Commission, 49–50
George Washington Bi-Centennial Quilt, 51
George Washington Quilt, 15
Gerald R. Ford Presidential Museum, 161
Gilbert, W. S., 82
Gilded Age, 68, 71–72, 91–93
Gillespie, Elizabeth Duane, 52–53, 58
Glenn, John, 139, 223
Glimpses of Fifty Years, 60
Godey's Lady's Book, 25, 54
Good Housekeeping magazine, 107, 112
Gordon, Beverly, 89
Gordon, Tammy, 141–42, 202
Grand Army of the Republic Quilt, 7, 8
Grand Central Terminal centennial, 217
Grant, Ulysses S., 22, 119, 147
Great American Quilt Festival, 202
Great Britain, 9, 11, 22, 85, 132
Great Depression, 109, 122
Great Exhibition of 1851, 9
Great Quilt Contest, 153, 194
Great Seal of the United States, 135
Gross, Joyce, 179, 194
Guermonprez, Trude, 188
Guracar, Genevieve, *174*
Gutcheon, Beth, *178,* 179, 180, 183, 187, 193, 197, 199

"Hail, Columbia!" (song), 46
Hall, Carolyn Vosburg, 186
Hall, Carrie A., 50
Halpern, Nancy, *187,* 188
Hampton Normal and Industrial Institute, 105
Hampton Roads. *See* Jamestown Ter-Centennial Exposition (1907)
Hanson, Marin, 78
Harding, Warren G., 120–21
Harding Jacquard Wool Blanket, 121
Harper's Bazar, 75, 96
Harper's Weekly, 37
Harris, Miranda, 225
Harrison, Benjamin, 46–47
Harry S. Truman Presidential Library & Museum, 123
Heard, Audrey, 183
Hedges, Elaine, 31, 91
Heinisch, Margarete, 215
Heller, Elsie G., 112
Henry, Patrick, 154
Heritage '76, 140–42
Hesse, Eva, 182

Hirschberg, Jeanne, 205–6, 207
historical context (of quilt culture)
- African Americans, 24–28
- celebrating US presidency, 46–50
- Indigenous fiasco, 21–22
- overview, 14–19
- quilts exhibited at Centennial, 35–46
- special days/buildings, 24–28
- textile industry, 31–35
- unifying America, 22–24

Hoffman, Susan, 183, 185
Holstein, Jonathan, 193–94
Home Magazine, 88
Honstain, Lucinda Ward, 18
Hood, Sarah, 223
Hoof, Gail van der, 193–94
Hoosier Suffrage Quilt, 120, *132*
Hoover, Herbert, 49, 121, 219
Hopewell Bicentennial Quilt, 157
Horizons '76, 140–42
Hortense Beck, *126*
Houck, Carter, 179
Houston, Sam, 115
Howard, Constance, 192
Howe, Julia Ward, 97
Humber, Mary Lou, 147
Huxley, Aldous, 183

IBM, 117
Ickis, Marguerite, 176
ideas/patterns (of Bicentennial quilts), sources of
- Bicentennial boost for quilts, 172–75
- group projects. *See* album quilts
- individual makers. *See* album quilts
- overview, 144–45
- *People's BiCentennial Quilt,* 170–72
- presidential quilts, 161–62
- red, white, and blue color scheme, 162–70

Illinois State Fair, 145
Independence Hall Quilters, 145, 147
Index of Bicentennial Activities, 11–12, 144
Indiana Bicentennial Barn Quilt, 221–23, *222*
Indian Reorganization Act, 125
Indian Self-Determination and Education Act of 1975, 118
Indigenous people. *See* Native Americans
Indigo Trapunto Quilt, 43
industries
- silk, 85–88
- textile, 31–35

Ingalls, J. F., 77
Ingram, J. S., *25*, 32
"International Exhibition 1876" (bandana), 38
International Temperance Conference, 10, 59–61

J. L. Simpson & Co., 66
Jacksonville Museum Quilters, 157, 161
Jacobs, Virginia, 191

James, Michael, 177, 181, 183, 185, 193
Jamestown Ter-Centennial Exposition (1907), 104–5
Japanese lacquerware, *81*
Japanese style (of crazy quilts), popularity of, 78–82
Jefferson, Thomas, 104
Joel Ellis Doll, 151
Johnson, Lyndon, 123
Johnson, Minnie, 120
Jones, John Paul, 154

Kansas State Fair, 139
Karasz, Mariska, 185–86
Keckley, Elizabeth, 28
Kelly, William D., 28
Kennedy, John F., 112, 123, *125*
Kensington Embroidery and the Colors of Flowers, 77
King, Martin Luther, Jr., 118, 148
Klein, Jody, 188
Knappenberger, Gertrude, 18
Knodel, Gerhardt, 179
Koeneke, Irene, 139
Korean War, 139
Kraak, Deborah, 34
Kratovil, Debby, *211*
Ku Klux Klan, 31
Kuthe, Mina K., 172

Ladies Society of the First Presbyterian Church, 47, 49
Lady Liberty Medallion Quilt, The, 203
Lady's Circle Patchwork Quilts, 151, 179
Lakota Sioux "Bicentennial" Quilt, 129
Langley, Tara, 221
Larson, Ed, 192
Latimer, Lewis, 29
Laura, Jean, 180
Laura Ashley Washington State Pictorial Quilt, 208, *209*
Laury, Jean Ray, 186–87, 197
lectures
- creating original quilt designs, 191–93
- quilt making and, 179–80

Leonhard, Emma Mae, *110*
Lesch, Alma, 180
Leslie, Frank, *32, 35,* 78
Lewis, Edmonia, 29
Liberty, term, 28
Liberty Bell, 14, *17, 107,* 140, 142, 161
Liberty Star Quilt, 132
Lincoln, Mary Todd, 28
Lincoln Flag Commemorative Quilt, 16
Lintault, Joan, 177, 182, 193
Lipsanen, Martha, 151
Log Cabin quilts, 64, 66
Louisiana Purchase Exposition, 101–4
Lowell Crazy Quilt, 39
Lutheran Community Services, centennial of, 227
Lutheran Community Services Northwest (quilt), *227*

Lyman, Marie, 179, 188

MacDonald, Linda, 192–93
Machinery Hall (US Centennial), 37, 86
magazines. *See entries by title*
Main Building (1876 Exhibition), 38, 53, 55–56, 74, 86, *95,* 96, 104
Malarcher, Patricia, 188
Mangat, Terrie Hancock, 180, 199
Manifest Destiny, 21–22
Marion, Rose, 102
Martha Washington, 40
Marvin, Florence Elizabeth, 78
Mary, Queen of Scots, 65, 99
Mary Strickland Quilts, 140
Mary Todd Lincoln Quilt, 28
Masonic Temple, 66
Masopust, Pasquini, 183, 199
May, Ann Baldwin, 172
May, Therese, 194
McCabe, H. C., 60
McCall Pattern Company, 179
McCrae, John, 131
McFarland, Nancy, 227
McKim, Ruby Short, 106, 176
McKinley, William, 100
McMorris, Penny, 197
McUne, George, 157
Memorial Hall (1876 Exhibition), 28–29, 38, *44*
Merced Express, 62
Midsummer Night's Dream, A (Shakespeare), 89, 91
Mikado motifs, 82, *83, 84*
Miller, Charles, 120
Miller, Joaquin, 17
Miracle, Cindy, 188
Mitchell, Eugenia, 151, 153
Montana Historical Society, 88
Moran, Edward, 202
Morris, Della May, 154, *158*
Moses, Robert, 111
moth, crazy quilt block with, *92*
Mountain Heirloom Quilt Faire, 147
Mountain in the Morning, 189
Mountain Mist, 141–42, 151, 162
Mount Rushmore National Memorial, 219
Ms. magazine, 142, 144
Mueller, Marie, 112
multitudinous quilts, 58–59
Mumford, John C., 63

Nadelstern, Paula, 177
NAMES Project AIDS Memorial Quilt, 8
Nashville, Tennessee. *See* Tennessee Centennial and International Exposition
National Association of Certified Quilt Judges, 153
National Bicentennial Quilt Contest, 144
national parks, centennial for, 219–21
National Quilting Association (NQA), 153
National Recovery Act, 122
National Woman Suffrage Association, 26
Native Americans, 47, 154, 157
  Anchorage, Alaska, centennial quilt, 221
  Arizona Centennial, 215–17
  Bicentennial ambivalence, 125–29
  Day of Rage, 148
  fiasco involving, 21–22
  and Jamestown Ter-Centennial Exposition (1907), 104–5
  and national parks centennial, 219–21
  Nineteenth Amendment centennial, 225–26
  Tuscaloosa, Alabama, bicentennial, 225
Nauman, Bruce, 188
Negro Building, 11, 94
  Jamestown Ter-Centennial Exposition (1907), 105
  Sesquicentennial International Exposition, *106,* 106–7
  Tennessee Centennial and International Exposition, *100,* 101
  Texas Centennial (1936), 109–11
New American Quilt, The, 194, 196–97, 199
Newman, Thelma R., *181,* 182
New Orleans, Louisiana. *See* World's Industrial and Cotton Centennial Exposition (1884)
newspapers, quilts in, 61–66
New World, celebrating discovery of. *See* World's Columbian Fair (1893)
New York City
  Grand Central Terminal centennial, 217
  Statue of Liberty centennial, 202–5
  World's Fair (1939–40), 111–12
  World's Fair (1964–65), 111–12
New York Dry Goods Company, 88
New York State Fair, 9
New York World's Fair (1939–40), 94, 111–12
New York World's Fair (1964–65), 114–15, 202
Nicholson, Eliza, 96
Nicolella, Jennifer, 223, *223*
1976, preparing for, 140
Nineteenth Amendment, 106, 130
Nineteenth Amendment centennial, 225–26
Nixon, Richard, 118, 123, 161
North, Tamar Horton Harris, 71
North Dakota Centennial Quilt, 1889–1989, 147
NQA. *See* National Quilting Association

Ohio Patchwork, 197
Ohio State Fair, 139
Oklahoma State Fair, 139
Old Oregon Trail, 121
Oregon Historical Society, 148
"Oriental" motifs, 78–82
Ornamental Stitches, 78
Orr, Anne, 106–7
Osage County Fair, 64

Pacific Mills, *34,* 58
Pajaro Valley Quilt Association, 151
Palace of Liberal Arts, *102*
Paris Silk Agency, *88*
Patrick, Mary Fay, 215
Patriotic Banner, 49
patriotic quilts
  after world wars, 139
  overview, 118–19
  Native Americans and, 125–29
  preparing for 1976, 140–42
  presidential quilts, 119–25
  World War I, 130–32
  World War II, 132–38
  women and, 129–30
Patriotic Yo-Yo Quilt, 137
patriotism, 6, 9, 17, 22, 25, 46, 49, 55–56, 88, 119, 122, 125, 129–30
Paul, Alice, *131*
PBC. *See* People's Bicentennial Committee
Peninsula Stitchery Guild, 192
Pennell, Peg, 219, 221
Penn's Treaty with the Indians (quilt), 106
People's Bicentennial Committee (PBC), 170
People's BiCentennial Quilt, The, 170, 170–72
periodicals
  creating original quilt designs, 186–91
  quilt making and, 179
Pezzicar, Francesco, 29, *30*
Pfeffer, Miki, 96
Philadelphia, Pennsylvania. *See* Sesquicentennial International Exposition; US Centennial
Philadelphia Centennial Commission. *See* US Bicentennial
Phoenix Silk Manufacturing Company, 37
Pictorial Sampler Quilt, 136
Pieced Centennial Flag Print Quilt, 40, 41
Pine Ridge Indian Reservation, 129
poppy, adopting as official flower, 131–32
Porcella, Yvonne, 193
Potwin, Charles, 205
Potwin Place Centennial Quilt, 205–6, *206*
Powell, Helen, 213
Power (quilt), 112
Powers, Harriet, 94
presidency, celebrating
  fundraising banner honoring Theodore Roosevelt, 47–49
  George Washington Bicentennial Commission, 49–50
  starting from 1789, 46–47
presidential quilts
  patriotism in, 119–25
  of US Bicentennial, 161–62
Presidents' Medallion Quilt, 49
Pride of Ohio, The, 139
Pryor, Beverly, 183
Przybysz, Jane, 202
Putnam County Bicentennial Quilt, 147
Puzzle of the Floating World, 197

Quigley, Shannon, *215*
Quilted Tapestries, 194

Quilters' Journal, 179
Quilter's Newsletter Magazine, 179, 193
quilting frame, 66
quilt making, rising phenomenon of
    Bicentennial commitment, 172–75
    books, 176–78
    creating original quilt designs. *See* books; classes; lectures; periodicals; workshops
    periodicals, 179
    Quilt National, 199
    quilts on view as work of art, 193–99
    workshops, classes, and lectures, 179–80
Quilt National (exhibition), 199
Quilts '76, 194
quilts, American history of, 230–31
    commemorative events of twentieth century, 200–229
    crazy quilts, 68–93
    historical context, 14–51
    idea and pattern sources of Bicentennial quilts, 144–75
    introduction, 6–12
    other exhibitions, 94–117
    patriotic quilts, 118–42
    rising phenomenon of quilt making, 176–99
    timeline, 8–9
    women at work, 52–66
quilts on view, 193–99
Quintessential Quilts: The Great American Quilt Contest, 153

Ramsey, Bets, 182
Randles, Virginia, 192
ratification stars, 130, *131*
Rauschenberg, Robert, 188
Razzle-Dazzle, *185,* 197
Read, S. H., 120
Reconciliation Quilt, 18
Reconstruction, 14, 29, 31
red, white, and blue, color scheme. *See* color scheme (of Bicentennial quilts)
Red, White, and Blue Quilt, *171*
Red Cross Quilt, *119, 135*
Reding, Kay, 157, 161
Reginato, Peter, 188
Reich, Sue, 58–59, 131
Remembrance Quilt, *125, 129*
Renshaw, Donna, 176–77
Republican campaign handkerchief, *121*
Revere, Paul, 154
Revolutionary War, 28, 154
Rifkin, Jeremy, 170
Robertson, Harriet, 37
Robertson, Maria Silsby, 37
Robinson, Blanche Wiggin Staples, 38
Rocky Mountain Quilt Museum, 151
Roosevelt, Franklin Delano, 111, 122
Roosevelt, Theodore, 47–49, 102
Ross, Betsey, 135, 154
Royal School of Needlework, *72–73,* 74–77, 99, 196
Rubin, Luana, 229

Samaras, Lucas, 188
San Antonio, Texas. *See* San Antonio World's Fair (1968)
San Antonio Tricentennial Quilt, *223,* 225
San Antonio World's Fair (1968), 115–17
San Francisco Art Institute, 140
Saville, Joy, 192
Schafer, Mary, 144
Scheidecker, Dora, 157, 161
Schulze, Joan, 191–92
Schwalb, Robin, 185, 226
Scranton, Kate, 65
Sears, Roebuck and Company, 107–9
Sears Building, *109*. *See also* Century of Progress (1933)
Seattle, Washington. *See* Century 21 Exposition
Semiferous Tubulae: mature, *182*
Senate Subcommittee on Federal Charters, Holidays and Celebrations, 141
Sesquicentennial International Exposition, 106–7
sewing machines
    advertisement for, *33*
    exhibiting, 31–35
Seymour, Laura Electa, 45
Shaw, Robert, 71, 75–76, 144
Shirey, David L., 197
Silber, Julie, 31
silk, industry of, 85–88
Silk Association of America, 86
Silk Industry in America: A History, Prepared for the Centennial Exhibition, The (Brockett), 86
silk remnants advertisement, *88*
silk-weaving mill, establishment of, 85–86
Singer Manufacturing Company, 31–32
Singer Sewing Machine Company, 77
Sioux Indian Life quilt, *126*
Smalley, Eugene, 96
Smith, Bertha, 123
Smith, Walter, 74, 82
Smithsonian Institution, 35
Smithsonian Institution Traveling Exhibition Service, 153
soft art, 186
"Song of the Centennial" (Miller), 17
Sonnemann, Nell Booker, 182
Sons of Liberty Bicentennial Quilt, 154, *158*
Southerners, patriotism of, 17–18
souvenirs
    bandana, *23, 24, 27,* 38, 40–41, *44,* 46, 99, 112, 117
    bookmarks, *6, 94*
    Centennial medals, 40
    handkerchief, 102, *105, 108*
    textile, 4, 37–38, 85, 102, 105, 112
    variations of, 38
Spanish-American War, 130
Speas, Jeanie, 188
St. Louis, Missouri. *See* Louisiana Purchase Exposition
St. Louis World's Fair. *See* Louisiana Purchase Exposition
Stamp Act, 154
"Star-Spangled Banner, The" (song), 46
state buildings (at 1876 Centennial), 24–28
state days, celebrating, 24
state fairs, 9, 11, 59, 61, 62, 99, 112, 144, 157
Statue of Liberty, *98*
Statue of Liberty Centennial, 202–5
stitchery, 77, 185–86, 191–92, 215
Stow, Ida M., 108–9
Stowe, Harriet Beecher, 92
Stride of the Century, *21*
suffragists, 129–30
Sukraw, Ernest, 135
Sullivan, Arthur, 82
Summer Olympic Games (1904), 102, *103*
Suplee, A. G., 32
Sweltering Sky Kimono, *198*

Taft, William Howard, 119, 121, 215
Take Me to the Fair (quilt), *116*
Taplin, George E., 89
Tennessee Centennial and International Exposition, 100–101
Texas Centennial (1936), 109–11
Texas Centennial Historical Contest, 111
Textile, Silver, and Copper Building (Jamestown Ter-Centennial Exposition), *104,* 105
Textile Arts Guild, 192
Textile History, 32
textiles, American industry of, 31–35
Therese, *195*
Thirteenth Amendment, 14, 217
timeline, 8–9
Tobacco Silks Quilt, *120*
Tournament of Roses Parade, 142
trade cards, 32, 77, 82, *84, 89*
Treaty of Washington, 22
Tricentennial quilt (of San Antonio, Texas), *223,* 225
Tulsa Race Massacre, commemorating, 226
Tuscaloosa, Alabama, bicentennial, 225
Twain, Mark, 147
twentieth century, commemorative events of
    Anchorage, Alaska, centennial quilt, 221
    Arizona Centennial, 215–17
    Ashland, Kansas, railroad centennial, 205
    California Sesquicentennial, 213–15
    Castine, Maine, bicentennial, 212
    Christopher Columbus quincentennial jubilee, 208–11
    Emancipation Proclamation sesquicentennial, 217–19
    Grand Central Terminal centennial, 217
    Indiana Bicentennial Barn Quilt, 221–23, *222*
    Lutheran Community Services Northwest centennial, 227
    national parks centennial, 219–21
    Nineteenth Amendment centennial, 225–26

overview, 200–202
Potwin Place, Kansas, centennial quilt, 205–6
San Antonio Tricentennial Quilt, 223, 225
semiquincentennial of USA, 229
Statue of Liberty centennial, 202–5
Tulsa Race Massacre, 226
Tuscaloosa, Alabama, bicentennial, 225
Washington State Centennial, 208
Wilmington, Delaware, sesquarcentennial, 206–7
Twentieth Century's Best American Quilts, The, 147, 154
Two Days in Tulsa, 226

Ulster County Bicentennial Quilt, 157
Ulster County Community College, 157
United States, quilting in. *See* quilts, America history
United States semiquincentennial, 229
Upton, Molly, 178–79, 183, 185, 187, 194, 197
Urmie, Tami L., 221
US Bicentennial, 2–3, 125–29, 194
idea and pattern sources of quilts of, 144–75
overview, 6, 8–12
patriotic quilts and, 118–42
people as making history, 170–72
preparing for, 140–42
presidential quilts of, 161–62
prompting quilt-making, 172–75
and rising phenomenon of quilt making, 176–99
themes of, 140
US Centennial
African Americans and, 28–31
fabrics, 14, *17*
fundraising events for, 54–55
historical context leading up to, 14–19
Candace Wheeler touring, 75, 77
celebrating US presidency, 46–50
charm quilts and, 58–59
colonial artifacts and activities at, *36*
Exhibition (1876), 72
booths at, *34*
exhibiting sewing machines at, 31–35
Japanese-style quilts at, 78–82
quilts exhibited at, 35–46
silk exhibition at, 85–88
souvenir textiles from, 40
special days/buildings at, 24–28
Women's Pavilion, 10, 32, 52–53, 55–58
and national mood of colonialism, 22
overarching theme of, 17
overview, 6, 8–12
possible inspirations during, 72, 82–85
quilt makers, 46
unifying America, 22–24

Veterans of Foreign Wars (VFW), 131
VFW. *See* Veterans of Foreign Wars
Victory Garden Quilt, 138
Victory Gardens, 138
Victory Quilt, 135
Victory quilts, 138
Vietnam Era Quilt, 174
"V" letter, 138
Vote, Housetop Variation, 175

Waldron, Sue, 205
Warner, Chase, 135
Warren Historical Commission, 144
Washington, Booker T., 105
Washington, George, 2, *6,* 14, 40, 47, 49–50, *98*
Washington, Martha, *14,* 49, 54
Washington State Centennial, 208
WCEC. *See* Women's Centennial Executive Committee
WCTU. *See* Women's Christian Temperance Union
We and Our Neighbors (Stowe), 92
Webster, Marie, 2, 106
Wednesday Friendship Quilters, 208
Weeks, Pamela, 2–3
Weise, Wenda von, 197
Wells, Yvonne, 225
Westphal, Katherine, 166, *169,* 193, 197, 202
Wheatley, Phyllis, 148
Wheeler, Candace, 72, *75,* 77–78, 97
Wheeler & Wilson, *32*
White House, 63, 100, 119–20, 123, 161
White House Birthday quilt, 161
Whitney Museum of American Art, 193
Willard, Frances E., 61
William, Joy, 221–23
Williams, Evelyn, 157, 161
Williams, Irene, *175*
Williams, Mollie, 63
William Simpson Sons, *34*
William Simpson & Sons, 58
Williamson, Jeanne, 180
Willimantic Linen Company, 89
Wilmington, Delaware, sesquarcentennial, 206–7
Wilmington Stamp, The, 207
Wilson, Edith, 120
Wilson, Edward Livingston, *95*
Wilson, Erica, 196
Wilson, Woodrow, 120
Windmill pattern, 123
Windmill Variation, 124
Winthrop, Robert C., 64
"Win with Ike" campaign handkerchief, *125*
Woman's Club of Minnesota Lake, 139
Woman's Department. *See* Cotton Centennial (1884)
women
charm quilts and, 58–59
at Cotton Centennial, 94–97
and fairyland imagery, 89–91
and fundraising events, 54–55
in Gilded Age, 91–93
International Temperance Conference, 59–61
Nineteenth Amendment centennial, 225–26
participation in Centennial celebrations, 52
and patriotic quilts, 129–30
and *People's BiCentennial Quilt,* 170–72
and quilts in newspapers, 61–66
and special days/buildings at Centennial, 24–28
at World's Columbian Fair (1893), 97–99
Women and Their Quilts: A Washington State Centennial Tribute, 208
Women's Alliance of the First Unitarian Society at Exeter (New Hampshire), 147
Women's Association of Macomb County Community College, 144
Women's Building, Tennessee Centennial and International Exposition, *100*
Women's Centennial Executive Committee (WCEC), 10, *52*
Women's Christian Temperance Union (WCTU), 10, 59–61, 97, 120
Women's Pavilion
San Antonio World's Fair (1968), 115–17
US Centennial, 52–53, *55,* 55–58
Women's Relief Corps, 8
Women's Silk Culture Association of the United States, 85
Wooster, Ann-Sargent, *181,* 182
workshops
creating original quilt designs, 191–93
quilt making and, 179–80
World of Tomorrow, The. See New York World's Fair (1939–40)
World's Columbian Fair (1893), 97–99, *99*
World's Fair. *See various fairs by name*
World's Fair Commissioners, 102
World's Fair Map Quilt (quilt), *115*
World's Industrial and Cotton Centennial Exposition (1884), 94–97
World War I, 11, 68, 106, 130–32
World War II, 11, 94, 111, 132–38
world wars, patriotic quilts after, 139
Wounded Knee Occupation, 129

Yabsley, Suzanne, 11, 109
250 Years of American Wilderness, *228–29*
yosegire, 80
yoyo quilt (National Recovery Act), *122*
Yu, Connie Young, 170

Zinn, Ethel, 123

Whether she's curating the USA's oldest quilts, teaching quilt design, or researching, **Sandra Sider** shines as a quilt historian. She served as curator of the Texas Quilt Museum for a decade, where the quilts exhibited under her direction dated from the 19th to the 21st centuries. Sider holds a graduate degree in art history, is a past president of Studio Art Quilt Associates (SAQA), and from 2019 through 2022 taught the History of Textiles course for the MFA Textiles program at Parsons School of Design.

She's published articles on fiber and textile art for more than three decades. Her more than one dozen books concerning quilting's relation to our society include *Deeds Not Words: Celebrating 100 Years of Women's Suffrage* and *Quarantine Quilts: Creativity in the Midst of Chaos*. www.sandrasider.com